Religion, Scholarship & Higher Education

Religion, Scholarship, & Higher Education

PERSPECTIVES, MODELS,

AND FUTURE PROSPECTS

Essays from the Lilly Seminar on Religion and Higher Education

edited by

ANDREA STERK

University of Notre Dame Press
Notre Dame, Indiana

Manufactured in the United States of America

The publisher thanks the Lilly Endowment for its generous support
in the publication of this book.

Library of Congress Cataloging-in-Publication Data
Lilly Seminar on Religion and Higher Education.
    Religion, scholarship, and higher education : perspectives, models and
future prospects : essays from the Lilly Seminar on Religion and Higher
Education / edited by Andrea Sterk.
        p.   cm.
    Includes bibliographical references.
    ISBN 0-268-04053-2 (alk. paper)—ISBN 0-268-04054-0 (pbk. : alk. paper)
1. Church and college—United States—Congresses.   2. Learning and
scholarship—United States—Religious aspects—Congresses.   I. Sterk,
Andrea.   II. Title.
LC383 .L49   2002
378'.014—dc21

                                                             2001004912

∞ *This book was printed on acid-free paper.*

Contents

Contributors

NANCY T. AMMERMAN is Professor of Sociology of Religion at the Hartford Institute for Religion Research at Hartford Seminary. Her research interests have focused on conservative religious movements and on the dynamics of religious organizations and their contributions to American society, a theme taken up in her 1997 book *Congregation and Community*.

RICHARD J. BERNSTEIN is Vera List Professor of Philosophy and Chair at the New School for Social Research in New York. His recent books include *Freud and the Legacy of Moses, Hannah Arendt and the Jewish Question,* and *The New Constellation: The Ethical-Political Horizon of Modernity/Postmodernity*. In spring 2001 he was a fellow at the Wissenschaftskolleg zu Berlin (Institute for Advanced Study) where he was writing a book dealing with modern conceptions of evil.

CLARKE E. COCHRAN is Professor of Political Science and Adjunct Professor, Department of Health Organization Management, at Texas Tech University. His primary fields of teaching and research are religion and politics, political philosophy, and health care policy. He is the author of *Character, Community, and Politics* (1982), *Religion in Public and Private Life* (1990), (co-author) *American Public Policy: An Introduction* (1999), and numerous articles. During 1998–1999 he was Senior Research Fellow in the Erasmus Institute, University of Notre Dame, and in spring 2001 he held the William H. Shannon Chair in Catholic Studies at Nazareth College, Rochester, N.Y.

BRIAN E. DALEY, S.J., is the Catherine F. Huisking Professor of Theology at the University of Notre Dame. His field of research is historical theology: more specifically, early Christian biblical interpretation and the formation of classical Christian doctrine in the fourth through seventh centuries. His books include *The Hope of the Early Church: A Handbook of Patristic Eschatology*, and he is currently working on a commentary of the Psalms drawn from early Christian homilies and biblical commentaries.

DENIS DONOGHUE is Henry James Professor of English and American Letters and University Professor at New York University. He is the author of more than twenty books, including *Adam's Curse: Reflections on Religion and Literature* (2001), *Words Alone: The Poet T.S. Eliot* (2000), *The Practice of Reading* (1998), and *Walter Pater: Lover of Strange Souls* (1995).

JEAN BETHKE ELSHTAIN is the Laura Spelman Rockefeller Professor of Social and Political Ethics at The University of Chicago. She is a Fellow of the American Academy of Arts and Sciences and the recipient of six honorary degrees. Her books include *Public Man, Private Woman: Women in Social and Political Thought* (1981), *Women and War* (1987), *Democracy on Trial* (1995), *Augustine and the Limits of Politics* (1996), and most recently, *Who Are We?* (2000).

SUSAN HANDELMAN became Professor of English at Bar-Ilan University in Israel in fall 2000 after serving as Professor of English at the University of Maryland, College Park since 1979. Her major academic interest is the relation of contemporary literary theory to Jewish thought, and her publications include *Fragments of Redemption: Jewish Thought and Literary Theory in Benjamin, Scholem, and Levinas* (1991) and *The Slayers of Moses: The Emergence of Rabbinic Interpretation in Modern Literary Theory* (1982). She has also recently co-edited *"Torah of the Mothers": Contemporary Jewish Women Read Classical Jewish Texts* (2000).

DAVID A. HOLLINGER is Chancellor's Professor of History at the University of California at Berkeley. His books include *Science, Jews, and Secular Culture: Studies in Mid-Twentieth Century American Intellectual History*. His current research concerns the children of Protestant foreign missionaries and their impact on American life.

SERENE JONES is Associate Professor of Systematic Theology at Yale Divinity School. She works in the fields of contemporary theology, feminist theory, and Reformed thought. Her most recent book, *Feminist Theory and Theology: Cartographies of Grace* (2000) maps out interconnections between recent works in feminist theory and the classical Reformed doctrines of faith, sin, and church. She is also the author of *Calvin and the Rhetoric of Piety* and is currently working on the interplay between theology and the law in contemporary culture.

ROGER LUNDIN is the Clyde S. Kilby Professor of English at Wheaton College. He is the author of several books, including *Emily Dickinson and the Art of Belief* (1998) and *The Culture of Interpretation: Christian Faith and the Postmodern World* (1993). He is currently directing a multiyear project on religion and American literature under the auspices of Christian Scholars Program of the Pew Charitable Trust.

JOHN MCGREEVY is John A. O'Brien Associate Professor of History at the University of Notre Dame. He is the author of *Parish Boundaries: The Catholic Encounter with Race in the Twentieth-Century Urban North* (Chicago, 1996). He is currently working on a study of Catholicism and American liberalism from slavery to abortion.

MARK A. NOLL is McManis Professor of Christian Thought in the history department at Wheaton College. His books include *Turning Points: Decisive Moments in the History of Christianity* (1997), *American Evangelical Christianity: An Introduction* (2001), and (as co-editor and editor, respectively) *Evangelicals and Science in Historical Perspective* (1999), and *God and Mammon: Protestants, Money, and the Market, 1790–1860* (2001).

FRANCIS OAKLEY is President Emeritus of Williams College and the Edward Dorr Griffin Professor of the History of Ideas at that college. He is a former Chairman of the American Council of Learned Societies and is currently President of the Fellows of the Medieval Academy of America. His most recent books are *Community of Learning: The American College and the Liberal Arts Tradition* (1992), and *Politics and Eternity* (1999). Forthcoming are his Sir Isaiah Berlin Lectures in the History of Ideas on "Conciliarist Constitutionalism in the Catholic Church: 1300–1870," delivered at Oxford University in fall 1999.

MARK R. SCHWEHN is Professor of Humanities and Dean of Christ College, the honors college of Valparaiso University. He is also the Project Director of the Lilly Fellows Program in Humanities and the Arts, an initiative designed to strengthen the quality and character of church-related higher education in the U.S. His publications include *Exiles from Eden: Religion and the Academic Vocation in America* (Oxford, 1993) and, most recently, *Everyone a Teacher* (Notre Dame, 2000).

ANDREA STERK is Assistant Professor of History at the University of Florida. A historian of Christianity, her primary research has focused on the relation between the monastic movement and ideals of leadership in the late Roman and early Byzantine world. She is also co-author of *John Comenius: The Labyrinth of the World* (1998).

JAMES TURNER is Cavanaugh Professor of Humanities and Professor of History at the University of Notre Dame and director of the Erasmus Institute. With Nicholas Wolterstorff he led the Lilly Seminar on Religion and Higher Education. His recent books include *The Liberal Education of Charles Eliot Norton* (1999) and *The Sacred and the Secular University* (with Jon H. Roberts, 2000).

ALAN WOLFE is professor of political science and Director of the Boisi Center for Religion and American Public Life at Boston College. He is the author or editor of more than ten books including *Marginalized in the Middle* (1997), *One Nation, After All* (1998), and most recently, *Moral Freedom: The Search for Virtue in a World of Choice* (2001). A contributing editor of *The New Republic* and *The Wilson Quarterly*, Professor Wolfe writes often for those publications as well as for *Commonweal*, *The New York Times*, *Harper's*, *The Atlantic Monthly*, *The Washington Post*, and other magazines and newspapers.

NICHOLAS WOLTERSTORFF, co-director of the Lilly Seminar, is Noah Porter Professor of Philosophical Theology at Yale University. His major publications include *Divine Discourse, John Locke and the Ethics of Belief, Thomas Reid and the Story of Epistemology, Until Justice and Peace Embrace*, and *Reason within the Bounds of Religion*. His primary areas of research are philosophy of religion, epistemology, political philosophy, and aesthetics.

ROBERT WUTHNOW is the Gerhard R. Andlinger '52 Professor of Sociology and Director of the Center for the Study of Religion at Princeton University. A specialist on religion and culture in the contemporary United States, his books include *After Heaven: Spirituality in America since the 1950s* (1998), *Loose Connections: Joining Together in America's Fragmented Communities* (1998), and *Growing Up Religious: Christians and Jews and Their Journeys of Faith* (1999). He is currently writing a book about spirituality and the arts and directing a research project funded by The Pew Charitable Trusts on the public role of mainline Protestantism.

Preface

Yet another book about religion and the academy or, perhaps worse still, the perilous plight of the American university? The wary reader has probably picked up this volume with a tinge of cynicism, if not disdain, and even the potential enthusiast for such topics may be slightly jaded by the recent stream of publications addressing such issues as secularization, de-Christianization, postmodernism, identity crisis, and a host of other ills allegedly afflicting the modern academy. It is the goal of this book neither to disabuse you of such concerns nor to propose a series of solutions to the challenges of higher learning at the start of the twenty-first century. It is rather to present the work of a diverse representation of academics, of varying religious and nonreligious persuasions, who have as a group debated and discussed strategy concerning these issues over the course of several years. Here I shall briefly introduce the nature and goals of this unusual gathering of scholars and outline the contents and distinctions of this collection of essays that has issued from their interaction.

The Lilly Seminar on Religion and Higher Education convened semiannually at different venues around the country over a three-year period ending in the fall of 1999. Funded by the Lilly Endowment, the project was intended in part to elucidate and synthesize the lessons learned from the endowment's broader initiative in this area. By drawing on some of those lessons combined with the experience and expertise of the Lilly seminar members, the primary aim of the seminar was to clarify, strengthen, and enrich the relation between religion and academic endeavor for the early decades of the new millennium; to formulate an agenda, as it were, for the next phase of developing links between religion and higher education.

Toward the fulfillment of these bold objectives a distinguished retinue of academics, both fresh voices and better-known scholars from a wide range of disciplines and institutional settings, were invited to participate in the seminar. While these individuals were all engaged in some way with issues of religion in American intellectual life, the group intentionally included a few who were keen skeptics about the whole project. Under the leadership of James Turner and Nicholas Wolterstorff, the final constitution of the seminar encompassed a rich mixture of Catholics, Protestants (both evangelical and mainline), Jews, and agnostics. Participants represented a variety of disciplines within the humanities and social sciences, a few administrators, and a broad spectrum of institutions: large and prestigious research universities, small private liberal arts colleges, religiously affiliated institutions, and divinity schools. To be sure, the membership could have been more diverse. The absence of natural scientists and representatives of the fine arts was at times keenly felt, as was the relative lack of skeptical voices. Despite these limitations the group benefited from a variety of backgrounds, ages, perspectives, and academic experiences that surely strengthened and sharpened the resulting discussions.

All but one of the essays in this volume were presented as formal or informal addresses to one of the seminar gatherings in 1998 or 1999. Readers who have followed the general discourse on religion and higher education in the past two decades will hear in these pages echoes of a generation of scholars who have helped to shape that conversation. Names like Charles Taylor and Alasdair MacIntyre in philosophy, Mary Douglas in anthropology, and George Marsden in history recur with some frequency throughout these essays. Even those authors who contest or challenge some of their ideas tacitly acknowledge an indebtedness to such foundational figures for reframing issues, posing questions, and positing theories that have prompted the academy to look afresh at its own identity and meaning and the possible roles that religion or religious perspectives may play in its future. Nor are many of the contributors to this volume themselves neophytes on the subject of religion and higher education. Several have written much longer articles or books about some of the topics addressed in this collection. So amidst the fresh voices and new approaches represented here there is also a familiar ring.

But this is not primarily a book about theory. What is distinctive of this volume amidst the recent outpouring of writings on related subjects is its orientation toward the personal and the practical. Though far from a collection of testimonials, which has alas become something of a scholarly genre of late, almost all the essays in this volume reveal elements of the author's own religious background or experience and an explanation of how these personal factors shape the way he or she approaches higher education in general or aspects of research or teaching in particular. Several contributors examine their own concrete projects or practices as scholars and teachers. While these essays are consistently descriptive rather than prescriptive, they provide suggestive models of scholarship or classroom teaching that, in diverse ways, reflect religious concerns and perspectives. Academics and administrators who have occasionally scratched their heads over what the theoreticians want, what the fuss is all about, or what their colleagues are actually doing to integrate a religious dimension into scholarship and teaching, will find the frank, practical tone of many of these essays refreshing.

The volume is divided into three sections. In Part I, on foundational issues, the lead essays of codirectors Wolterstorff and Turner show the authors switching disciplinary hats. Philosopher Nicholas Wolterstorff reflects on the history of recent developments in higher education and specifically in the philosophy of science (from Kant and Weber to Thomas Kuhn) in order to elucidate the process by which the very notion of religiously based scholarship has come to be taken seriously by academics even at major "secular" universities. James Turner's essay poses the philosophical question of whether religious intellectual traditions have anything of value to offer the scholarly enterprise at the start of the twenty-first century, a question he answers affirmatively, albeit in the cautious tone of a historian. Alan Wolfe turns to the subject of religious institutions of higher education, signaling their distinctive opportunities in contemporary academic culture and considering the options they face in responding to the pressures toward orthodoxy on the one hand, and fulfilling their potential for pluralism on the other. If these first three contributions appear cautiously optimistic about the future prospects of religion or religiously informed scholarship in the academy, David Hollinger's essay will no doubt give the reader pause. Hollinger reminds us of historical and epistemological reasons why mainstream academia has come to maintain a certain critical distance from religion in general and Christianity in particular, and warns against efforts to reform higher education in a more religious direction. Mark Schwehn responds to some of these concerns and reflects on the very nature of the university, which, he suggests, both religious and nonreligious members of the seminar were seeking to preserve against a different set of threats.

Part II addresses the theme of religion and scholarship, the subject of a larger conference sponsored by the seminar in order to inform its final year of deliberations. Several contributions to this section were originally presented in this context. The essays are of two types, though both focus on disciplinary issues. John McGreevy, Nancy Ammerman, Roger Lundin, and Brian Daley address the disciplines of history, sociology, literature, and historical theology respectively, providing, as it were, a survey of the state of the discipline with respect to religion and research. The last three essays present specific examples of scholarship grounded in or informed by religious perspectives. Clarke Cochran discusses ways in which the Roman Catholic notion of sacramentality has informed his recent work as a political scientist while Serene Jones describes how classical Christian theology has shaped her work in feminist theory. Richard Bernstein's contribution, which outlines his ideal of a democratic society and its broad implications for academic culture, might well have been included in Part I. But in order to demonstrate its specific application to scholarship and religion, Bernstein presents an engaging account of how he came to write his recent books on Hannah Arendt and Sigmund Freud. The questions and hypotheses he poses in these works, he explains, were clearly influenced by his own identification with the Jewish tradition. Indeed, for reasons McGreevy discusses in his essay, it is often difficult to separate foundational issues from specific disciplinary approaches.

Part III takes up the theme of teaching, specifically the question of whether teaching should reflect the religious perspective of the teacher. Contributors to this section come from diverse institutional settings: research universities, a Christian liberal arts college, a divinity school, and a large state university. As several authors emphasize, both context and subject matter significantly influence the way one answers the question posed. The approaches in these essays vary considerably. Mark Noll speaks primarily of the task of a teacher of history, particularly within the setting of a Christian college. Denis Donoghue leads us through the text of a poem in order to illustrate his approach to the teaching of literature and a few of the problems he has encountered along the way. Robert Wuthnow discusses the breadth of roles and responsibilities that he faces in his job as a professor of sociology—advising graduate students, supervising junior papers and senior theses, teaching a variety of types of classes within the department—and the different ways in which his religion may influence his teaching in these different settings. Jean Bethke Elshtain describes the standard curriculum in political theory and reflects on how religious convictions, like other kinds of beliefs and concerns, almost inevitably influence the choice of material one includes in a syllabus. Susan Handelman brings two distinctive dimensions to her discussion of teaching—the perspective of an Orthodox Jew whose pedagogy has been inspired in part by the Jewish mystical tradition, and a focus on the voices of undergraduate students. Handelman reminds us that "underneath those pulled-down baseball caps and Walkman headphones" students are often passionate in their beliefs or unbelief, seriously struggling with issues of truth, faith, and doubt; and they may even have something of value to say to the academy about learning.

Did the Lilly Seminar succeed in its grand design? Did it adequately address the themes and subthemes one would need to examine to enact reforms in the world of higher education? In his concluding reflections Francis Oakley, speaking from a wealth of experience as a scholar, teacher, and college president, discusses a few of the important "failed issues" of the seminar before summarizing some key lessons learned from each of the three years of the project. Nicholas Wolterstorff wraps up the volume with an epilogue from the perspective of the codirectors presenting a particularly important contribution of the Lilly Seminar to the broader discourse on religion, scholarship, and higher education. The significance of the lessons and contributions featured in these two closing essays can only be assessed over time. But beyond the strictly measurable results of such an initiative, the relationships formed over the course of three years of deliberations may prove in the long run most valuable and most influential in the academic arena. Ongoing friendships and relationships of respect that developed among leading academics across institutional, disciplinary, religious, and philosophical lines were for most of the seminar members one of the great legacies of the project. Most participants, both believers and agnostics, came away with the sense that there needs to be more cooperation across religious and secular lines in order to preserve the university at its best.

Finally, a few words of gratitude are due to the Lilly Endowment for its generosity and its willingness to support the kinds of intellectual projects whose results are often less tangible. The seminar also benefited from the vision and experience of Craig Dykstra and Jeanne Knoerle, who not only represented the endowment but were active participants in our meetings. Donna Ring consistently went beyond the call of duty in making those meetings as comfortable and conducive to productive discussion as any academic gathering could hope to be. She has now put the detailed reports of the six seminar meetings on a website (www.nd.edu/~lillysem/), so curious readers can access accounts of the lively discussions that followed some of the presentations included here.

It is our hope that this volume representing contributors from a wide range of perspectives and institutional contexts will find an equally wide-ranging audience. For readers who are suspicious about the project of religion and higher education, it may serve to allay some doubts. For those seeking constructive examples of the integration of religion in the scholarly enterprise, it may help to foster similar creative models. If it has either of these effects, or if it simply serves to inform and deepen the quality of ongoing discussion, the Lilly Seminar will have accomplished much.

Andrea Sterk

PART I

Foundational Issues & Concerns

Scholarship Grounded in Religion

NICHOLAS WOLTERSTORFF

Forty years ago, when I was a graduate student at Harvard and beginning my career as a philosopher, the question of the possibility and desirability of religion-based scholarship would have been asked only in certain liberal arts colleges with religious orientations. Now it has become a topic for open conferences sponsored by major foundations at major universities. What has caused the topic, of whether it is possible and desirable for scholarship to be grounded in religion, to emerge from small pockets of inquiry out into the open public arena?

I will be telling a story—narrating the main developments in a stretch of recent history. But let me announce in advance what will in any case soon become evident: I will not be telling the story as a historian would tell it. I do not bear fresh and startling news from the archives—for the reason that I haven't visited any archives. My story was composed in the proverbial posture of the philosopher: sitting in a chair, thinking, using my memory, such as it is. The narrative will necessarily be sketchy. After offering the narrative, I'll conclude with some brief suggestions as to how we should conduct ourselves in the situation in which we now find ourselves.

I

I remember well the basic thrust of the philosophy of science course I took from Karl Hempel when I was a graduate student at Harvard, and of the various public lectures on philosophy of science that I attended. Teacher and speakers were all engaged in the project of trying to display the *logic* of science—or in case the speaker was one of those who thought that the logic of the social sciences was different from that of the natural sciences, engaged in the project of trying to display the *logics* of science. The thought was that there is some entity called "science" with which we are all acquainted, that this entity has a nature or essence, that one ingredient of that essence is a *logic* or *logics*, that we know a priori the essential features of this logic, that for some reason science as it actually is conceals this logic from us, and that it is the noble and challenging task of the philosopher to display that logic—to reveal the hidden. We talked in my day about how terribly difficult it was to accomplish this revealing of the hidden. Philosophy of science, we told ourselves, is extremely hard work; that's why only the brightest and the best go into it. In my day we all furrowed our brows over the infamous "problem of the counterfactual." Though scientists use counterfactuals all the time, how they fit into what we knew to be the *logic* of science was not at all evident.

In retrospect it's clear to me that my teachers were assuming a certain understanding of the relation between philosophy and science—a Kantian understanding. Kant was the first to articulate explicitly the *angst* of the philosopher in the modern world: given the growth of the "special sciences," what's left for philosophy to do? Kant's answer was that whereas it is the business of the special sciences to deal with contingency, it remains the task of the philosopher to explore issues of *modality*—that is, issues of possibility and necessity. The assumption of my teachers, that it is the province of philosophers to reveal the logic of science, was a descendent of that Kantian view.

Beyond operating with a certain understanding of the relation between philosophy and the "special sciences," my graduate school teachers were also making certain assumptions about the place of science in modern culture. I doubt that any of them had read Max Weber; I certainly don't remember any of them mentioning him. Nonetheless, it's my judgment that the assumptions they were working with on this score have never been better articulated than they were by Weber, who set them in the context of his theory of modernization.

Weber was convinced that the essence of modernization is to be located in two related phenomena. Modernization consists, in the first place, in the emergence of *differentiated spheres* of activity—specifically, in the emergence of the differentiated *social* spheres of economy, state, and household, and in the emergence of the differentiated *cultural* spheres of science, art, law, and ethics. The picture which underlay Weber's thought at this point was the neo-Kantian picture according to which individual spheres of activity, each with its own dynamics, reside in the very nature of things, albeit hidden and concealed throughout most of history. What Weber added to the neo-Kantian picture was the claim that it is the dynamic of rationalization which, after de-magicalizing the world and confining the ethic of brotherliness to the realm of the private, brings these spheres to the light of day by differentiating them from each other and securing the relative independence of action within these spheres from outside interference.

I submit that Weber is here articulating a way of thinking deep in the practice and mentality of modernity. In earlier days and places, what we now call art was inextricably intertwined with other social and cultural phenomena; then, beginning in the West in the eighteenth century, the arts became a distinct sphere within society and culture, and artistic activity was liberated from external demands of church and state. Art "came into its own." So too for *Wissenschaft*. In earlier days and places, learning was likewise inextricably intertwined with other social and cultural phenomena; then, beginning in the West in the seventeenth century, learning began to "come into its own," led forward into the promised land by the new natural science: it became possible to identify a certain sociocultural sphere as that of *Wissenschaft*, and activity within this sphere became liberated from external demands. None of my professors would have been able, or if able, willing, to articulate their assumptions with anything like Weber's grand sweep; nonetheless, there can be no doubt that they thought along these lines. And so do most of us; witness how we think of what we call "academic freedom" and "artistic freedom."

The second main aspect of Weber's theory of modernization was his account of what transpires within these various social and cultural spheres, once they have been differentiated from each other and activity within them freed from external influence. Activity within the spheres becomes autonomous, self-normed; it begins to follow its own internal logic. Weber thought that these internal logics are all manifestations of *rationalization*. Rationalization thus plays the double modernizing function of accounting for the emergence of these differentiated spheres and of being what happens within these spheres once they have been differentiated and action within them allowed to become independent and autonomous. The fundamental dynamic of action within our modern capitalist economies is rationalization, just as the fundamental dynamic of action within our modern bureaucratic states is rationalization; but so too, Weber argued, the fundamental dynamic of thought within modern science is rationalization, oriented as that thought is toward prediction, grounded as it is in sensory experience, and intertwined as it is with technology. Given these views, the history of science becomes the story we have all heard, namely, the story of the gestation and birth of science as we now know it. The narrative begins with conception among the ancient Babylonians and Greeks, it continues with agonized stirrings among the medievals, it waxes lyrical when finally birth occurs with the publication of Newton's *Principia*. There are other ways to tell the story; that's the ever-so-familiar Weberian way.

My judgment, in retrospect, is that my graduate school teachers were not only working with a roughly Kantian picture of how philosophy differs from science, and with a Weberian picture of the place of science within culture; they were also working with this Weberian picture of science as having an interior logic. They were not alone in that. Characteristic of the modern academy in general has been a regnant understanding of the structure or, if you will, "the logic" of well-formed *Wissenschaft*. The past quarter-century has witnessed the shattering of that regnant self-understanding; that's what makes the academy today very different from what it was forty years ago. We want to understand the causes of this shattering; but for that, we'll have to catch at least a glimpse of what was shattered: the once-regnant understanding by the modern academy of the inner structure of well-formed *Wissenschaft*.

Perhaps the deepest component in this understanding was the conviction that well-formed learning is a *generically human* enterprise. To put the point pictorially: before entering the halls of learning we are to render inoperative, for the time being, all our particularities—of gender, of race, of nationality, of religion, of social class, of age—so as to allow only what belongs to our generic humanity to be operative within those halls. My graduate school professors, if not totally mystified by such projects as Afro-American history, feminist epistemology, Muslim political theory, and liberation theology, would have regarded these as *bad* history, *bad* epistemology, *bad* political theory, *bad* theology. They would have dismissed them as *biased;* learning practiced *qua* some particular kind of human being is malformed learning. The project of the academy is to construct an edifice of *objective* learning, that is, learning open to the facts by virtue of being generically human. Such learning can be expected eventually to gain the consensus of all normal adult human beings knowledgeable in the discipline. When learning is rightly conducted, pluralism in the academy is an accidental and temporary phenomenon.

A second component in this self-understanding of the modern academy was a distinctive hierarchy of the academic disciplines. We're all familiar with it. At the top were the physical sciences and mathematics; these were the paradigmatic disciplines. At the bottom were the humanities; the social sciences occupied a position somewhere in between. Theology? If one thought of theology at all, the place one assigned it depended on whether one judged it to have been rationally grounded or not. If it was, it belonged somewhere among the humanities. If not, it was off the ladder.

What underlay this hierarchy was of course a certain understanding of what constitutes well-formed *Wissenschaft*—an understanding which, I would say, first came to articulate expression in the writings of John Locke and his cohorts in the Royal Academy. The thought was that mathematics and the natural sciences have already attained the status of well-formed *Wissenschaft*, whereas the other academic disciplines have yet to do so. When their "Newtons" appear and their revolutions take place, they will join mathematics and natural science at the top. "The logic" of science is not something unique in principle to the natural sciences and mathematics; it is the logic which any academic discipline will exhibit once it attains the status of a well-formed *Wissenschaft*. Until that new day arrives, we can compose a hierarchy of the disciplines in terms of how far they are from meeting the ideal.

The two matters already mentioned—well-formed *Wissenschaft* understood as a generically human enterprise, and the assumed hierarchy of the disciplines—are background and consequence of what was understood to be the method of science. On this there was, I would say, somewhat less consensus than on those other two matters. Nonetheless, there can be little doubt that the dominant view was that the method of well-formed science is *foundational*—more specifically, *classically* foundationalist. On this occasion I refrain from explaining what constitutes classical foundationalism; for the purposes at hand, explaining it won't be necessary.

Before moving on to the next part of my story we should note how, on this once-regnant self-understanding of the academy, a person's religion was seen as related to his or her practice of learning. Obviously it was not regarded as a particularity which appropriately shapes the practice of learning. Within the bounds of that shared conviction, various options were proposed and explored. Some thought of Christianity and other religions as appropriately providing *motivation* for engaging in learning—which one then practices in generically human, foundationalist, fashion. Others held that religion has nothing at all to do with learning, but belongs to some other sphere of human life, possibly to its own unique sphere—though Weber himself seems to have thought of it as a remnant of the unrationalized rather than as a differentiated action-sphere of its own. But also, from the Enlightenment onwards, there have been those who were convinced that it is possible to construct a rationally grounded theism—even a rationally grounded Christianity. Such a theism, or such a Christianity, would rightly occupy a place in the academy. The conviction that theism in general, and Christian theism in particular, is rationally grounded, was widespread among American academics until the early years of the twentieth century. Then it began to fade. The disturbed relationship between religion and the academy which has characterized so much of our own century is due, as I see it, in great measure to the fading of that conviction. If religion lacks rational grounding—so it has been assumed—it has no place in the academy.

II

This self-understanding of the modern Western academy, whose major contours I have outlined, has been shattered over the past quarter-century. Let me schematize what happened into what I will call "the first revolution" and "the second revolution."

First to go was the conviction that the method of well-formed *Wissenschaft* is classical foundationalism. The emergence of meta-epistemology, among philosophers, played a significant role in this development. The course I took in epistemology as a graduate student was, to my mind, stupefyingly boring; requirement satisfied, I opted for the exhilarations of metaphysics. I did not understand at the time why it was so boring. Now I do: classical foundationalism was simply taken for granted as *the* structure of justified belief, so much so that it wasn't even identified as such; and we confined ourselves to worrying one and another problem within classical foundationalism. I remember the day when we were all instructed to press one of our eyeballs so as to induce double vision, and then invited to reflect on what was to be made of such vision. I did not succeed in getting any double images. But I silently concluded that there was something wrong either with my eyeball or with my pressing of my eyeball; accordingly, conceding that epistemology was about normal adults, I went along with the supposition that the double vision everybody else was apparently getting posed an important problem—albeit, to my mind, a boring one.

Then, starting about twenty-five years ago, epistemology became interesting. Rather than just taking for granted that to be an epistemologist is to think along classically foundationalist lines, philosophers stood back to survey the alternatives available for the structuring of epistemological theories. Classical foundationalism came to be identified as just one among others—albeit, the alternative we had all been taking for granted. Having been thus identified, it was then held up for appraisal, whereupon it came to seem to almost everybody thoroughly implausible as an account of justified belief and knowledge.

I am inclined to think that a different development was even more decisive, however, in shattering the reigning ideas about the method of well-formed *Wissenschaft*. Also around twenty-five years ago, a group of scholars who were trained as natural scientists, philosophers, and historians—all of those—began to study episodes from the history of modern Western natural science so as to compare the *regnant self-understanding* of natural science with its *actual practice*. What they over and over bumped up against was reputable, even admirable, episodes from the history of modern Western natural science which simply did not fit the self-understanding of natural science as a classically foundationalist enterprise. Thomas Kuhn became the best known of these. In his now-famous book, *The Structure of Scientific Revolutions*, Kuhn argued that revolutions in science do not occur because some new theory is discerned to be more probable than the old theory on evidence accepted by all parties; nor—to bring Karl Popper into the picture—because the old theory has been falsified. Instead, something like a conversion takes place. Kuhn himself borrowed religious language at this point.

Three things are worth noting about this Kuhnian development. In the first place, the fact of such discrepancy between self-understanding and actual episodes tells us something important about the workings of natural science. Rather often it is assumed by those who talk about the workings of science that there is such a thing as *the* scientific method, that natural scientists somewhere learn this method, and that in their work they apply the method learned. But if that were how things go, there would be no discrepancy between self-understanding and actual episodes, other than discrepancies which result from failed attempts to apply the method. But the new historians were not inviting us to look at the falls and fumbles of modern natural science; they were inviting us to look at some of its great celebrated achievements. *These* were the episodes that did not fit the regnant self-understanding; *these* were the episodes that were not implementations of the supposed scientific method. Science does not come about by scientists being taught *the* scientific method and then applying that method. The practice of science proves much more intuitive than that.

Second, to interpret the historical evidence as showing that much admirable natural science has not in fact followed what everybody had supposed to be the method of science, namely, classical foundationalism, required a fascinating alteration of mentality from that characteristic of my graduate school teachers. My teachers never denied—in fact they freely conceded—that actual natural science does not appear to be classically foundationalist. But from these appearances they did not conclude that it does not in fact have that structure; they concluded instead that we philosophers had to work hard to show that it really does, appearances not withstanding. The new historians were saying that the appearance is the reality; nothing is hidden.

Why did this alteration in interpretation take place around twenty-five years ago, when protests to the same effect by Heidegger, by the American pragmatists, and by numerous others over many years, had had negligible impact? I think it was above all the wealth of historical detail provided by the new historians that produced the alteration. Before the new historians came along, the history of natural science, in discussions concerning the method of science, served mostly as a reservoir of examples for illustrating conclusions arrived at a priori. The new historians drew their conclusions about the methods of science from their detailed study of its actual practice. They didn't think; they looked.

Perhaps the most important thing to observe about this Kuhnian development, though, is this: when finally one gives up dismissing appearance in favor of some hidden reality, and instead concedes that there really is discrepancy between self-understanding and actuality, one can then say either "So much the worse for actuality" or "So much the worse for the self-understanding." For centuries, whenever discrepancy was acknowledged between regnant self-understanding and the actuality of some segment of academic learning outside the natural sciences, the response had been: "So much the worse for the actuality." Now the response was different. No one said, "So much the worse for modern natural science." Everyone said, "So much the worse for the received self-understanding of natural science." That shows the enormous cultural prestige of natural science as it has actually developed. It was that very prestige which was crucial to the shattering of the self-understanding. When the paradigmatic disciplines proved not to fit the received self-understanding of well-formed *Wissenschaft*, then something deep had to go. The prestige of the natural sciences insured that it was the received self-understanding that went.

An inevitable consequence was that the old hierarchy of the disciplines came unstuck. For suppose that one has worked with some a priori notion of the method of well-formed *Wissenschaft*, suppose that one has interpreted the success of the modern natural sciences, and the relatively high degree of consensus within them, as an indication that those disciplines have followed that method, and suppose that one has located the other disciplines, in their present form, somewhere lower in the hierarchy for the reason that they do not follow that method. And now suppose that one is forced to surrender that a priori notion of the method of well-formed *Wissenschaft*, and led to the conclusion that probably there is no such thing as *the* method. That is our situation today. Then the old hierarchy of the disciplines begins to creak and totter. The conviction that the humanities—the interpretative disciplines—are inferior to the natural sciences loses its grounding.

It is these dynamics that are being played out in the academy today. The passion for hermeneutics is no accident. Literary critics, instead of waiting for the appearance of the Newton who will revolutionize their discipline into a well-formed *Wissenschaft*, are declaring that their discipline is OK as it is. The science ideal is losing its grip. What else could it do but lose its grip, when we no longer believe that there is such a thing as *the* method of well-formed *Wissenschaft*, which, supposedly, the natural sciences instantiate?

III

I move on, now, to the second revolution: the repudiation of the conviction that well-formed academic learning is a product of our generic humanity.

Historically, the academy in the modern West has been populated in overwhelming proportions by white Eurocentric bourgeois males. Slowly, as the result of various liberation movements in society generally, the proportion has been changing, so that now significant numbers of the once-disenfranchised enjoy positions within the academy. Some fifteen or twenty years ago their numbers reached a critical mass, so that they were emboldened to say what they had long felt if not thought, or thought if not said; namely, that it is sheer pretense to present the learning of the academy as generically human in character. The learning of the modern Western academy reflects the particularities of those who have peopled it. The reason for the dominance in society generally of its learning is not that it so successfully renders the truth of the matter as any objective human being would see it; the dominance of the learning is due in good part to the social dominance of its practitioners.

Here too, as with the point of discrepancy discussed earlier, various options were available to the person who acknowledged discrepancy between self-understanding and actuality. One could insist on the importance of the traditional self-understanding and urge that we do all in our power to *make* the learning of the academy live up to its self-professed ideal of being generically human. Alternatively, one could repudiate that traditional self-understanding as misguided in one way or another. Having done that, one could in principle go on to argue for the perpetuation of the hegemony of white Eurocentric bourgeois males in the academy, openly acknowledging that the learning they produce is not generically human; or one could argue for the right of other particularities to engage in learning from their own perspective. I know of no one who has openly chosen the former of these.

The debate today is thus a two-sided debate between those who continue to embrace the traditional ideal of generically human learning, and who insist that the academy should live up to that ideal, and those who reject the ideal and argue that particularist learning of many forms should be allowed to flourish in the academy. Typically those who defend this latter position argue that there never was and never can be such a thing as generically human learning; the ideal of such learning is and always has been illusory. The learning of the academy is unavoidably particularist; best to acknowledge that, shed one's illusions, and act accordingly. The pluralization of the academy is not a matter of happenstance but of essence. And in fact the past two decades have seen the flowering of particularist scholarship to a truly astonishing degree. Liberation theology, feminist psychology, black history, on and on—where not very long ago the very phrases would have grated on our ears, now, no matter how we evaluate the substance, the phrases along with the reality have become familiar.

I judge this second revolution to be considerably more fundamental than the first. The first helped to prepare the way for the second; but the disturbance caused by giving up various illusions about the method of natural science in particular, and of well-formed *Wissenschaft* in general, was minor compared to the disturbance caused by the widespread acceptance of the thesis that learning in general never has been, and never can be, a generically human enterprise, and the embrace of particularist learning and the pluralizing of the academy which flows from that.

IV

It's time I laid my cards on the table. I embrace both of the revolutions to which I have called attention. I do not believe that there is a sociocultural sphere of *Wissenschaft* following its own internal logic, that that logic was first instantiated in natural science in the eighteenth century, that the other academic disciplines continue to await their Newtons, and that, until their Newtons appear, they are consigned to a lower rung on the hierarchy of the academic disciplines. Neither do I believe it possible nor, if possible, desirable, to render inoperative during our practice of learning all our particularities of religion, gender, class, and so forth, so as to function just as generic human beings. Accordingly, it is my view that when considering the question before us, whether scholarship shaped by religion has a place in the academy, we must understand the academy in this new, postrevolutionary, way. Does scholarship grounded in religion have a place in that form and understanding of the academy which is today slowly coming to birth?

My answer is that it does. As I see it, what ought to replace the old picture of the academy as a generically human, foundationalist, enterprise, is a picture of the academy as a locus of what might be called "dialogic pluralism": a plurality of entitled positions engaged in dialogue which is aimed at arriving at truth. Those who see the world through religious eyes belong in that dialogue.

On this occasion I unfortunately lack the space to explain and defend the position I have just espoused. Before I close, however, I do feel compelled to make clear that though I am a firm defender of what I have called particularist learning, I nonetheless disagree with much of what is regularly said or assumed nowadays by my cohorts—especially by those who call themselves "perspectivalists," using the word in the Nietzschean sense.

It is regularly said or assumed nowadays that reality is never present to us, forever screened from view by concepts. I disagree. The fact that I perceive what is before me under the concept of a podium does not prohibit its being a podium that is perceptually present to me. It is regularly said or assumed nowadays that embracing the legitimacy of particularism in scholarship requires becoming a global antirealist—requires holding that there is no way things are except relative to our conceptual schemes. I disagree. The fact that we cannot render inoperative our particularist identities so as to function just *qua* human beings in no way implies that there's not a ready-made world awaiting our discovery, nor does it imply that truth in beliefs consists in coherence rather than in correspondence between the content of one's beliefs and the facts. It is regularly said or assumed nowadays that each "perspective" is as good as any other. I disagree. A good deal of what many believe is such that they are not entitled to believe it. It is regularly said or assumed nowadays that the academy is nothing but a constellation of clusters of power, and that claiming knowledge is a scarcely concealed device for gaining power over others. I firmly disagree. I do not deny that power is often used illegitimately in the academy; Calvinist that I am, I expect it! Nonetheless I insist that often when we give reasons for and against some position, and when we claim to have achieved knowledge, we are not just exerting power. Sometimes our reasons are good ones; sometimes our knowledge-claims are true. It is regularly said or assumed nowadays that it is impossible for those who embrace one particularity to talk and reason with those who embrace another. I disagree. Of course it's true that when talking across the particularities which reflect our identities we often reach a stalemate; but that's not how it always goes, and when it does go that way, our challenge and calling is to seek a way of overcoming the stalemates. It is regularly said or assumed nowadays that the reason for allowing standing in the academy to the particularities of the once-disenfranchised standing is either that their power makes it advisable or that equity requires it. I disagree. Equity does indeed require it; but what's more important even than equity is that those with a particularity distinct from one's own are often capable of discerning dimensions of reality that escape those who share one's own narrative identity. Not only justice but truth requires it.

My disagreements with my fellow particularists are thus multiple and deep. Nonetheless, I too hold that we cannot render inoperative all our particular identities as we engage in academic learning. Nor, I have just suggested, should we do so if we could. For particularity is not always obstructive bias. Augustine was right: particularities sometimes enable access to reality—including then, so I would argue, certain religious particularities. *Credo ut intelligam.* I believe so that I may understand.

2 | Does Religion Have Anything Worth Saying to Scholars?

JAMES TURNER

Although probably not ignorant or stupid by the standards of the world at large, neither am I broadly cultivated, widely learned, or philosophically acute. Hence I approach with trepidation the subject of this brief essay, because those extraordinary qualities are the minimum requirements for adequately carrying out the assignment I have perhaps foolishly taken on.

This assignment is to argue the following proposition: that research in the humanities and social sciences will benefit if scholars today pay renewed attention to deploying within their different disciplines the *intellectual* traditions associated with Judaism, Christianity, and Islam. The qualifier "intellectual" requires emphasis because religions are complex, lived webs of ritual, spirituality, custom, creed, institutions, mores, morals, and much more. The object of scrutiny in this essay is *not* Judaism, Christianity, or Islam, but rather the thickets of ideas that have grown up, as it were, around and within these religions and that can be explored by any inquirer, regardless of whether she or he is personally involved with the faith in question.

The listing of these three faiths is not meant to disparage the intellectual traditions of other faiths that might also prove helpful. It is simply to point to three historical facts: (1) the overlapping intellectual entailments during many centuries of each of these religions with the others; (2) the highly rationalized character of some traditions within each; and (3) the contributions of all three over the past two millennia to the evolution of the European university culture—latterly exported to other continents—out of which emerged the diverse academic disciplines practiced today.

This discussion is a very different kind of enterprise than that undertaken by other authors in this volume who are concerned with intellectual consequences stemming from personal faith or personal experience of religion. I am concerned with intellectual consequences of what may be regarded as impersonal traditions, intellectual resources potentially available to anyone, without regard to individual faith or background. That is, in the same way that a Thatcherite neo-liberal can read Marx with comprehension and even learn from him, so an atheist can read Maimonides and still learn from him. Yet is this true? Can the atheist really learn from Maimonides—or only *about* him? That is the question. Put differently, are there academic grounds, not religious ones, for encouraging what would amount to partial integration of the intellectual life of religion with the intellectual life of universities? I say "partial" because collapsing the one into the other, even if it were possible, would hardly benefit either.

This massive question being posed, realism requires that I immediately back away from most of it. A short essay can do no more than offer sketchy observations. Limitations of my own background and reading mean that even these inadequate comments will draw mostly on Roman Catholic examples. Narrow, this approach confessedly is. But perhaps the narrowness is not crippling since, after all, Catholic traditions in their origins developed from Jewish ones, and they frequently overlap Protestant and Orthodox ones.

A famous example provides a good starting point for my reflections. In *Sources of the Self*, Charles Taylor makes the point that "it was Augustine who introduced the inwardness of radical reflexivity and bequeathed it to the Western tradition of thought. The step was a fateful one, because we have certainly made a big thing of the first-person standpoint. . . . It has gone so far as generating the view that there is a special domain of 'inner' objects available only from this standpoint; or the notion that the vantage point of the 'I think' is somehow outside the world of things we experience."[1] If Taylor is right, one of the most deeply formative concepts underlying our thinking today has a Christian origin. Now, one might plausibly respond to this claim, "Okay; so what? Where the idea came from matters not a whit, except to historians. It now exists and functions in our thinking in purely secularized form, stripped of any religious implications or connection with a God."

This answer seems to me partly true, but also too easy. For, as Taylor goes on to note, Augustine developed his "radical reflexivity" precisely as "a step on our road back to God."[2] It strains credibility to claim that this telos left no permanent mark whatsoever on the character of Western subjectivity. Yet the very fact that the Christian origins of subjectivity have, so to speak, gone underground may hide such distinctive marks from us. Were scholars to excavate and explore the specifically religious lineaments of subjectivity, they might help us better to understand prevailing notions of self-consciousness and inner life, whether in psychology, philosophy, or other disciplines.

One could make analogous observations about less world-shaking but nonetheless consequential topics. Caroline Bynum, in her eulogy at the memorial service for the distinguished medieval historian David Herlihy, spoke of Herlihy's role as the great pioneer of women's history in medieval studies. She traced his innovations back to their source in Herlihy's interest in the discourse of spiritual friendship of men and women in the monastic tradition.[3] Simply as the origin of a historiographic innovation, this connection deserves note. But I wonder *how* this specific context shaped Herlihy's thinking and *whether*, therefore, the conceptual apparatus of gender in medieval studies is inflected by these Catholic intellectual traditions. Or, to turn to another discipline, the social efficacy of symbolism in cultural anthropology, from Malinowski onward, is hard to imagine without the precedent of Jewish and Christian thought. But has anyone asked how these roots nourish and limit the anthropological category?

What I am suggesting is neither religious studies nor theology but something distinctly different: trying to forward, through research within so-called secular academic disciplines, the rediscovery and reappropriation of the efficacy of Catholic and other monotheistic religious traditions, *for the benefit* of those academic disciplines. Paradoxically, the full development of "secular" knowledge may now require reversing the secularization of knowledge.

Were such a shifting of gears to occur, the benefits might well go beyond fuller comprehension of "how we think now." Researchers in the various academic disciplines might actually discover, or rediscover, intellectual resources that enable them to work out new lines of thinking, develop approaches to problems that could not evolve from standard sources in their fields. David Herlihy's research in women's history already hints how this could happen, though in that particular case one suspects that medieval history could not in any case have long remained untouched by the revolution in women's studies. A better example may be the rapid and rather remarkable development of just-war theory in political science in the past two or three decades. In the wake of the Vietnam War, American political theorists found themselves searching for better tools for analyzing the circumstances under which military force might become a valid option for a government. Scholars such as Jean Bethke Elshtain found such instruments not in the "secular" toolbox of their discipline but in ancient Jewish and Christian thinking about the use of force and violence by the powers-that-be: in Elshtain's case, especially Augustine's writings. As a result, just-war theory has been habilitated as a key discourse within political science and seems even to have affected war planning in the Pentagon.

It is not hard to imagine other possibilities. The principle of subsidiarity, as developed in Catholic social teaching, played a pivotal role in the working out of the constitutional arrangements of the European Union. Might that principle, and other Christian teachings on the nature and limits of state power, prove more broadly helpful to political scientists? They now cope with a world in which regional devolution, on the one hand, and supragovernmental entities like the UN and NGOs and multinational corporations, on the other, make hash of the traditional idea of sovereignty as the dominant category for understanding "the state." Where does sovereignty reside in the European Union? Roman Catholic thinking, never friendly to the notion of sovereignty (in part because national states threatened the universal church's own claims), makes available more flexible ways of conceptualizing government power. Likewise, the rout of Marxism leaves mainstream political economy with only an individualistic idea of property unencumbered by social obligations. Kathryn Tanner of the University of Chicago has suggested that Christian traditions provide a starting point for alternative and more complex ways of defining property, which could enrich the thinking of economists and make it more responsive to real-world conditions.[4]

I am neither a political scientist nor an economist, and am incompetent to judge whether these diverse suggestions would in fact prove rich in consequences within these disciplines. In any case, one objection to such a call for a revival of attention to Catholic (and, more broadly, Abrahamic) intellectual traditions is immediately obvious: a skeptic might plausibly retort that the whole business amounts to much ado about nothing. Scholars can already graze in whatever meadows they wish, munching on Maimonides and Anselm just as easily as Nietzsche and Bourdieu. No bar obstructs the exploration of the intellectual traditions of Western monotheism, as indeed the examples of David Herlihy and Jean Elshtain make clear. And, anyway, what gives Judaism, Christianity, and Islam primacy? Could not the same claims be made about Hinduism or Buddhism or Confucianism? And, if so, am I not, in the end, just urging scholars to keep their intellectual horizons open to all kinds of possibly fertile ideas from outside their disciplines? Who would say no to that—or to mother-hood and apple pie?

These are well-aimed questions, but they miss the target. True, there is no formal bar to the use of any intellectual tradition whatsoever in con-temporary scholarship. Neither is there any official obstacle to first-string linemen on the Florida State University football team majoring in astro-physics. Few, however, are observed to do so, for the culture of big-time college football does not nourish in its inhabitants an interest in the more rigorous and arcane sciences. There is likewise, I believe, a scholarly cul-ture that tends to assume that religion is a dead force intellectually: that its traditions, however interesting as objects of study for historians or an-thropologists, do not speak to live issues in scholarship today. A scholar of literature is far more likely to recur to Nietzsche than to Augustine; a po-litical scientist is far more likely to pay attention to John Rawls than to John XXIII. It is probably not accidental that the scholars mentioned above as explorers of the intellectual potential of religious traditions all have personal allegiances to religions. And precisely because Western monotheism now lies beyond the pale of the academy, it "has going for it," in Kathryn Tanner's words, "a strangeness, an ability to startle."[5]

To be sure, Buddhism might also startle. But Buddhism was not con-tinually and thickly implicated in the formation of the Western intellectual traditions from which spring all contemporary academic disciplines. West-ern monotheism was. For this reason, the intellectual traditions of the Abrahamic faiths have "the potential" (again quoting Tanner) "to demand attention from a Western audience."[6] They are (one could argue further) likely to adapt more easily to the discourse of academic disci-plines and to apply more directly to actual questions raised in academic re-search even today.

I am far from proposing some Great Instauration, still less a *Novum Or-ganum*. I am simply suggesting that academic work would benefit very substantially from a self-conscious, well-planned return to the sources, from a deliberate, thoughtful effort to recover and reappropriate for con-temporary scholarship the intellectual traditions of Judaism, Christianity, and Islam.

Nor do I think that scholarship would be the only beneficiary. I have been writing as a scholar, with the interests of scholarship in mind. But I am also a Christian, a Roman Catholic. The thinking of my church—and, mutatis mutandis, that of other denominations in the United States—has proceeded for the last century in odd isolation from the intellectual life of universities. The drafters of, for instance, papal encyclicals and national pastoral letters have not (at least not in recent decades) ignored non-Catholic and nontheological thinking. But these ecclesiastical writers have not lived in day-to-day contact with it; they have had, so to speak, to strain to bring together two discourses not routinely on speaking terms. This relative isolation has impoverished theological and moral reflection. Were academic work systematically more involved with Catholic intellectual traditions, were the gap between the intellectual world of religion and the intellectual world of universities more effectively bridged, the thinking of the academy would be more accessible to the intellectual workers of the church. The thinking of the church might eventually grow more nuanced, more supple, more in touch with the culture it hopes to influence.

The persisting suspicion of religion within the academy has good historical grounds, as no one knows better than a historian of higher education such as myself. The dissolution of the Christian framework of academic inquiry opened important new paths of knowledge; the relaxing of the Protestant grip on American higher education opened colleges and universities to groups formerly excluded or demeaned, notably Jews and Catholics. It would be dangerous to forget why tension exists between religion and academic knowledge. But it would be ironic as well as foolish to allow a justified cautiousness to block potential paths to knowledge today. If we could allay the tension and open the doors, both religion and the academy might be the better for it.

Notes

1. Charles Taylor, *Sources of the Self: The Making of the Modern Identity* (Cambridge, Mass.: Harvard University Press, 1989), 131.

2. Ibid., 132.

3. Personal information.

4. Kathryn Tanner, "Economies of Grace," working draft presented to the Erasmus Institute's fellows' seminar, April 1999.

5. Ibid., 1.

6. Ibid.

The Potential for Pluralism

Religious Responses to the Triumph of Theory and Method in American Academic Culture

ALAN WOLFE

Theory and Method in the American Academy

The recent death of Isaiah Berlin, together with the publication of a biography of him and a collection of his representative essays, suggests that, despite his failure to publish a systematic treatise, Berlin was among the most original philosophical voices of this century.[1] An appreciation of his work leads inevitably to a concern with pluralism, raising the question of whether human beings are better off attempting to maximize one particular good to the best of their ability or trying to live with diverse, sometimes mutually exclusive, goods, even if the cost of doing so is the inability to maximize any of them.

Berlin was a defender of pluralism not only in politics but also in understanding. He argued that, just as we seek diverse goods, we should also appreciate diverse ways of knowing the world. Indeed one of the least appreciated aspects of Berlin's writings are his passionate statements about what could be called, in contemporary parlance, academic culture. Berlin himself was trained in the hothouse environment of analytic philosophy at Oxford but eventually decided that its rigorous pursuit of relatively narrow questions did not fit his way of thinking about the world. He is often credited with developing the field now called "the history of ideas" as an alternative. At the time he did so, there was no real place for such an academic discipline at Oxford, leaving Berlin, although he was honored with extraordinarily prestigious positions from a relatively early age, somewhat marginal to the academic disciplines of his time. As his biographer makes clear, Berlin's fame rested largely on activities outside the academy: wartime work in Washington, BBC broadcasts, and an insatiable appetite for hobnobbing with influential figures.[2]

Perhaps because of his experiences outside of academia, Berlin became an effective critic of what might be called the imperial pretensions of academic theory. His study of Marxism, combined with his experiences as a child in St. Petersburg, had already led him to be critical of totalizing theories which ambitiously seek to explain the entire world through one causal law of history. But, in typical fashion, Berlin did not merely identify such efforts at totalization as synonymous with Marxism but instead tried to delineate a particular style of thought attractive to people with many different objectives but united in their commitment to the relentless pursuit of one idea. Condorcet and Comte, not Karl Marx, are in many ways Berlin's real target. Of Comte, Berlin writes that his understanding of the social sciences aimed at "one complete and all-embracing pyramid of scientific knowledge; one method; one truth; one scale of rational, 'scientific' values." "This naïve craving for unity and symmetry at the expense of experience," Berlin concluded, "is with us still."[3]

For Berlin all such attempts to reduce our understanding of human beings to one system threatened to deprive people of their freedom. Individuals must, in Berlin's view, have the freedom to make choices, for without that freedom they cannot be considered responsible. Yet totalistic theories of society, certain as they are that they have uncovered the secrets of how societies "really" work, base themselves on the denial of human choice. If people really understood what the social scientist does they would avoid ignorant and ill-informed choices—at least according to the social scientists. "The more we know," as Berlin summarizes their viewpoint, "the greater the relief from the burden of choice."[4] Worried about the arrogance and unfreedom of imperialistic social science, Berlin discovered in humanistic thinkers a tragic sense of life that warned against making individuals perfect—all too perfect. This did not lead him to conclude that social scientific knowledge was illegitimate or wrong. "It is plainly a good thing," he wrote, "that we should be reminded by social scientists that the scope of human choice is a good deal more limited than we suppose."[5] The obvious way to preserve the value of social science theorizing while also recognizing its limits was to be pluralistic. Because human beings are complicated creatures who desire contradictory goods, the study of human beings must itself be a complicated affair, devoted to many, sometimes incompatible, ways of knowing. No one approach to the understanding of human beings ought ever to be permitted to drive all others out of existence.

Yet a case could be made that, in the contemporary academy, something like this has indeed taken place. I am not referring here to scientific disciplines. The study of nonhuman phenomena (or creatures) does not raise issues of pluralism in the same way as the study of human beings, since the former not only fail to desire contradictory goods, they also, in some cases, fail to desire any goods at all. Scientific disciplines do have bitter controversies over method. Even when data is "hard," moreover, interpretation can be "soft." In science, like in every other field of knowledge, academic freedom and a willingness to consider divergent points of view are requirements for the pursuit of truth. But science is not, and need not be, pluralistic once truths are established, for the task of the scientist is to build upon fact in order to reach the next level of analysis. The social sciences, by contrast, have both an explanatory and a normative character, and to the degree that the latter plays a role—which it must if the subjects under study are norm-making and norm-altering creatures—pluralism of method and approach becomes essential. Unfortunately, developments in the social sciences in recent years can only be described as a setback for pluralist ways of understanding.

The example of the lack of pluralism in the contemporary academy comes from the field of political science, more interesting because the theory in question—rational choice theory—is one that, seemingly in contradiction to Berlin's fears, prides itself on its commitment to human freedom. Arising out of micro-economics, rational choice theory has its roots in versions of libertarianism distrustful of government and dedicated to advancing freedom of choice as a normative goal. Yet when adopted by political science departments as a model for how scholarship ought to be conducted, the success of rational choice theory does seem to confirm Berlin's fears. For one thing, this theory is reductionist, constantly seeking to show why behavior which might seem to contradict its premises—altruism, for example—can nonetheless be explained in terms of rational choice.[6] In its unwillingness to recognize other forms of behavior than the one it prefers, rational choice theory demonstrates quite well the illiberalism of certain forms of liberalism, as if the wide variety of human behavior throughout the world has to be channeled into one thing and one thing only.

At the same time, rational choice theory has little respect for pluralism in the organization of academic life. Departments committed to rational choice theory generally can never have enough rational choice theorists. Political science being what it is, there will in any department be some individuals who are not committed to rational choice: political theorists for example. But it is possible to redefine political theory as "formal theory," thereby bringing a rational choice perspective to that aspect of the discipline. Or if tenure has insured that the political theorists in a department otherwise committed to rational choice are feminists or Straussians, they can essentially be left alone while the serious business of political science takes place elsewhere. But whatever the strategy, pluralistic departments of political science are unlikely to result once strong commitments to rational choice have been established. Since this theory and only this theory is presumed to be the basis for a proper understanding of human political behavior, hiring people with a different orientation—say, a historical or institutional understanding of politics—seems a silly waste of valuable resources.

I confess to being flabbergasted by the popularity of rational choice theory. As a participant in the radical attack on "behavioral" political science in the 1960s, I was certain that the sheer irrelevance of the research then undertaken was matched only by its inability to establish findings beyond the obvious.[7] I neglected what could be called "sociology of knowledge" reasons for the perpetuation of scientific models as the proper way to study politics. Large numbers of students were attending graduate schools, hoping to become professors in the rapidly expanding universe of higher education. Social science research was increasingly being funded by federal agencies. Graduate education came to wag the tail of undergraduate education. The only research model which seemed to be compatible with the evolving structure of academic organization in the United States was a form of knowledge production emphasizing the publication of journal articles rather than books, based on research carried out by teams, and emphasizing quantity of publication over quality.

My own attraction to the social sciences came about as a result of an undergraduate course I took at Temple University which introduced students to works of social criticism by scholars such as David Riesman, C. Wright Mills, and William F. Whyte. (I am teaching very much the same course now.) As someone "politicized" by the civil rights movement and Vietnam, furthermore, I was attracted to the political sociology then being practiced by scholars like Seymour Martin Lipset and Daniel Bell. Although

I imagined myself in those days far too radical to be comfortable with their centrist political viewpoints, I viewed them as first-rate scholars and writers, dealing with important subjects in well-researched and well-written books. They also taught at America's leading universities, leading me to conclude that work along the lines they did was the key to academic success.

Only much later did I learn how marginal many of these scholars were to their universities and their disciplines. Riesman, a lawyer without a social science doctorate, was all but ignored by Harvard's majordomo, Talcott Parsons. Daniel Bell and Nathan Glazer had worked in journalism, making them always somewhat tainted among professional academics. Lipset wrote books, when it was far more prestigious within the academic world to publish articles in refereed journals. Reinhard Bendix, like other European émigrés and refugees who had studied in the shadow of Max Weber and Karl Mannheim, could never be replaced. To my somewhat naïve eye, American social science departments were pluralistic because Columbia had both Paul Lazarsfeld and Robert K. Merton to do the science and C. Wright Mills to do the social criticism, while Harvard had both social relations and social studies. But such pluralism was more of a façade than a reality, since rarely did one faction hold the other in any respect.

Academic pluralism, if that is what it was, also proved to be tenuous. Once upon a time the fields with which I identify—sociology and political science—were also bifurcated geographically. There was something called "Midwestern social science." Led primarily by Michigan and Wisconsin, political scientists at Big Ten universities concentrated on studies of the American electorate, developing comprehensive data bases and taking the lead in article publication. Ivy League and West Coast universities, by contrast, were more "book" oriented and more likely to contain at least a few scholars who leaned in the direction of becoming public intellectuals.[8] Over the past twenty years, however, the coastal universities have been thoroughly "midwesternized." Harvard's sociology department never replaced Riesman, Bell, and Glazer after their retirements. With the exception of Orlando Patterson, who has been in the department for nearly thirty years, and Theda Skocpol, who was tenured only after a lawsuit and who has in any case moved into political science, Harvard's sociology department built itself up by recruiting full professors from

Wisconsin, North Carolina, Northwestern, and Ohio State. Much the same took place at Columbia (where Herbert Gans and Allan Silver no longer fit the department's profile) and Cornell (the home of Robin Williams). With a few exceptions—the University of Virginia, New York University, Berkeley—there is generally only one way to be considered professionally serious in the social sciences, and that is the one rooted in a model borrowed from the natural sciences.

I have no doubt that a great deal of good has emerged from the efforts I have described to make the social sciences more rigorous. Much of our understanding of social life has been enriched by systematic efforts to gather data that are then treated rigorously so that ideas about reality can be tested against measured dollops of that reality. Even the sociology of religion, a subject matter that comes closest to exploring the most subjective and meaning-laden aspects of human experience, can benefit from an emphasis on rational choice, as witnessed in the work of Rodney Stark.[9] Social science without the quantitative imagination would be hardly worth having. But neither would social science without the sensibility of a David Riesman or Daniel Bell. Because social science studies human beings, creatures who, as Isaiah Berlin insists, pursue many competing goods, they can only be studied by methods which also reflect many different, and sometimes contrasting, understandings of their actions. If pluralism in method and approach ought to be the guiding way to organize academic life in the social sciences and the humanities, that test has been failed.

Religious Institutions as One Exception

As a student entering college in the somehow appropriate year of 1960, I knew that there were religious institutions of higher education, although it never occurred to me to think about attending one. Catholic universities, in the circles in which I traveled, were best known for their basketball teams, while their academic qualities, as far as I could see, lay more in conveying dogma than in understanding the world. (Villanova, St. Joseph's, and LaSalle were the leading ones around where I grew up.) I barely knew that Protestant institutions existed, and when I discovered one for the first time, called David Libscomb College in Nashville, and learned of the strict rules governing campus life, I could not believe that the place was in the twentieth century. As for Jewish universities, they were not even on my family's radar screen, since the whole point of being Jewish was to succeed in secular America. Call this prejudice, if you want, for no doubt I knew too little about what was actually happening in those places for which I had so little respect. But I also do not think my reaction can be completely attributed to ignorance. There was something insular about many of those institutions at that time. They did make claims to already know what they needed to know, making instruction seem more like the conveyance of dogma than the search for understanding. It was more important for them to keep the loyalty of their alumni than to attract the best faculty. If one were looking for a model of how to educate people broadly so that they could, upon graduation, go out into the world not only learned but with strong critical sensibilities, one would hardly think first of faith-based institutions.

There are ironies in the transformation of religious colleges and universities over the past thirty years fully as surprising as those by which the 1960s generation of student radicals became the apologists for the 1990s university. At the time I was active in protesting the nature of political science, I would have been aghast had anyone told me that someday I would be relatively sympathetic toward religious institutions of higher learning. But now, as I try to survey the American academic landscape, the conspicuous exception to the antipluralist pattern I have been describing are America's faith-based colleges and universities. Here one can find an academic culture less completely transformed by the single-minded drive toward theory in the humanities and data in the social sciences witnessed elsewhere in American academic life. While there will always be exceptions, philosophy departments at many institutions of higher learning which take their religious mission seriously continue to be interested in Continental philosophy and thus are relatively untouched by the emphasis in the rest of the discipline on analytic methods or the clarification of scientific concepts. A concern with religious themes in poetry, the novel, works of art, and music makes it difficult for departments in the humanities to treat those forms of "cultural production" as if their actual content was irrelevant to the questions we have about them. And political science departments in many faith-based colleges pay more attention to political theory and to the actual institutions of politics in the real world than political science departments in the secular culture, often, in the process, resisting some of the trends toward empirical methods and formal theorizing.

This is not to say that faith-based institutions can be characterized as pluralist. Many of them insist on the priority of the faith which guides them, inevitably assigning second-class status to approaches or beliefs associated with other faiths—or with no faith at all. Careful to preserve the tradition, religious institutions are less impressed by work that offers itself as the "cutting-edge" of new ways of theorizing the world. Often unable to compete with the salaries paid to academic superstars in the humanities, religious institutions try to do the best with what they have. If they retain more of a commitment to the liberal arts and to general education than the more prestigious private universities, this may be because they are more successful in recruiting excellent undergraduates than graduate students. The potential for pluralism, in other words, can be found at faith-based institutions almost in spite of themselves. Sometimes, nonetheless, religious colleges and universities will find themselves with highly ranked departments aggressively competing for prestige on the terrain established by secular institutions: Notre Dame's sociology department, for example, one of the best in the country, is widely regarded as a quantitative department. Still, if one wants to find a version of the academic culture which existed before the totalizing tendencies of recent years—one which has all the attractions of a skepticism toward academic pretension, as well as all the problems of a certain insecurity and insularity—then one must turn to faith-based colleges and universities.

No one knows whether religious institutions will continue to serve as a viable alternative to the dominant academic culture in America. There clearly are forces urging them not to do so. George Marsden has written about the pressures that follow when religious institutions opt to modernize and to join the academic mainstream.[10] But there are also threats from the other direction, ones which do not challenge the stature of these institutions as alternatives—quite the contrary, for they insist on their theological character—but may challenge their ability to be a *viable* alternative in an otherwise secular culture. Most prominent among them is the question of *Ex Corde Ecclesiae,* which seeks to strengthen the specifically Catholic character of American Catholic colleges and universities. But it is not just Catholic institutions that may be facing pressure to become more orthodox. All institutions of higher learning are dependent on their core constituencies for financial support. Public institutions have to worry about state legislatures. Elite private universities study the mores of suburban families with as much zeal as those families study the admissions processes of elite private universities. And the future of faith-based institutions will inevitably be linked to the nature of the faith-based communities they serve. Among Jews, therefore, Yeshiva University will respond to the resurgence of orthodoxy and ultraorthodoxy in ways that may strengthen the historic mission of the institution but which will also insure its isolation from the mainstream of American academic life. Even Brandeis University, which historically has been suspect among the most orthodox Jews, will find its character altered by the strength of religious traditionalism. Brandeis' secular orientation was at its strongest when assimilation and intermarriage marked the Jewish experience in America. Now when Jews can attend any university for which they can qualify, Brandeis, to carve out a market niche, needs to protect its reputation as a general university while appealing to those Jews in search of reaffirmations of their faith.

Protestant colleges also find themselves the beneficiaries of a return to religion in the secular culture. Parents dissatisfied with binge drinking, fraternities, and the peer pressure to which young people are so vulnerable are increasingly looking to evangelical colleges as an alternative. Campuslife issues have an unpredictable relationship with curricular issues, but there can be little doubt that traditionalism in the office of Dean of Students will have an impact on faculty culture as well. Max Weber wrote about the paradox of success: John Wesley worried that Methodist piety would produce people so economically successful that they would lose their taste for Methodist piety.[11] In some ways, faith-based institutions face the opposite problem: they cannot be pious enough, at least in the eyes of their natural constituents, but responding to their piety can further isolate them from what passes for success in the academic culture. Religious colleges and universities do not face conflicts between their mission and the forces of modernization at only one time. These are ongoing tensions, and the next time they are resolved it may be more in the direction of faith than it was when Northwestern or Emory were making their decisions to join with the dominant secular culture.

Caught, as they always have been, between the forces of modernization and the attractions of faith, religious institutions face a future that no one can predict. Yet if there are to remain alternatives to the dominant secular culture, the future of those institutions is important to all students of higher education and not just those seeking to protect and preserve faith-based communities. I can envision three ways in which faith-based colleges and universities will respond to their present dilemma of choosing between pressures toward orthodoxy and fulfilling their potential for pluralism. I will call these rejectionism, parallelism, and opportunism. In the final section of this paper, I want to make an argument in favor of the last of them.

Three Responses

By rejectionism, I mean the option of joining with assertions of orthodoxy in an effort to return religious institutions to a position of instruction in the faith. There will be some, strongly committed to their faith, who will view pressures toward orthodoxy as positive developments and will feel obligated to encourage them. I wonder, however, whether rejectionism, whatever one's views about it, is even possible, at least for all those religious institutions which are not at the margins of American academic life. To have some sense of the viability of rejectionism, we all ought to watch with care the response of America's leading Catholic colleges and universities to *Ex Corde Ecclesiae.*

The response to this point has certainly not been one of universal praise. The Jesuit magazine *America* has called the latest draft of norms "unworkable and dangerous."[12] The president and former president of two of America's most prominent Catholic universities similarly found the document "positively dangerous" to Catholic institutions of higher education and warned of "havoc" if it were implemented.[13] From the perspective of someone like myself, who is not Catholic but who admires much of the scholarship at Catholic universities, the bishops' recommendations as written appear to make it impossible for Catholic colleges to preserve their character as it has evolved over the past three or four decades, making the price of rejectionism high indeed. But this is a matter that clearly will have to be worked out between the bishops and the presidents, trustees, and theology faculty of Catholic universities, and one can only hope that whatever resolution finally emerges, it is one that respects the pluralism these institutions have embodied. The great fear, by contrast, at least on my part, would be one in which these colleges were tempted to return to orthodoxy.

If there were such a rejection of modernity in favor of faith, it would certainly not be the first time. The American academic environment has always been capacious enough to include at least a few institutions which reject much of the world around them, such as Grove City College in Pennsylvania which consistently turned down federal funding as a way of avoiding what it considered to be intrusive federal regulation. One can easily imagine Protestant and perhaps some Jewish colleges responding to new pressures for orthodoxy by withdrawing from the world in ways familiar to us from the writings of Max Weber.[14] But they are almost certain to be small in number, which means, for many institutions, the search for other alternatives.

A second possible response to the situation in which religious colleges and universities find themselves would be to protect what I will call parallelism. By parallelism I mean the existence of more than one kind of academic culture within an institution, but structured in such a way that these various subcultures have little in common with each other but instead operate as if they were on parallel tracks. The temptations of parallelism can be found among those committed to a particular version of what George Marsden has called "the outrageous idea of Christian scholarship."[15] I have in mind the version that finds attractive the development of various kinds of "perspectivism" in the contemporary university. Not displeased to witness the collapse of Enlightenment projects based on the unity of knowledge, such scholars, while not necessarily attracted to feminism or multiculturalism, argue that such movements are correct to emphasize the partiality of knowledge in the contemporary world. Since the university acknowledges no one overriding truth, it follows that a Christian way of understanding the world constitutes a particular perspective which has just as much legitimacy as any other way of understanding the world.

The point I want to make about this attraction to perspectivism is not an epistemological one but a sociological one. Whether or not the philosophical claims undergirding perspectivism can be sustained, the concrete result of its appeal is to generate a series of academic subcultures each of which is committed to a particular approach but, because of its self-referential quality, has little to say to others who work from a different perspective.

The issue, in a word, is not whether there are feminist or Christian ways of knowing, but whether there are feminist or Christian ways of granting tenure. For the creation of parallel subcultures within the university usually leads to a situation in which each subculture generates its own journals, its own circles of prestige, its own career paths, and, finally, its own claims to be the sole judge of those working within the parallel tradition.

When many parallel subcultures exist side by side in the contemporary university, the result is clearly not rejectionist. Advocates of particular points of view, including Christian points of view, accept rather than dismiss the forms and functions of the contemporary university: they emphasize the importance of the academic vocation, are committed to scholarship, and try to influence national debates about subjects of importance to them. But while such approaches are not rejectionist, neither are they pluralist. One does not, from a position of parallelism, enter the fray of academic debate prepared to have one's first assumptions open to scrutiny of others. Interaction with others outside one's perspective is not so much a situation of give-and-take as it is a kind of, at best, peaceful coexistence. Ways of knowing are not dissimilar from ways of life. And if ways of life are at stake, then the impulse of parallelism is defensive and protectionist. Parallelism survives by a kind of mutual suspicion. Its approach is not so much to welcome other points of view as to encourage a situation of academic laissez-faire which allows one point of view to exist so long as it agrees not to challenge the existence of other points of view.

Catholic universities have become homes for many types of parallel subcultures. It may make sense, therefore, for those responding to such pressures as *Ex Corde* to react by emphasizing the importance of parallelism to such institutions; indeed *Ex Corde* itself, with its proposed way of treating theology departments at Catholic colleges and universities in a way different from other departments, seems to endorse one version of parallelism. It may be that parallelism is an attraction in Catholic colleges because such colleges have always been to some degree parallel to other academic institutions in America. Not so long ago, after all, Catholic universities embodied a conservative alternative to the dominant liberal culture of the American academy, and one that was therefore attractive to dissenters seeking a place in a general system of higher education to which they felt marginal.

Yet this situation is no longer the case. Many religious institutions have willingly joined a national academic culture that has committed itself to such notions as academic freedom and hiring through merit. In some cases, Catholic commitments to liberalism go much further; indeed the position of the Catholic bishops on both domestic and foreign policy, with the exception of abortion, is closer to the left end of the contemporary political spectrum than to the right. The dilemma facing Catholic colleges and universities is that forms of parallelism have been essential to their growth into institutions of national prominence. They could rest at that point; after all, there is enough parallelism in secular research universities, usually embodied in feminist and multicultural perspectives, to enable Catholic colleges and universities to claim equality with them. But why should equality necessarily be enough?

There is, I believe, a third option facing Catholic colleges and universities as they struggle with the latest stage in the never-ending quest for the proper identity. I will call this option opportunism. I intend this term to be taken positively. Secular institutions, I have argued in this paper, are committed in theory to pluralism but rarely practice it; members of departments, whatever their orientation, usually like to hire people exactly like themselves and universities like to compare themselves to other universities like themselves. Religious institutions, by contrast, are not pluralistic in theory but have been forced by circumstances to have a potential for pluralism in practice. By opportunism I mean an effort to try to fill that potential.

This is not an opportunity all such institutions will welcome. Surely many, if not most, religious institutions have a greater obligation to the life of their faith than they do to the reform of American higher education. The fact that the leading secular universities have in many cases developed their own forms of dogma, complete with strict professions of faith, suspicion of outsiders, and arcane rituals is no reason why religious institutions, whose purposes are generally not pluralistic, should fill the resulting gap. Since appeals to live by one's principles are hard to resist, moreover, there are many reasons to believe that an atmosphere emphasizing greater religious orthodoxy is not one that would result in a search to fulfill pluralist potential.

Still, I think it would be a sad day for higher education if the lack of pluralism in the secular culture were matched by a lack of pluralism in the religious culture. Should that occur, we would indeed have a culture war in higher education, one in which the certain loser would be those, including myself, who think that culture wars of all kinds are far less preferable than efforts to live side by side with cultural and moral differences. But I do not think I would be the only one whose interests would not be served by such a situation. Should it come to pass that secular universities will continue down one path while faith-based colleges continue down another, both will be harmed.

I am not one of those writers prone to find fault with the modern research university. In my experience, faculty who pursue an active research agenda are often among the most stimulating and worthwhile teachers, while those who have given up on research all too often have given up on teaching—and on service to their communities—as well. Nor do I join with those critics of the research university, from the right or from the left, who mock its scholarship and consider its way of doing business as little more than serving the needs of a tenured, and out of touch, professorate. But not everything in the contemporary university is as good as it can be. In particular, undergraduate education is often given less consideration in tenure decision than work with graduate students, even as the tuition of the undergraduates pays for the whole thing. There is, moreover, a failure of too much academic research, particularly in the humanistic disciplines, to speak to the important issues facing our culture with which all citizens, including even professors, ought to be concerned. Finally, I find considerable truth in the arguments of David Damrosch, who uncovers in the mores of the contemporary university a kind of isolation, one that in turn can breed an atmosphere of resentment and irresponsibility.[16]

An engagement with religious traditions, as well as a willingness to live side by side with religious institutions, can, I believe, serve as a partial corrective to some of these tendencies. (I say partial because, suspicious of overzealous efforts to root out wrongdoing, I think some of them will never, and probably ought never, be changed.) One gift that religion can offer the humanities and social sciences is memory. All too much academic research, I believe, is committed to innovation for the sake of innovation, as if it will inevitably be the case that the newest ideas are the best ideas. This may well be true in the sciences, but when the history of sociological (or economic or political) thought is viewed as a curiosity of little relevance to what contemporary social scientists are doing, the results are often as trivial as they are arrogant. One of the enduring lessons I take from the Lilly Seminar on Religion and Higher Education is Mark Noll's comment that the Christian has an affinity with history, for his religion is a historical religion. Academics who knew more about the histories of their disciplines—let alone the histories of their universities—would be less likely to exaggerate their own innovations.

In addition, religious scholars and religious institutions can help prevent the academy from insulating itself against the larger questions of meaning and purpose within which it exists. In theory, America's tradition of separation of church and state ought to lead religious institutions to a withdrawal from society, while America's other great tradition of land-grant universities ought to lead secular institutions to an engagement and involvement with the social problems of the day. Yet in some ways the reverse has taken place. Big Ten universities, in emphasizing a highly professional and scientific model of academic success, prize detachment, while religious institutions, arising out of a need to define for themselves what kinds of institutions they are, are constantly reworking mission statements in an effort to emphasize their relevance to the society around them. One could, of course, argue that for the university, mission statements are inappropriate; the university ought to do what it does rather than try to articulate what it does. But I think that if research universities worried more about what kinds of goals they have, they would be more likely to look favorably on research with public relevance, emphasize their commitments to undergraduate students, and even try to make a place for public intellectuals as well as for scholars.

Any benefits which might flow to secular universities from greater respect for people and institutions committed to their faith are more than matched by the gains which religious institutions would obtain from engaging with secular universities on their own terms. For whatever they are worth, I offer my personal impressions of the faith-based scholarship and commentary with which I have become familiar through my involvement with the Lilly Seminar. The most striking characteristic of this work is its oscillation. One voice in which religious scholarship speaks is an insecure voice, as if those who are engaged in such work feel a need to prove that they really do belong in the academy after all. Despite our faith, this message reads, we do pretty good work and you, the nonreligious folk presumed to sit in judgment over us, really ought to recognize this. Yet, on other occasions, religious scholars speak out of a sense of superiority, that because of their communities of faith, they have managed to avoid the ills plaguing everyone else in academic life, especially the isolation, competitiveness, and lack of purpose they see around them. One advantage of the opportunistic response I am advocating might be to tone down both attitudes: to give faith-based scholarship enough security so that it feels less need for a defensive stance and to give it enough respect for what happens in the secular university to recognize how much academics of all persuasions have in common.

An even greater benefit which might flow to religiously based institutions of higher education, if they took advantage of the opportunity to fulfill the pluralist potential they have been given, would be the avoidance of self-referentialism. A by-product of the paucity of pluralism in secular universities, I have argued, is the proliferation of academic subcommunities: whatever their other differences, postmodernists, rational choice theorists, Straussians, feminists, and critical race theorists tend to judge each other but to resist judgment from others. (Indeed one can foresee, if it has not already occurred, each of these subcommunities breaking up into sub-subcommunities, each with its own standards and prerogatives.) Despite, or perhaps because of, this sense of being a persecuted minority that can be found among religious scholars, a place can be made at the academic table for them. They would then become one more academic interest-group complete with their own journals, prestige circles, and professional associations.

This is a tendency that ought to be resisted for the same reason that postmodernists should not be allowed to be the sole evaluators of other postmodernists. In the social sciences (and to a lesser degree the humanities), an earlier generation's striving for objectivity has lost its legitimacy. There is something of value in that loss, for the notion that human beings could be studied without taking into account that human life is in significant measure moral and value-preferring proved to be naïve indeed. But one can also go too far in the other direction, as various Foucauldians have with their tiresome repetition that knowledge is political, a half-truth which in turn becomes the rationale for engagement in scholarship that is rarely tested against the criticism that comes from people outside the circle of like-minded believers. Given a history of religious sectarianism, there are certainly built-in tendencies for religious scholars to erect walls around their own work, to distrust the views of outsiders, and to use their work to reaffirm their faith. I leave it to others to wrestle with the complicated issue of how they can balance their faith-commitments with their commitments to truth. But so long as truth is part of the equation at all, they will suffer from a lack of exposure to criticism which comes from uncomfortable, sometimes even unwanted, sources. The lack of such criticism, I believe, is what gives so much trendy academic work its character as seemingly daring yet bloodless, unorthodox yet thoroughly predictable, and politically motivated without political content. It would be a terrible shame if the religious scholarship I have come to admire and respect were to duplicate, in form if not in content, work like that.

There is strong reason to believe that what Christopher Jencks and David Riesman in 1968 called "the academic revolution" is over. Those who know that book will recall that its title was not meant to refer to the student rebellions of the period but to a transformation of the university in which faculty professionalism would become the model of academic organization. Jencks and Riesman wrote their book with a strong commitment to the kind of academic pluralism I have been advocating, which explains why they spent so much time in women's colleges, black colleges, and religious institutions. The authors were not very hopeful about the prospects for Protestant institutions, noting in passing that such colleges could only survive by opposing the world of capitalist rationality that Protestantism did so much to create. In writing about Catholic higher education, about which they had more sympathy, Riesman and Jencks wrote that "there is as yet no American Catholic university that manages to fuse academic professionalism with concern for questions of ultimate social and moral importance,"[17] a goal, they believed, such institutions should seek to reach.

One can argue about whether religious institutions of all types ever did combine professionalism with ultimate questions in the way Jencks and Riesman hoped that Catholic institutions would. My sense is that while the task of balancing these competing goods is enormously difficult and sometimes impossible, faith-based institutions have done at least as well as, if not better than, secular institutions. The question now is whether they will continue along those lines or will move either in the direction of copying secular universities or in the direction of returning to their religious roots. Oddly enough, both of the latter directions, however opposite from each other, share the fact that neither is as pluralistic as the continuing struggle to reconcile objectives that work at cross-purposes.

Notes

1. Isaiah Berlin, *The Proper Study of Mankind: An Anthology of Essays* (New York: Farrar, Strauss, and Giroux, 1998); Michael Ignatieff, *Isaiah Berlin: A Life* (New York: Metropolitan Books, 1998).

2. Ignatieff, *Berlin*, 221–43.

3. Isaiah Berlin, "Historical Inevitability," in his *The Proper Study of Mankind*, 121.

4. Ibid., 156.

5. Ibid., 149.

6. An extensive critique of rational choice theory is contained in Donald P. Green and Ian Shapiro, *Pathologies of Rational Choice Theory : A Critique of Applications in Political Science* (New Haven: Yale University Press, 1994).

7. My own participation in the radical caucus within political science is described in Alan Wolfe and Marvin Surkin, eds., *An End to Political Science: The Caucus Papers* (New York: Basic Books, 1970).

8. Alan Wolfe, "Books Versus Journals: Two Ways of Publishing Sociology," *Sociological Forum* 5 (September 1990): 477–89.

9. Rodney Stark, *The Rise of Christianity: A Sociologist Reconsiders History* (Princeton: Princeton University Press, 1996).

10. George M. Marsden, *The Soul of the American University: From Protestant Establishment to Established Nonbelief* (New York: Oxford University Press, 1994). See also Philip Gleason, *Contending with Modernity: Catholic Higher Education in the Twentieth Century* (New York: Oxford University Press, 1995).

11. Max Weber, *The Protestant Ethic and the Spirit of Capitalism* (London: George Allen and Unwin, 1976), 175.

12. *America*, November 14, 1998.

13. J. Donald Monan, S.J., and Edward A. Malloy, C.S.C., "Ex Corde Ecclesiae Creates an Impasse," *America*, January 30, 1999.

14. Max Weber, "Religious Rejections of the World and Their Directions," in Hans Gerth and C. Wright Mills, eds., *From Max Weber: Essays in Sociology* (New York: Oxford University Press, 1946), 323–59.

15. George M. Marsden, *The Outrageous Idea of Christian Scholarship* (New York: Oxford University Press, 1997).

16. David Damrosch, *We Scholars: Changing the Culture of the University* (Cambridge: Harvard University Press, 1995).

17. Christopher Jencks and David Riesman, *The Academic Revolution* (Garden City: Doubleday, 1968), 405.

4 Enough Already

Universities Do Not Need More Christianity

DAVID A. HOLLINGER

Universities have reason to be proud of having created, within the most Christian of all industrialized societies of the North Atlantic West, a rare space in which ideas identified as Christian are not implicitly privileged. Our leading colleges and universities once shared in a pervasive Protestant culture, to which they owe a great deal. Now, however, mainstream academia maintains a certain critical distance from the Christian project. This critical distance is consistent with the drift of science and scholarship in the North Atlantic West. Not everyone is happy about this critical distance. The very topic "Religion and Higher Education" generally carries an implication that something is amiss. Higher education has gone too far in a secular direction, it is sometimes complained, and now pays too little respect to religious commitment in general and to Christian commitment in particular. I find this complaint hard to credit.

In defending mainstream academia's critical distance from Christian commitment here, I will not be suggesting that the men and women who are caught up in secular academia's workings are able always to live by the rules of fairness they espouse. Nor is my point that modern learning has so fully exhausted the intellectual resources of the classical religious traditions that it can responsibly pay no attention to them. I stress these disclaimers because I find that anyone who resists the movement to bring more Christian commitment back into academia is accused of being an uncritical defender of the status quo. At issue, rather, is *whether these imperfect academic communities can be improved by diminishing the critical distance from Christian cultural hegemony that they have achieved only after a long struggle.*

I put the question in this way because without this question there turns out to be little to discuss. I assert this with some conviction after three years of conversation within the admirably collegial Lilly Seminar. The overwhelming majority of the members of this seminar displayed a commitment to Christianity (I believe I was one of only four out of thirty who did not). Within this majority, a great many displayed a persistent if elusively articulated sense that American higher education was too aloof from religious commitment. Just where and how is this aloofness problematic? To this question the seminar was not able to come up with a coherent, agreed-upon answer. Of specific complaints from one concerned Christian or another there was no shortage, but most of these complaints proved too weak to generate sustained support even from coreligionists. Everyone in the seminar agreed, to be sure, that crude religion bashing could not be defended, that the serious academic study of religion should be higher than it now is on the agenda of several scholarly disciplines, and that this society needs a variety of kinds of institutions of higher education, including some that are religiously affiliated. And almost everyone agreed, after some friendly interrogation, that Christians were so well treated in the United States, even in elite academia, that it was a mistake to represent Christians as "victims." Many of the seminar's most animated discussions were well off the topic. It was common to grouse about this or that aspect of contemporary American academic life—its failure to live up to its own stated ideals was a favorite theme of some—but eventually someone would point out that what we were discussing was not much related to religion.

So, one might ask, what's all this about? The Lilly group was a seminar in search of a problem. But every now and then the search succeeded. In almost every such moment, a close reading of the transcripts will confirm, the problem proved to be some version of the question I have italicized above.

Here, in this post-seminar volume, I want to sketch several of the arguments I made during the seminar. In so doing, I will voice a skeptical perspective on the higher-education-and-religion conversation as it is now being pursued in the United States.

Many of those who want to reform academia in a more religious direction turn out, upon scrutiny, to be hoping to change the structure of plausibility taken for granted by the prevailing epistemic communities, but are slow to articulate and defend this program of reform. This initiative should be brought out into the open and debated. To do so, we need to begin with a familiar distinction.

Motivation and warrant; origins and verification; discovery and justification. These are three versions of an old distinction about science and scholarship that was drawn too sharply by the logical positivists, and by some of the theorists who preached against "the genetic fallacy." We now are quick to acknowledge that our decisions about what shall count as a standard for true belief may owe something to what motivates us to make a claim, or to hope that the claim may be proven true. And we are quick to acknowledge, too, that the prevailing modes of warrant in the epistemic community within which we work may also become part of our motivation for advancing a claim: we may be motivated to advance certain ideas because they are likely to be found true within a community whose approval we desire. But once these and other such caveats are entered against the old distinction, it can serve us well when we talk about religion and contemporary learned communities.

The personal circumstances of any individual inquirer exercise an important influence over what topics he or she will pursue and what approaches to those topics he or she will find attractive. There is no reason to doubt or lament this fact about inquiry. An individual's religious orientation may help to motivate an inquiry, a working hypothesis, and/or a specific claim one hopes to vindicate. But when it comes to warranting the claims made, what matters most are the rules, formal and tacit, of the relevant epistemic community. Those rules are of course contingent, and often contested. But that such rules exist, and are important, will be understood by anyone who has sat on a journal's editorial board, served on a prize committee, attended a tenure meeting, dispensed grant money, or helped an academy decide who should be elected to membership. If those rules fail to reflect a given religious orientation, then that religious orientation loses its salience in the warranting process. Even if an individual or a particular group finds that biblical evidence, or the evidence of immediate religious experience, helps to convince them of a particular truth, other kinds of evidence will be required to persuade the larger epistemic community of sociologists or physicists or historians.

I stress the cogency of this simple distinction between motivation and warrant because so many people have proven eager to avoid it. Often, the initiative to change warranting rules is obscured when a Christian believer says he or she simply wants to be able to declare a worldview openly. That sounds like an affirmation of a motive, and a request to be heard sympathetically when one affirms the motive publicly. When asked if this is all that's meant—when invited, that is, to accept the distinction between motivation and warrant, and to keep religion on the one side of it—some will see the point and say, "yes, the warranting process, if it is to work in a community that includes nonbelievers as well as believers, must operate by that community's structure of plausibility." Fair enough. Yet others will equivocate. It's "more complicated," they will say. They will complain that the rules of the mainstream academic communities are too narrow. There almost always follows a call for "tolerance," for a more "pluralistic" setting in which a variety of outlooks are entertained.

Pluralism in this context usually means accepting forms of evidence and reasoning that were once plausible within disciplinary communities in the social sciences and humanities but are no longer. There was once a time when scholars in the North Atlantic West took for granted a shared Christianity. In that bygone era, the boundaries of the epistemic community and the boundaries of the community of faith were largely coterminus. But now the boundaries of the epistemic communities that define discussion in the learned world are no longer coterminus with the Christian community of faith, and this fact appears to create discomfort on the part of some Christians. There are good reasons, too obvious in the intellectual history of the last three hundred years to bear repeating here, why the prevailing epistemic communities now have the boundaries that they do, and why these communities, as a consequence of their relative de-Christianization, no longer count biblical evidence and other religious experience particular to Christianity as relevant to the assessment of a truth-claim or an interpretation. At issue, then, is not whether learned communities should be tolerant or intolerant, pluralistic or nonpluralistic, flexible or inflexible, open or repressive; at issue rather is the specific direction the always ongoing revision of the epistemic rules of these communities should take.

An incident that took place during a meeting of the Lilly Seminar can illustrate the importance of the motivation-warrant distinction, and can also illustrate the ease with which this distinction can be obscured or evaded by well-meaning discussants who are eager to get Christianity more involved in the academic process. A speaker criticized the political science discipline, and presented his critique as growing directly out of his Catholic commitment. I asked him to specify the relevance of Catholicism to the critique. Was it simply a personal context in which he had developed the critique, and indeed a motive for thinking in this direction?

Was the critique one that only Catholics would be able to develop? Could non-Catholics accept the critique (it was manifest by this time that many non-Catholics in the room accepted the critique, so the significance of this question was all the more apparent)? Could the critique be justified on grounds that had nothing whatsoever to do with Catholicism? If the latter, was the relevance of Catholicism not confined to the context of motivation, and largely irrelevant to the context of warrant?

The speaker and several others struggled for some time with these questions. Several were determined to keep Catholics in possession of the critique, while eager to see it shared with the rest of the world. Eventually, one position won strong support in the group. It was as follows. Sure, non-Catholics can appreciate and make use of this critique, but if they detach it from the matrix out of which it came they will be failing to credit Catholicism for producing the critique. Catholicism is the inspiration for something valued by the larger community; hence the nurturing of Catholicism is in the interests of the larger community. We do not want to cut off this source of inspiration, which might happen if we neglected the tree from which the fruit was picked. This tree is likely to bear other good fruit. The questions I had raised, while provocative, were beside the point. What really mattered was the connection between good ideas and their matrix.

This position is remarkable in several respects. First, it invites the retort that when ideas we like come from matrices we dislike we do not make the nourish-the-tree argument. An example is the Nazi campaign against cancer and tobacco, many features of which prefigured programs that are now counted as wholesome in medical and public-health communities of the United States. We do not say, "Hey, this cancer breakthrough shows that the Nazi tree could bear good fruit, so let's see if trees of the fascist species bear other good fruit in regard to, say, race or retardation or government organization." Second, the position does not take into account the possibility that a lot of non-Catholics might have come up with the same ideas on their own, which would diminish the argument for watering the Catholic tree. The harvest of many orchards needs to be assessed before we can be sure just where our agricultural energies are best spent. Third, the position takes no account of the distressing possibility that when the entirety of the cherished tree or orchard's harvest is assessed, it will be found to produce as much noxious fruit as sweet. Most matrices for cultural production have negative as well as positive potential. Fourth, the position finesses the motivation-warrant issue by (a) agreeing that the critique might be justified within a community of warrant that recognizes no Catholic principle, while (b) demanding that the larger community give points to the Catholics for coming up with the critique that proved of value to the larger community. This proposed trade-off concedes that whatever gives an idea any claim to a distinctly Catholic character is no reason for a larger community to accept that idea, but expects in return that the larger community will continue to recognize the idea's Catholic character. This move neutralizes the potential of the motivation-warrant distinction to sever from the faith community an idea that promises to enhance the standing of that faith community in the larger world.

This last point invites elaboration. The greater proportion of the inventory of valuable ideas that can be traced to Christianity, the less sense it makes for the prevailing epistemic communities to maintain the critical distance from it that distinguishes them from their counterpart communities of past centuries. Hence there is a tendency to credit religion in general and Christianity in particular with producing and sustaining a host of valuable aspects of contemporary culture, title to which might well be claimed, or at least respectfully shared, by other parties. At work here is a familiar dynamic in the struggle for possession of cultural capital. It works as follows.

Ideas the value of which is recognized in a large social arena will be claimed by particular groups as their own contribution. One of the means by which groups achieve, maintain, or lose relative power in a multigroup arena is to be identified or not identified with highly valued items in the common cultural inventory. What endows an item with the capacity to function as cultural capital is the prestige it enjoys among many groups. This dynamic has been especially visible in recent years among ethno-racial groups, rather than among religious groups. Consider the following well-known examples. Some Afrocentrists claim the culture of ancient Egypt as the contribution of a descent-community that embraces African-Americans of the present day. Some educators have asked that the Iroquois Federation be given credit for having inspired vital aspects of the constitution of the United States. An earlier example is the assertion that democracy is owed to the sturdy Saxons of the primeval German forests who then carried it to England and finally to America. Another is Madison

Grant's notorious insistence that Jesus Christ belonged not to the Jewish community of descent but to that of the Nordics, by way of the Savior's long-obscured Greek ancestry.

I choose extreme examples to identify the dynamic, not to deny that some claims of this order are true. Indeed, Christianity itself is so massive a presence in the last two millennia that it is not difficult to proliferate credible and convincing claims about how many of the things almost everyone today appreciates came to us through a Christian chain of cultural transferal. The point of understanding the dynamic is not to turn us away from honest inquiries into the historic path by which valuable practices, artifacts, ideals, and doctrines have been created, transferred, preserved, and critically revised. Rather, the point is to be better able to approach critically claims of this kind in a context in which the party making the claims is concerned about its standing in relation to other groups, in this case non-Christian groups. Do we owe Catholicism credit for our colleague's critique of political science? The question needs to be considered in relation to this dynamic.

The need to keep this dynamic in mind is all the more compelling when we see someone assigning to their favorite group credit for cultural commodities that are highly generic. The rule of thumb is this: the more generic the commodity claimed, the more suspect the claim should be. It is common to hear Christianity associated with a set of general virtues, including humility, generosity, decency, charity, and spirituality. Now, Christianity's ordinance has been so large that it is indeed within a Christian context that millions of people have seen the generic virtues articulated and exemplified. When you practice the classic virtues especially well, someone will say, honestly and without artifice, "Oh, you *are* a good Christian!" When you hear that you are likely to be quite far removed from the faculty club. But I invoke this charming mode of praise to call attention to a presumption that has proved durable even in some academic circles. The presumption is that behaving well and being religious and being Christian are somehow part of the same thing. Another episode from the Lilly Seminar can illustrate this presumption.

One member of the seminar expressed the concern that without the sustaining influence of religious communities, academia was having a hard time transferring "spiritual values" from one generation to the next. This person backed off when he was reminded that lots of non-Christians, even atheists, had proven capable of practicing these virtues as well as Christians could, and even of transferring them to their young. But what I found remarkable was that so able and sensitive a scholar could write and speak as he did in the initial iteration. He was not engaged in a power ploy, I'm sure, but he inherits and sometimes works within a frame of reference that, when it operates in an arena of diverse religious orientations, functions to advance Christianity by reserving to it a unique leadership role in the wholesome project of enabling people to be good.

A closely related incident, this about cosmology rather than ethics, betrayed the same presumption that Christianity owns the title to some very generic cultural material. In this instance, a member of the seminar observed that the knowability of the world and the capacity of humans to grasp parts of its nature were distinctly Christian presuppositions, and that historians, in particular, simply could not do their job effectively without this Christian cosmology. When I asked this colleague if Thucydides and Gibbon and Perry Miller operated on Christian presuppositions despite their lack of Christian commitment, he said yes. Christianity has title, it would seem, to metaphysical and epistemological realism. This view was met with some skepticism in the seminar.

But even many of those who were skeptical about this particular example remained attracted to the basic outlook I have been analyzing here, which can be seen as a fallback position on behalf of the cultural project of Christianity. It is a "fallback" position in the sense that this project, after loosing influence over the rules by which truth is established, lays a more adamant claim to being the inspiration, indeed the cultural matrix, out of which arises those truths that do not actually conflict with the project as understood by its current supervisors. Hence there is now so much more talk of Christianity as a set of insufficiently tapped resources, not as a standard for belief. This is another step in the historic process of secularization.

I have been proceeding here in the mode of the "hermeneutics of suspicion," but only for the purposes of bringing out aspects of the conversation on religion and higher education that are often hidden. In concluding, I want to pull back from this mode and call upon my religiously committed colleagues to recognize the virtues of the critical distance mainstream academia now maintains toward Christian commitment. Now that academia is emancipated from a Protestant hegemony, the evils of which surely require no belaboring here, it has proved to be a setting in which Catholics, Protestants, religious Jews, agnostics, atheists, and more recently Muslims are able to work together in creating good science and scholarship, and in sustaining good teaching programs for graduate and undergraduate students. I believe we should rejoice in this.

Unless we suppose that the religious believers who function well in this environment are somehow less authentic in their faith commitments than those who do not so function, we must surely consider the possibility that the line dividing religious from irreligious scholars is not terribly important, after all, for the purposes of higher education. If it is more important for such purposes—I am not talking about life as a whole, but about higher education—than I grant here, surely our reformers need to provide an analysis of those of their coreligionists who live so successfully within the present system. Is their religion less authentic than that of the reformers?

I sometimes think that our reformers are in the thrall of a parochially Pauline model of religious authenticity. Diaspora Judaism represents an interesting contrasting model, eschewing evangelical modes. And there are other styles of religious commitment and practice. The choice between models of religious authenticity is relevant to teaching as well as to science and scholarship. I am often dismayed at the loose talk about "formation" that I hear from religiously committed colleagues. I wish these colleagues would attend more to the intellectual content of the subject matter they teach, and less to their own conceptions of the moral needs of their students.

Perhaps our reformers need to be reminded that Christianity marched into the modern era as the strongest, most institutionally endowed cultural program in the Western world. Its agents tried through a variety of methods, some more coercive than others, to implant Christian doctrines and practices in as much of the species as possible. Yet as the centuries went forward, this extraordinary presence in world history lost some of the ground it once held. Christianity after the recent end of the century prophesied in 1900 as "the Christian Century" is less triumphant in the North Atlantic West than it was in 1500 or 1700 or 1900. The fate of Protestant culture in the United States is but a fragment of this larger drama of the transformation of the North Atlantic West from a society heavily invested in the cultural program of Christianity to a society in which Christianity found it harder and harder to retain the spiritual capital of its most thoughtful and learned members.

If Christianity's continuing adherents include some of the world's most thoughtful and learned men and women—as I believe they do—let them continue to bear witness as they will. But let's not forget that outside secular academia, Christianity continues to be the cultural norm, not the exception, in the United States. Even today, our society is one in which voters in 2000 could choose between two more-Christian-than-thou presidential candidates: one, George W. Bush, who declared his favorite philosopher to be "Christ," and another, Al Gore, who claimed to solve ethical dilemmas by applying the old formula of Charles Sheldon, "WWJD" (What Would Jesus Do?"). Enough already.

Universities should not surrender back to Christianity the ground they have won for a more independent, cosmopolitan life of the mind. There are plenty of things wrong with higher education in the United States today, but a deficiency in Christianity is not one of them. Of all the parties to our cultural conversation, none has had a greater abundance of opportunities to be heard in the United States than Christianity.

Where Are the Universities of Tomorrow?

MARK R. SCHWEHN

For the past three years I have been engaged in conversation with colleagues around the country about the relationship between Christianity and higher learning in the United States. This conversation, the Lilly Seminar, has included a wide range of subjects among a fairly diverse group of scholars; and as a result of this extended inquiry, my own thinking about the proper configuration of this discourse has changed. The several questions that defined the conversation within the Lilly Seminar on Religion and Higher Education can best be understood and pursued, I believe, if they are construed as part of a larger inquiry into the fate of the university in our time. The modern research university that many of us have come to know and to love is, by comparison to other institutional forms of higher education, very young. By contrast, the university under some description or another is very old, stemming from the high Middle Ages. Thus, one way of assessing the significance of the Lilly Seminar would be to wonder about how well it prepared us all to think about the following question: to what extent and in what ways will the present-day university need to draw upon its roots as a religious undertaking in order to preserve its integrity, even, some would say its very nature as a university?

As of this writing, the stream of articles about the perilous condition of the academy continues unabated. If anything, the flow of discourse has increased, propelled by the relatively new emphasis upon the university's captivity to a growing number of rich and powerful clients that are often as indifferent to the university's own purposes as they are passionately interested in the knowledge it might produce for them.[1] One has the distinct sense that the character of knowledge, its production, distribution, and "ownership" are being defined by processes and powers remote from the precincts of the ivy towers. And one has also the concurrent sense that those who still dwell within the walls of the academy are fast losing entirely whatever sense of common purpose and identity remains among them.

Some Lilly Seminar members construed George Marsden's remarkable book *The Soul of the American University* to be a story of the growth of the modern research university in the United States that is told in such a way so as to predict that university's present, perilous condition. According to this interpretation, *The Soul of the American University* is a narrative of declension. The seeds of the university's present failures were sown in the early years of its growth. In the course of its successful liberation from Protestant hegemony, higher learning in America may have gained the world, but it lost its soul in the process. Many of those in the seminar who have read Marsden to be saying this or something like it, such as David Hollinger and Jim Turner, have taken issue with this so-called "declension model."

I share some of these reservations. A decline is always relative to some particular quality or quantity, of course, and with respect to "Protestant hegemony," no informed observer would deny that there has been a relative decline of Protestant domination of higher learning in this country over the course of the last century. Disagreements arise over the question of whether such decline should be lamented or celebrated, or, to put the matter more judiciously, whether such decline should be regarded as being better or worse for American higher education generally. Marsden's book invites attention to these latter questions without at all resolving them. *The Soul of the American University* charts one rising action, the growth and development of the modern research university in the United States, and one concurrent falling action, the decline of Protestant hegemony over higher learning, without taking a decisively clear position on the precise causal connections between the two developments.

Indeed, I wonder whether, in view of Marsden's own historical analysis, a Christian *university* under the auspices of "traditional Protestantism" was ever *possible* in the post–Civil War United States. In Marsden's earlier work, especially in his lead essay in *The Secularization of the Academy*, he treats modernity in a manner like that of the sociologist Anthony Giddens, as being a juggernaut that simply overwhelms institutions of higher learning, whatever their origins, once they decide to become universities. "More than anything else," he writes, "what transformed the small colleges of the 1870s into the research universities of the 1920s and then into the multiversities of the late twentieth century was money from industry and government for technical research and development."[2]

In *The Soul of the American University,* however, Marsden seems to want to place a somewhat greater emphasis upon the active complicity of liberal Protestants in bringing about the secularization of the academy than upon their being victims of it. Yet although he works hard to develop a feeling of contingency, a sense that the process of secularization or the disestablishment of religion *could* have been otherwise, this effort is undermined by his elaborately defended decision to exclude from his discussion any sustained attention to either Catholic institutions of higher learning or to the myriad Protestant church-related colleges, many of which have persisted from their founding in the nineteenth century to the present day. Though his restriction of attention to the "flagship" universities is otherwise sensible and salutary, these omissions make it nearly impossible for the reader to imagine any plausible *historical* alternative to the scenario Marsden so ably presents.

When Marsden does turn his attention briefly to other Christian institutions that might be viewed as alternatives to the American university, the results are not encouraging. So, for example, he looks very briefly at Abraham Kuyper and the Free University of Amsterdam as an "alternative to the American model," but his examination here is so hurried as to tacitly concede the irrelevance of the Dutch Calvinist experience in Europe to the American context. The Roman Catholic church in America did manage to maintain a distinctive identity during the period of liberal Protestant capitulation to secularism but, according to Marsden, "at the price of accepting Roman authoritarianism and severe restraints on its intellectual life." The difficulties with "strongly religious" colleges even today, much less during the period 1870–1920, are sometimes buried in Marsden's notes, as when he admits that academic due process is often absent from such schools and "dictatorial rule is particularly common."[3]

Marsden confesses in his admirably candid introduction that his point of view is "that of a fairly traditional Protestant of the Reformed theological heritage." And he goes on to acknowledge the influence exerted upon him by his years of teaching at Calvin College. One might wonder what Marsden would say about the following thought experiment. Calvin is strongly tied to its sponsoring church body, it is Christian in the "traditional Protestant" sense of the term, and it has undeniably produced and nurtured an impressive number of distinguished scholars whose works are widely respected throughout academe. But could Calvin add a school of law, a medical school, and several Ph.D. programs while maintaining its present Christian identity? Or would its inevitable reliance on increased government funds, its need to recruit a talented faculty in many specialties and subspecialties, its subjection to a bewildering array of accrediting agencies, and its search for sources of support well beyond the confines of the Christian Reformed Church lead automatically to the kind of liberal Protestantism that Marsden criticizes, and beyond that to secularization?

The most plausible answer to this latter question for Marsden would seem to be yes, for as he notes in *The Secularization of the Academy*, "Protestants in America are divided about evenly between evangelicals and moderate-liberals. Yet *neither group supports any major universities that are Protestant in any interesting sense*."[4] In sum, while Protestantism might have been a midwife to the modern university in the United States, and though the distinctive character of higher learning in this country has been for most of this century marked by this contingency, it is possible to argue on the basis of Marsden's own analysis that no credible version of the university *could* have survived the twentieth century under exclusively Protestant ministrations.

Some of Marsden's critics were perhaps too harsh in noting what they took to be another shortcoming of his position. They suggested that he at times seems to be arguing that Christians should strive to "retake the English Department." I myself doubt that Marsden entertains even mildly imperial ambitions. Indeed, most of his critics have forgotten that he insists throughout *The Soul of the American University* that the Protestant establishment was elitist in the bad sense of that term, and that it was socially exclusive and distressingly imperialistic in ambition. Instead of endeavoring to reclaim lost territory, Marsden suggests that Christian scholars should invoke the kind of perspectivism that is fashionable among some postmodernists to claim a legitimate place within the decidedly pluralistic house of learning that is the American university.

While I have my doubts about the prudence of Marsden's invocation of postmodernism to legitimate the presence of articulate Christian voices within the secular academy, I agree completely with him about the need for institutional pluralism within American higher education. I think it is a mistake for all colleges and universities to become more and more like one another in the sense of "distributional pluralism," i.e., in terms of some allegedly ideal standard of internal diversity among faculty and students. Colleges and universities that are linked in serious ways to particular church bodies will not attract faculty and students whose demographic profile coincides exactly with the profile of the nation as a whole. And this will apply as much to schools, public and private, that define themselves by their mission to serve a particular geographical region as it will to schools that define themselves by their mission to serve a particular religious constituency. Church-related colleges and universities should be encouraged publicly to state the ways in which they seek to integrate the life of the spirit with the life of the mind and the extent to which a religious worldview shapes the curriculum and organizes the various fields of study at the school. These complicated relationships will work out very differently within the several Christian denominations. There is, as everyone well knows but frequently forgets, a good deal of pluralism *within* Christianity.

For the record, I view my own sense of calling as a scholar who happens to be a Christian as twofold. First, I have found that my own intellectual gifts are more actively engaged in shaping an institution of higher learning that is in important respects different from the dominant model. But, second, I resolutely oppose a sectarian retreat into an intellectual enclave. I believe that faculty and students in Christ College at Valparaiso University must constantly seek to engage a larger and larger intellectual public with the fruits of their research and teaching. Nor should any of them claim within those larger publics a kind of epistemic privilege for their points of view. Christians must draw upon whatever resources they have at their disposal in order to engage others who do not share their assumptions but who share with them a commitment to learn the truth of matters.

My own book, *Exiles from Eden*, sought to reflect upon some of the same large issues that George Marsden and others have treated historically and institutionally, by construing the secularization of the academy as a vocational problem, i.e., by thinking critically about how the "secularization of the academy" transformed the meaning and the significance of academic work. This issue arose for me first on a personal level, as I began to sense an inner conflict between the ethos that I had imbibed in graduate school and a deeper sense of calling that had impelled me to go to graduate school and to strive to become a college teacher in the first place.

I argued first that the dominant conception of the academic vocation in colleges and universities today is based upon a transmutation, even an inversion, of Calvinist concepts of the calling. According to this twentieth-century view, most clearly articulated by Max Weber in his 1918 address, "Wissenschaft als Beruf," the work of the academic consists primarily, sometimes exclusively, of the project of making knowledge, not transmitting knowledge and skills, much less in forming character.[5] Moreover, the Weberian project of making knowledge is based upon an attenuated conception of rationality as purely instrumental, and it is directed toward the end of "mastery of the world." After an analysis and critique of this concept, I tried to remind readers that for most of Western history religion and higher learning were interdependent in ways that have in many places been largely occluded by Weberianism and have therefore escaped the notice of many present-day analysts of the university.

I then proceeded to develop a redescription of the academic vocation that reckoned seriously with Weber, in part by recovering some of the more venerable notions of the nature and purposes of academic inquiry that his celebrated address so thoroughly and effectively undermined or ignored. I sought to restore to the academic calling a kind of religious piety, thereby altering its Weberian character by redirecting its moral trajectory. For Weber, the point of academic life was *making* knowledge; under my redescription, it became *seeking* the truth of matters. Instead of Weberian *mastery* of the world through calculation and control, academics ought, I argued, primarily to seek understanding of the world through communal inquiry. This latter endeavor follows quite naturally, I suggested, from the affections of awe, wonder, and gratitude that together constitute piety. Finally, I tried to absorb the means-end rationality that defined the academic mind for Weber into a far more capacious epistemology that views qualities of character, mind, and spirit as integrally related to one another.

Under this description, the principal task of academicians would not be to enable students to master life technically but to enable students to achieve a kind of excellence that harkens back in some respects to the Platonic Academy. That model of excellence fully integrated moral and intellectual virtue. Leon Kass has cast this same objective into a more contemporary idiom by saying that colleges and universities ought to provide education "in and for thoughtfulness."[6] The word "thoughtfulness" conveys, as Kass noted, both the notion of being filled with reflections about important matters of human concern and the notion of being considerate of others. The same double meaning applies to the corresponding vice: to be thoughtless is to be both foolish and inconsiderate. I extended Kass's analysis by suggesting that one cannot be truly thoughtful in either of the two senses he has specified without being thoughtful in the other sense as well.

Exiles endeavored to show that practices of communal inquiry are alive and well in many academies, secular as well as church-related, universities as well as colleges. So a large part of *Exiles* was an appeal to all academics to discover in what they already do or in what they most deeply long for the traces of older models for the aims, the purposes, and the character of higher learning. *Exiles* also wondered, however, whether the several virtues that are essential to communal inquiry could be sustained indefinitely in the absence of those communal practices, stories, rituals, and beliefs that had at one time given meaning and strength to such virtues as charity and humility. I referred to these latter virtues as "spiritual," leading David Hollinger to inquire about what exactly I meant by the use of that term.

For most of *Exiles*, I used the term "spiritual" in a precise, historical sense as a way of reminding readers that virtues like charity and humility arose originally within religious communities. But then I did explicitly shift to an understanding of the term in accordance with Charles Taylor, who uses it, in *Sources of the Self*, to refer to those ultimate horizons that give shape and meaning to our lives. When I wrote the book, I did not believe, nor do I believe now, that only religious people are humble, charitable, and otherwise virtuous. I did, however, write explicitly from the vantage point of a particular religious tradition. And that particular tradition, Lutheranism, is highly suspicious of all human claims to righteousness, especially of religiously-based claims to it.

I will close with a prediction, something ordinarily forbidden to historians. I do not think that the next century of higher education will be marked significantly by arguments between religious folks and secular folks, between people like myself and Nicholas Wolterstorff and Mark Noll on the one hand and Alan Wolfe and Richard Bernstein and David Hollinger on the other. Instead, I think, as I stated at the beginning of these reflections, that the real threats to higher learning come from vast changes in the way that knowledge is understood, transmitted, produced, and sold. And these changes are being driven by technological and economic forces at tremendous speeds. I rather suspect that the devout Christians and the resolute secularists in the Lilly Seminar, belonging as most of them do to the same generation, seek, from slightly different motives, to preserve the best of university life and culture against some of the more menacing onslaughts of global capitalism. All of us will insist, for example, on the public character of all research, and we will resist for as long as we can the notion that the research we and our colleagues do at the university should be sold privately to the highest bidder and kept secret, if only for a time, from the larger world of scholarship. We may even have occasion to revisit the ancient monastic prohibition against selling knowledge for money. And we may agree at last that even the modern secular academy that many of us have loved was bound more deeply to a kind of asceticism than any of us had realized.

We may notice as well that it may be true but increasingly unhelpful to stress the fact that disciplinary specialization is *the* salient condition of academic life and that the university should, by implication, be a kind of Institute for Advanced Studies writ large. This account of the university, if it slides imperceptibly from description to prescription, can aid and abet the disappearance of a vital discourse that construes or anyway strives to construe the specialties as parts of a whole rather than as haphazard annexations to an institute. In his own contribution to this volume, David Hollinger clearly and forcefully outlines a number of distinctions that are, I agree, crucial to intellectual engagement within the academy. These distinctions between motive and warrant, discovery and justification, etc. that David and I both honor apply most saliently *within* epistemic communities called disciplines, not so saliently with respect to discourse about the relationships among the disciplines, about their proper arrangement, their bearings upon one another, and the relationship between any such account and the view of what should constitute a proper university education.

In the course of his argument, David lumps together several very different university activities, *not all* of which can be accurately characterized in terms of the epistemological distinctions he introduces. Tenure meetings within departments, editorial board decisions about articles submitted to a particular professional journal, and intradisciplinary disputes belong in one category; tenure decisions within university-wide committees, ACLS panels deciding on grant proposals from multiple disciplines, and juries to award prizes to *the* best book by a university press are in another category altogether. In the former category, professional judgment reigns supreme, subject to all of the distinctions Hollinger makes between motives and warrants, discovery and justification, etc. In the latter category, something like practical wisdom or just plain wisdom is involved. Questions like, "Whom do you trust and on what grounds?" arise. Character matters, not so much the character of the author of the book or proposal, but the character of the letters of support and appraisal, the character of those writing such letters, and the character of one's colleagues on the evaluation committees. Is this physicist engaged in special pleading for his discipline, or does he really believe that this woman is the best person in the field? Does the university really need at this point all three of the top people in some subspecialty or other?

This is the old Socratic insight once more. Engagements within the various specialized domains are one thing. But engagements among them are not finally managed or manageable by inventing yet another specialized domain for the management of discourse among or about the various domains. And insofar as the university has lost the capacity to renew and strengthen and transmit *this* discourse (let's call it philosophy in the old sense) and *this* virtue (let's call it wisdom) it has ceased being a university and it has lost the capacity to renew itself. It must finally give up the game utterly to outside clients who will, largely through money, set the priorities, determine the hierarchy of disciplines, and define the character of our knowing and the purpose of our knowledge.

Notice that in the course of these predictive and critical comments about the shape of the future argument about the university, it has not been necessary for me to have recourse to theological or Christian language. I will nevertheless find myself drawing upon Newman and MacIntyre in these conversations, whereas Wolfe or Bernstein might draw upon Plato or Aristotle. Whatever the case may be, the philosophical ties among those of us in the Lilly Seminar who love and seek to preserve the university at its best are far stronger than the religious differences that occasionally divide us. That reassuring discovery was the most important lesson I learned in the seminar.

Notes

1. Cf. Eyal Press and Jennifer Washburn, "The Kept University," *Atlantic* (March 2000): 39–54.

2. George M. Marsden, "The Soul of the American University: A Historical Overview," in George Marsden and Bradley J. Longfield, eds., *The Secularization of the Academy* (New York: Oxford University Press, 1992), 20.

3. George M. Marsden, *The Soul of the American University* (New York: Oxford University Press, 1994), 442, n.10. For the other citations in this paragraph see 214 and 272 respectively.

4. Marsden, "The Soul of the American University," in *The Secularization of the Academy* 9 (emphasis added).

5. See Max Weber, "Science as Vocation," in H. H. Gerth and C. Wright Mills, trans. and eds., *From Max Weber: Essays in Sociology* (New York: Oxford University Press, 1977), 129–56.

6. Leon Kass, "The Aims of Liberal Education," address delivered at the University of Chicago, September 25, 1981.

PART II

Religion & Scholarship
Disciplinary Perspectives

6 | Faith Histories

I find the topic of whether religiously informed historical scholarship can or should exist a perilous one. This is not simply because my distinguished colleague George Marsden has powerfully shaped this field of inquiry with his history of religion and the American university and his recent essay on Christian scholarship. And it is not because of the presence of others here; I think especially of my friend Mark Schwehn, who has thoughtfully considered this topic.[1] And it is not because I am a Catholic faculty member at a Catholic university, giving this presentation to an audience that includes departmental colleagues, notably our host, James Turner, acquaintances from across the university, and the stray dean. It is 3:00 P.M. on a Saturday afternoon, near the end of a long day, but for at least one person in this room the stakes suddenly seem high.

Instead, the topic is a perilous one because I am a historian. What this means is that like many of my colleagues I've never taken a course on method, and tend to view historical method as an extension of common sense; never felt a particular philosophical orientation was a precondition of good historical work; never felt embarrassed by such increasingly quaint phrases as "empirically sound" and "objective." I've used the term "theoretical" as a less than flattering adjective. History as a discipline, I think it's fair to say, has rarely raised its analytical sights to what Robert K. Merton once called the middle range of causal explanation. We attempt to explain segregation in the late nineteenth-century South but rarely move to apartheid more generally; we devote a lifetime to the origins of the French Revolution without comparing it to Russian or Iranian counterparts. And most historians, myself included, work below this level of generalization.

But even historians have found themselves shaken by the perspectival winds sweeping through the human sciences over the past scholarly genera-tion. Forty years ago Yale's Edmund Morgan, one of the craft's foremost practitioners, put his generation's conventional wisdom this way. Historians, he warned, should be suspicious of loyalty oaths—here Morgan invoked the specter of McCarthyism. But they should also be cautious of ways in which membership in a political party might produce biased work, just as adherence to a specific religious creed might distort the historical enterprise.[2]

Morgan wrote three years before the publication of perhaps the most influential book of the twentieth-century human sciences, Thomas Kuhn's *The Structure of Scientific Revolutions*. Kuhn famously viewed scientific knowledge itself as bounded by a community of inquirers. He later came to disavow virtually all nonscientists who spoke in his name, but Kuhn's own efforts to historicize the physical sciences, coupled with Michel Foucault's assertion that all knowledge is tied to power, have had considerable influence on history, philosophy, literary study, and anthropology.[3] Compare Morgan's fear of partisanship with one of the most influential historians of the past fifteen years, Joan Scott. The goal of her scholarship on gender and French history, Scott argues, is "avowedly political: to point out and change inequalities between men and women." Both a "radical feminist politics and a more radical feminist history," she concludes, "require a more radical feminist epistemology."[4]

Scott is exceptional in her philosophical acuity, but a much sharper sense of perspectivalism—that all knowledge is ineluctably situated in a particular time, place, and set of power relationships—has moved closer to the center of the historical enterprise. I've encountered this most vividly over the past few years when teaching entry-level seminars for graduate students. At about week four each year one student, when confronted with differing interpretations of, say, the New Deal or gender in colonial New England, will assert that scholarly difference of opinion is simply "politics," or "power." It is impossible, the student will assert, to adjudicate between competing accounts. Neither account is more compelling, neither is more persuasive.

A related impulse is evident in the vigorously gerundive book titles we've become familiar with over the past two decades—the imagining of nationalism, the inventing of race, the creating of sex, the constructing of class. The making—it seems—of just about everything. These conspicuous gerunds urge readers to search for the power relationships behind seemingly neutral, falsely objective social categories, and cumulatively these titles possess what in retrospect may seem a period flair.

Finally, a cluster of recent books on the historical profession—itself an intriguing phenomeon—is suggestive. The most notable of these is Peter Novick's provocative disciplinary history, centered around the century-old pursuit of historical objectivity, a quest Novick sees as always quixotic and now irrelevant.[5] Historians are still a good distance from the angst of anthropology—in Clifford Geertz's recent memoir he slyly remarks that the first entry in the index to most anthropological works is now: "anthropology, crisis of"—but we think about matters of perspective more than we used to.[6]

These extended (and yet too brief) preliminary remarks only suggest how difficult it is to follow the logic of today's program. We cannot separate foundational issues from specific disciplinary matters, precisely because the most compelling advocates for a religious "perspective" have used the opening created by the postmodern or historicist turn to press their case.

To be more specific I'll quote my colleague George Marsden, who in his *The Outrageous Idea of Christian Scholarship* moves directly from Thomas Kuhn to the following observation:

It is now commonplace among contemporary scholars, including many moderate liberal scholars, to acknowledge that . . . pretheoretical influences such as social location substantially shape interpretations in the humanities and social science. Almost everyone concedes, for example, that being an African-American or Native American makes a difference in how some things are perceived. One might think, therefore, that it would be relatively easy to gain agreement that, since strongly held religious views are often part of one's social location, religious perspectives should be accepted as playing potentially legitimate roles in academic interpretations.[7]

The rest of my presentation is a gloss on this statement. At the outset I should emphasize my admiration for Marsden's work, an admiration deepened by a conversation about today's presentation. Those historians who casually welcome perspectivalism based on gender or race but then describe Marsden's advocacy of Christian scholarship as "surprising" and "disturbing" risk defending an incoherent position.[8]

But I'm not convinced that framing religious perspectives as yet another assault on universal reason is the best strategy. (And I should add here that for practical reasons I limit my observations to Christianity, and at times even Catholic Christianity, the religious tradition I know best.)

Two points seem to me crucial. The first centers on what might seem a recondite historical problem. How are we to characterize the seventeenth- and eighteenth-century Enlightenment? If we follow Alasdair MacIntyre's influential formulation, and Marsden does so explicitly, "the Enlightenment project" is a failed attempt first to separate theology from morality, and then to ground morality in a putatively universal and secular human nature. The legacy of Hobbes, Diderot, Voltaire, and Kant, then, is to pit religious knowledge against genuine verifiable knowledge, and the long-term result is the marginal role that religion plays in the Oxford, Harvard, and Stanford of today.[9]

I'm hardly equipped to disagree with MacIntyre's general interpretation and I number myself among the many scholars attracted to his compelling blend of philosophy and history. But it's worth emphasizing that MacIntyre's Manichean separation of Christianity and Enlightenment is, historically, uncertain. Another colleague, Father Robert E. Sullivan, has recently made this point in a superb review essay: that scholarship over the past generation has emphasized the *importance* of Christianity for eighteenth-century thinkers as diverse as Samuel Johnson, James Madison, and Vico.[10] We now recognize several Enlightenments, stretching from German Pietists and Jews to Portuguese Catholics. The plural form— Enlightenments—allows us to see that many of the most prominent participants, especially if we look beyond Paris, saw the attempt to ground morality in a universal human nature as a distinctly religious project.[11] The view of religion and modernity as locked in mortal combat is a legacy of nineteenth-century readings of the eighteenth-century past, readings subtly updated by our own contemporaries such as MacIntyre working from a Catholic neo-Thomist model, and Peter Gay writing from an explicitly secular vantage point.[12] That faculty in the core arts and science programs of elite universities rarely engage in theological inquiry seems to me indisputable; that this unfortunate lack of theological engagement was an inevitable and necessary extension of the Enlightenment is an open question.

This dispute has implications for today's discussion. If we ignore the most extravagant claims made by Enlightenment enthusiasts, we are left with more defensible notions. One of these is that an Enlightenment legacy enduring into the late twentieth century is mutual criticism among scholars committed to a common search for the closest approximation to truth. These scholars especially value what Thomas Haskell terms "asceticism" or the ability to detach oneself from one's own commitments long enough to fully understand and criticize others. By asceticism Haskell does not mean a specious, never to be achieved, neutrality. Instead he asks those drawn to the postmodern view whether they really believe that historical scholarship is indistinguishable from propaganda, or that historical empathy and methods cannot cross cultural divides.[13]

Haskell emphasizes that a provisional detachment results in what every historian recognizes, the powerful argument that demonstrates full understanding of other positions even as it makes a convincing case for an alternate view. I concede that the ability to make this sort of broadly compelling argument is not widely shared. But it exists. Anyone reading François Furet on the French Revolution, Caroline Bynum on medieval notions of the body, or C. Vann Woodward on the Reconstruction South has the exhilarating sense that an entire generation's research agenda has shifted. Such books allow historians to sustain a judgmental vocabulary. By that I mean the ability to say a certain book is excellent, persuasive, or compelling; or to say that a certain book is inadequate, unconvincing, partial. Allied disciplines seem to me to be edging toward a moment when one's theoretical predispositions (dispositions often formed in a moment of panicked groupthink during the first year of graduate school) crudely determine readings of particular texts. There is less room for craft, for an admittedly partial but still serious barrier separating intellectual commitments and scholarly subject matter.

My point is that the ability to persuade is in part a Christian virtue, as the very term *asceticism* implies. Indeed, the Jesuit theologian Bernard Lonergan's discussion of historical consciousness independently emphasizes one of Haskell's terms—"detachment"—and stresses its moral importance. The late Joseph Cardinal Bernardin also urged Catholic intellectuals to be "ascetic in [their] use of explicitly religious appeals" when addressing a neutral state and diverse public.[14]

If Christianity and Enlightenment are intertwined in the eighteenth century, then, notions of objectivity may be more than scholarly conventions tied to a discredited Enlightenment past. I need to be clear on this point: no one denies that invocations of objectivity have frequently disguised interest, in matters ranging from financial audits to historical scholarship. What needs reaffirmation is that claims to objectivity are not always, or only, masks. Instead, the pursuit of objectivity is a practice and a belief worth preserving, for religiously motivated scholars as much as or more than anyone else. The philosopher Charles Taylor, writing of his own Catholic convictions, argues that "the nature of philosophical discourse (as I see it anyway) [is] to try to persuade honest thinkers of any and all metaphysical or theological commitments."[15] Historians, I think, should agree, especially since our peculiar challenge is to render understandable subjects whose experiences inevitably differ in great measure from our own.

The immediate objection to this formulation frames my second point. Let us return to Professor Marsden. To repeat:

> Almost everyone concedes, for example, that being an African-American or Native American makes a difference in how some things are perceived. One might think, therefore, that it would be relatively easy to gain agreement that, since strongly held religious views are often part of one's social location, religious perspectives should be accepted as playing potentially legitimate roles in academic interpretations.[16]

Professor Marsden's language here is cautious—"*almost* everyone," "*a* difference," "*some* things," "*potentially* legitimate." But I think we need to probe further. Does the experience of "being" an African-American or Native American—or a woman, or a white male, or a lesbian—"actually" make a difference in how things are perceived? To the extent that historical scholarship differs from parliamentary representation, no. Experience itself is of course never unmediated, but my emphasis here is on the multiple identities we all claim.[17] To say a scholar is an African-American is important, but what "perspective" does an African-American Christian woman from Minnesota, who vacations on Martha's Vineyard, represent? The confidence that so many perspectives are incommensurate seems to me a conceit that our scholarly descendants will find amusing. Affirmative action as a remedy for past discrimination—which I support—should not be confused with the more dubious argument that differences based on race or gender automatically lead to untranslatable worldviews, even for scholars speaking the same language, raised in the same city, in the same country, at the same historical moment.[18]

To make the point in another way, many of the women who have spear-headed the flourishing of feminist historical scholarship over the past generation came to their convictions, as we all do, through a combination of personal experience and intellectual insight. But feminist scholarship has succeeded precisely to the extent that it has convinced men and women who are *not* feminists that ideas about gender shape the emergence of the modern welfare state or eighteenth-century notions of civic virtue. Likewise, actual experience as an African-American may have prompted some African-American scholars to emphasize the importance of slave autonomy more than their white colleagues, but they have achieved enduring recognition only after convincing scholars from all backgrounds. Those scholars who claim privileged cognitive access inaccessible to non-Latinos or non-Christians or nonworkers remain, rightly in my view, on the margins of the profession.[19]

The situation for religious historical scholarship is not exactly analogous. Most immediately, experience in a religious community is often, as Marsden correctly points out, a "social location" comparable in importance to experience as a man or as a Native American. I know my own work on twentieth-century Catholic parishes and race relations was shaped by a gradual realization that my entire world until the age of eighteen had been drawn within a tightly connected familial and parish milieu. And I suspect many scholars of religion—from whatever background—can tell similar birth narratives.[20] But of course any such historical work becomes persuasive to a broad audience only when scholars from different backgrounds find a particular argument well reasoned, the marshalling of evidence compelling. The historical study of monasticism undoubtedly benefits from the scholarly perspective of those who have lived as monks, but it does not depend upon it.[21]

Equally important, many religious traditions are at once ascribed and chosen in a way not typical of ethnic identities. Christian faith is at once a social experience *and* a set of beliefs, a field of practices *and* doctrines. Sir Thomas More and Henry VIII shared certain social experiences common to Christians in late medieval England, but they became divided over matters of fairly abstruse canonical and theological interpretation. Experience within a religious community will provide insight for future historians of that community, but only immersion in a chosen religious intellectual tradition offers a new angle of vision on common problems, or the ability to recognize a problem not previously understood as such.

Here I agree wholeheartedly with Professor Marsden that a more self-conscious reappropriation of religious intellectual traditions is a necessary prerequisite for religiously informed historical work. This seems especially important because we now work in an academic culture far less tightly bound to the central texts of the Judeo-Christian tradition, from the Hebrew Bible through Augustine's *Confessions* to the classics of Protestant and Catholic reform. Secular intellectuals—the famous brigade of atheists for Reinhold Niebuhr—will no longer do our historical work for us, and Christian commonplaces like the redemptive value of suffering, the persistence of sin, and the importance of community are in the process of becoming countercultural.[22]

This very intellectual isolation means new opportunities. A Christian understanding of the integrity of the self, for example, offers a powerful challenge to widespread Foucauldian assertions that the self is merely a product of colliding discourses. (And here I think Alasdair MacIntyre's discussion of Foucault is a model.)[23] At the same time, the multilayered Catholic discussion on the relative merits of autonomy and authority checks those too quick to define authority as power, and autonomy as freedom.[24] One thinks in this regard of how John Noonan glides from study of the twists and turns of Catholic dogma on bribes, contraception, and usury to analysis of Supreme Court decisions. Defenders of both court and church (and Noonan is both) prefer the term development over change, and are too sophisticated to reflexively equate dogma with control.[25]

Other examples: the intense emphasis over the past century in Catholic theology and philosophy on the social dimension of life—evident in discussion of the sacraments as well as political economy—have helped both historians and ethicists view the human person as embedded in networks and communities stretching across the globe.[26] It is unsurprising that Catholic scholars were among the first to posit the existence of a North Atlantic world in the eighteenth century, that they resisted viewing the nation-state as the culmination of human history, and, at their best, remained determinedly multilingual and comparative in approach.[27] The very international dimension of the Christian experience, and in its Catholic variant the attempt to achieve doctrinal homogeneity across diverse cultures, is suggestive. Such work places debates about American multiculturalism in a fresh context, and might also inform the theme of cultural contact so pervasive to recent historical work on periods ranging from late antiquity forward.[28]

Perhaps the most suggestive example of Catholic intellectual life moving beyond the theological guild is in the field of cultural anthropology, where Mary Douglas and Victor and Edith Turner have inspired a generation of practitioners in all areas of the human sciences. Scholars have so absorbed these insights that the vocabulary of Douglas and the Turners—taboo, ritual, pilgrimage, *communitas*—has become utterly familiar. Peter Brown has recently reminded us, however, of how fresh Douglas's work seemed in the late 1960s, of his stunned realization that Douglas had discovered a "universal law of gravity" applicable to historical periods ranging from late antiquity to the present. Brown also emphasizes that Douglas's enormously influential discussion of "popular" culture rested upon the fierce discussion within Catholic circles about how to implement the reforms of the Second Vatican Council. This interplay of theological and disciplinary concerns continues. Douglas has recently published a discussion of whether the Catholic church should ordain women priests that doubles as a reflection on gender differentiation in a modern society.[29]

Questions of audience and translation are always crucial. Insofar as Catholic or Christian historians direct their books and articles only at each other, the standardized biblical and theological vocabulary available to them increases even as their readership plummets. Few now favor this option, but viewing the modern academy as a place where work from a religious, or African-American, or feminist perspective proceeds along parallel tracks, checked only by a grudging tolerance for certain procedures, is barely more appealing. Far better, I think, to cultivate religious intellectual traditions and then to make the historical views that spring from those traditions accessible to a broad range of readers. These religiously inspired views and practices will not, necessarily, differ from those of non-Catholic, non-Christian historians. John Noonan is not the only historian to write sensitively about the development of doctrine; Mary Douglas is hardly unique in her concern for ritual. Even so, the ongoing de-Christianization of American intellectual life means that distinctiveness is possible; but only if Catholic scholars, at least, become more self-conscious about how theological presuppositions can provide new vantage points for weary problems.

Making these views accessible to a broad audience requires a certain asceticism of its own, and some theologians would view the translation of Christian perspectives into a public language as an inevitable distortion of Christian content. Historians, fortunately, are incapable of settling that dispute. Still, the position that scholarly objectivity needs to be nurtured by historians does have a respectable theological pedigree. In the Catholic tradition, surely, it derives from a conviction, recently reaffirmed, that reason is universal, and that its proper use can lead to faith.[30] Perhaps the most well-known epigram of our most famous Christian historian, Augustine, remains "I believe in order to understand." But Augustine also emphasized the importance of understanding, "the better to believe."[31] One signal contribution that religiously minded historians might make in the present academic climate, ironically, is to reaffirm the moral importance and autonomy of understanding.

Notes

Thanks to Father Robert E. Sullivan for a close, informative reading and many suggestions. Thanks also to Scott Appleby, Cathy Kaveny, Mark Schwehn, Chris Shannon, Jim Turner, and Bill Tobin.

1. George M. Marsden, *The Soul of the American University: From Protestant Establishment to Established Nonbelief* (New York: Oxford University Press, 1994). Mark R. Schwehn, *Exiles from Eden: Religion and the Academic Vocation in America* (New York: Oxford University Press, 1993); Schwehn, "Christianity and Postmodernism: Uneasy Allies," in *Christianity and Culture in the Crossfire*, David A. Hoekema and Bobby Fong, eds. (Grand Rapids: Eerdmans, 1997), 155–68. On the topic of history more specifically, see *Religious Advocacy and American History*, Bruce Kuklick and D.G. Hart, eds. (Grand Rapids: Eerdmans, 1997).

2. Morgan in *Yale Alumni Magazine* (November, 1959): 10–13, as cited in Eric Cochrane, "What Is Catholic Historiography?" *Catholic Historical Review* 61 (April 1975): 182.

3. Steve Fuller, "Being There with Thomas Kuhn: A Parable for Postmodern Times," *History and Theory* 31 (3) (1992): 241–45.

4. Joan Wallach Scott, *Gender and the Politics of History* (New York: Columbia University Press, 1988), 3–4. See also Ann-Louise Shapiro, "Introduction: History and Feminist Theory, Or Talking Back to the Beadle," *History and Theory* 31 (4) (1992): 1–14.

5. Peter Novick, *That Noble Dream: The "Objectivity Question" and the American Historical Profession* (Cambridge: Cambridge University Press, 1988); Joyce Appleby, Lynn Hunt, and Margaret Jacob, *Telling the Truth About History* (New York: Norton, 1994); *Imagined Histories: American Historians Interpret the Past*, Anthony Molho and Gordon S. Wood, eds. (Princeton: Princeton University Press, 1998); David Harlan, *The Degradation of American History* (Chicago: University of Chicago Press, 1997). Special issues of various professional journals suggest the fascination. See, as one example, two hundred and ninety-two pages on "The Practice of American History," in the *Journal of American History* 81 (December 1994).

6. Clifford Geertz, *After the Fact: Two Countries, Four Decades, One Anthropologist* (Cambridge: Harvard University Press, 1995), 97–98. Jane Kamensky also cites this remark in her engaging essay "Fighting (Over) Words: Speech, Power, and the Moral Imagination in American History," in *In the Face of the Facts: Moral Inquiry in American Scholarship*, Richard Wightman Fox and Robert Westbrook, eds. (Cambridge: Cambridge University Press, 1998), 117.

7. George M. Marsden, *The Outrageous Idea of Christian Scholarship* (New York: Oxford University Press, 1997), 27.

8. Thomas Bender, "Politics, Intellect, and the American University, 1945–1995," *Daedalus* 126 (Winter 1997): 28. Also see Thomas Bender, "Putting Religion in Its Place," *Culturefront* 3 (Fall 1994): 77–79.

9. Alasdair MacIntyre, *After Virtue* (Notre Dame: University of Notre Dame Press, 1984), 36–78. More specifically on the university, MacIntyre, *Three Rival Versions of Moral Enquiry* (Notre Dame: University of Notre Dame Press, 1992).

10. Robert E. Sullivan, "The Birth of Modern Christianity," copy in possession of author.

11. J. B. Schneewind, *The Invention of Autonomy: A History of Modern Moral Philosophy* (Cambridge: Cambridge University Press, 1998), 8.

12. Sheldon Gilley, "Christianity and Enlightenment: An Historical Survey," *History of European Ideas* 1 (1981): 103–21. Also see Dorinda Outram, *The Enlightenment* (Cambridge: Cambridge University Press, 1998).

13. Thomas L. Haskell, *Objectivity Is Not Neutrality: Explanatory Schemes in History* (Baltimore: Johns Hopkins University Press, 1998), 145–73. I should emphasize here my admiration for Haskell's work and his influence on my thinking.

14. Bernard J. F. Lonergan, *Method in Theology* (New York: Herder and Herder, 1972), 231. Insightful on Lonergan and the question of objectivity more generally, Philip Gleason, *Keeping the Faith: American Catholicism Past and Present* (Notre Dame: University of Notre Dame Press, 1987), 202–25. See also Joseph Cardinal Bernardin, *A Moral Vision for America* (Washington, D.C.: Georgetown University Press, 1998), 149.

15. Charles Taylor, "A Catholic Modernity?" in *A Catholic Modernity?* James Heft, ed. (New York: Oxford University Press, 1999), 13.

16. Marsden, *The Outrageous Idea of Christian Scholarship,* 27.

17. Provocative on experience is Joan Scott, "The Evidence of Experience," *Critical Inquiry* 17 (Summer 1991): 773–97.

18. David A. Hollinger, *Postethnic America: Beyond Multiculturalism* (New York: Basic Books, 1995), 19–50; Robert N. Bellah, "Is There a Common American Culture?" *Journal of the American Academy of Religion* 66 (Fall 1998): 613–25.

19. For a prominent example, Molefi Asante, *The Afrocentric Idea* (Philadelphia: Temple University Press, 1998).

20. John T. McGreevy, *Parish Boundaries: The Catholic Encounter with Race in the Twentieth-Century Urban North* (Chicago: University of Chicago Press, 1996). Marsden also makes this point in *The Outrageous Idea of Christian Scholarship,* 70.

21. A point made in Jean Leclerq, O.S.B., *The Love of Learning and the Desire for God* (New York: Fordham University Press, 1961), viii.

22. David A. Hollinger, *Science, Jews, and Secular Culture: Studies in Mid-Twentieth-Century American Intellectual History* (Princeton: Princeton University Press, 1996), 29.

23. MacIntyre, *Three Rival Versions of Moral Inquiry,* 196–215.

24. Exemplary on this issue is Wilfrid M. McClay, *The Masterless: Self and Society in Modern America* (Chapel Hill, N.C.: University of North Carolina Press, 1994). On the philosophical subtext, Charles Taylor, *Sources of the Self: The Making of Modern Identity* (Cambridge: Harvard University Press, 1989).

25. John T. Noonan, *The Lustre of Our Country: The American Experience of Religious Freedom* (Berkeley: University of California Press, 1998); Noonan, *Contraception* (Cambridge: Harvard University Press, 1986); Noonan, *Bribes* (New York: Macmillan, 1984).

26. A point made by J. Bryan Hehir, "The Church in the World: Responding to the Call of the Council," in *Faith and the Intellectual Life,* James M. Heft, ed. (Notre Dame: University of Notre Dame Press, 1995), 107–8. A classic expression of the social emphasis in Catholic theology is Henri DuLubac, S.J., *Catholicism: A Study of the Corporate Destiny of Mankind* (New York, [1938], 1958).

27. Carlton Hayes, *The Historical Evolution of Modern Nationalism* (New York: Richard Smith, 1931); Hayes, "The Church and Nationalism—A Plea for Further Study of a Major Issue," *Catholic Historical Review* 27 (April 1942): esp. 12; Bernard Bailyn, "The Idea of Atlantic History," *Itinerario* 20 (1996): 22–23. On languages, see the reflection on Eric Cochrane in Anthony Mohlo, "The Italian Renaissance, Made in the USA," in *Imagined Histories: American Historians Interpret the Past,* Anthony Mohlo and Gordon Wood, eds. (Princeton: Princeton University Press, 1998), 282.

28. Think, for example, of the sixteenth- and seventeenth-century Jesuits in New France and China. Influential studies touching upon these themes are John Demos, *The Unredeemed Captive: A Family Story from Early America* (New York: Knopf, 1994) and Jonathan Spence, *The Memory Palace of Matteo Ricci* (New York: Viking Penguin, 1985).

29. Peter Brown, "The Rise and Function of the Holy Man in Late Antiquity, 1971–1997," *Journal of Early Christian Studies* 6 (1998): 353–76, esp. 359–60; Mary Douglas, *Purity and Danger: An Analysis of Concepts of Pollution and Taboo* (New York: Praeger, 1966); Mary Douglas, "Sacraments and Society: An Anthropologist Asks What Women Could Be Doing in the Church," *New Blackfriars* 77 (December 1995): 28–40; Mary Douglas, "The Garden of the Beloved," *Heythrop Journal* 36 (1995): 397–408; Victor Turner and Edith Turner, *Image and Pilgrimage in Christian Culture: Anthropological Perspectives* (Oxford: Oxford University Press, 1978); Victor Turner, "Ritual, Tribal and Catholic," *Worship* 50 (November 1976): 504–26.

30. *Fides et Ratio* (Washington, D.C.: National Conference of Catholic Bishops, 1998).

31. *The Works of St. Augustine: Sermons II (20–50) On the Old Testament,* Edmund Hill, O.P., tr. (Brooklyn, N.Y.: New City Press, 1990), 241–43.

7 | Sociology and the Study of Religion

NANCY T. AMMERMAN

Perhaps no single field has so clearly articulated and embodied the secularization of the academy as sociology. Born in the political and social upheavals of late-nineteenth-century Europe, sociology's first conceptual challenges surrounded the transition from traditional to modern societies. On the one hand, Max Weber was convinced that religion—specifically Calvinist Protestantism—had been instrumental in making this transition possible.[1] But on the other hand, he and others were equally convinced that religion would not survive its own creation, that the world would become an "iron cage" dominated by the logics of technology and the market, not by sacred ritual or divine command.

All of the early theorists in sociology were interested in explaining what would likely happen to religion under conditions of modernity. One of the earliest, August Comte, simply posited that sociology would take the place of theology and philosophy as the "queen of the sciences" and the explanation for human conditions.[2] Somewhat similarly, Karl Marx hoped that when workers were able to act in their own behalf, as full participants in the creation of the social order in which they lived, they would no longer need the veil of mystification and false comfort provided by religion.[3]

Weber's verdict, however, is the most far-reaching and carefully argued. He wrote extensively about religion. His accounts of the various world-religions are magisterial, describing in vivid detail the power of religion as a cultural system, the ways of life it engendered, the power of its leaders, and the ability of religious visions to compel quiet (and not so quiet) revolutions.[4] Still, the sheer logical and technological prowess of the "rational-legal" mode of social organization was, in Weber's mind, destined to overpower both traditional and "charismatic" modes of authority. A rational ordering of the world and means-end logic would so outperform the alternatives in accomplishing human goals that mystical and supernatural powers would simply vanish from sight.[5]

Durkheim's vision was somewhat different. He was not so convinced that the world would become the sort of disenchanted realm Weber envisioned. Just as aboriginal groups needed the "collective effervescence" of ritual and the power of the totem in establishing identity and norms for the group, so modern people would need some functional equivalent.[6] Eventually, he hoped, primitive and nationalist forms of religion would be replaced by a "cult of humanity," where the idea of the sacred worth of the individual would bind the world's people together into one grand, universal whole.[7] Traditional religious institutions would disappear, but something like religious ideas and functions might remain.

By the 1950s, the theories of Talcott Parsons had extended Weberian and Durkheimian ideas, and those who still thought they ought to pay some attention to religion took their cue from him. Where does religion go in this modern, differentiated, privatized world? It retreats into individual meaning systems, said Parsons, following Durkheim, or is diffused into generalized cultural values.[8] This emphasis on values coincided nicely with the available research technologies of the day. In those postwar years, sociologists were perfecting their use of survey research, asking thousands of individuals every year about their opinions, beliefs, attitudes, and behavior. With Chi square tables and correlations in hand, they tried to sort out grand cultural patterns based on the cognitive constructs that lurked in the minds of survey respondents.

A decade later, Parsons was passé, and critical sociology seemed more attuned to the conflict-ridden sixties. Attention to beliefs, values, and attitudes had passed from the scene, as well. No need to study religious "attitudes"; critical sociologists, following Marx, knew that behavior is really governed by situations and interests, not by cognitive constructs. That critical moment coincided, of course, with the beginnings of declining memberships in the mainstream American Protestant churches (a pattern long in place on the other side of the Atlantic). That religion was becoming irrelevant in American society seemed evident to sociologists eager for human empowerment and social transformation.

By the time I was picking a dissertation topic in the late 1970s, the prevailing culture in the field was pervasively secular (even if the culture we were studying was not). When I announced that I wanted to do a dissertation on fundamentalism, my professors were not so much opposed as quizzical: "Religion. Hmm. How quaint. I suppose one could study that." Religion had simply passed off their radar screens as a subject of study.

Because the modernization process was so central to Western experience, and because these early theorists had so clearly tied secularization to modernization, it is impossible to understand the history of sociology without attention to both the substance and the situation of these founding theories. When sociologists *have* asked questions about religion, the questions have largely been shaped by modernist assumptions. For instance, sociologists have often looked for the effects of higher education on orthodox religious beliefs and on participation in religious activities. Indeed, rather consistently, people with higher levels of education are found to be less likely to hold traditional religious tenets or to have high levels of religious participation. This is sometimes complicated by social class effects—people who are better educated also tend to be better off, and those who are better off tend to be joiners of all types of community organizations, including religious ones.[9] In spite of this, the finding has endured; education is one of the strongest predictors of decline in individual religious beliefs and attachments.[10] Just as Weber might have predicted, the modern modes of thought represented by higher education seem to erode the power of traditional religion to define the contours of the world we know.

In a more Durkheimian vein, other researchers went looking for the individualized "meaning systems" the modern world was predicted to produce. While not ignoring the continuing presence of religious institutions, recent studies of "spirituality" and "seeking" track the extent to which autonomous modern individuals assume that they can and should construct for themselves whatever religious system they adopt.[11] When 78 percent of Americans tell pollsters that a person can be a good Christian or Jew without attending church or synagogue,[12] they are often speaking from the experience of their own institutional disaffection and spiritual pastiche. And as the modernization theorists would have predicted, those least embedded in traditional local communities and familial networks are also least committed to involvement in a parish.[13] Autonomy and mobility have taken individuals increasingly outside traditional religious communities and into a vast religious (and secular) marketplace of ideas.[14]

Both the founding theories and subsequent research, then, have maintained sociology's strong attachment to the notion that modern technology and modern ideas will inevitably erode the power of religious ideas and religious institutions. Two important implications follow: Education itself is a secular enterprise, and attention to the study of religion is attention misplaced. Other essays in this collection focus on the first of those implications. The second is my focus here. The assumption that modernization would mean secularization has had important effects on the field of sociology itself and especially on the study of religion as a social phenomenon. Because many sociologists assumed that society was (or would soon become) secularized, attention has simply gone into other pursuits.

The Current State of Affairs

Just what is the current situation for sociology's study of religion? Has religion indeed disappeared as a subject of study? Assuming that we might gain some indication of research activity from what is published in three of the leading journals in the field—*American Sociological Review*, *American Journal of Sociology*, and *Social Forces*—I surveyed all the issues of those journals from 1994 to 1998. While my counts may have missed a few articles in which attention was given to religion, it appears that, over that period, these three journals have published a total of about thirty articles in which religion was a major topic. That constitutes about 4 percent of the total number of articles published. Similarly, our disciplinary journal of book reviews, *Contemporary Sociology*, has published over 3,000 reviews during that time, about 4 percent of which were of books primarily dealing with religion.

While that is a relatively small percentage, several other subfields might have done similar counts with similar results. There are simply too many subfields in this now highly specialized discipline for any one focus to gain dominance. The most numerous topics in journals and among published books in the field are race, gender, stratification, economic development, national and global political institutions, family and work, demography and immigration, and the like. The study of religion is a relatively small, but persistent, presence in the books and journals that gain attention in the discipline at large.

As with most subspecialties, the study of religion in sociology is often isolated, rarely overlapping with other empirical questions. That is, only rarely does an article or book explicitly on one of sociology's "hot" topics also address the role of religion—as in an exploration of gender roles or economic development that takes religion into account, for instance. The reverse, however, is not true: Books and articles on religion *do* address many of the otherwise hot topics. A survey of recent titles catalogued by OCLC under "American Religion" revealed that nearly one-third of those books dealt with race, gender, and ethnicity as they affect American religion.[15] Historians, religious studies scholars, theologians, and others are actively seeking to understand the relationship between religion and these social realities, but when they do they must usually extrapolate from social research and theory that does not itself address religion. That is, there is attention *from* religion *to* sociology, but not often in the other direction.

More commonly, sociology books and articles on religion address issues that at least on the surface appear to be only of relevance *within* the study of religion: changing attitudes among American Catholics, the takeover of the Southern Baptist Convention, ordination of women clergy, and such. The titles of many sociology of religion books do not automatically signal to others in the larger field that they are of relevance to people who study social movements, organizations, families, economic development, and the like. As in much of the rest of academe, we are often specialized in ways that fail to signal the overlapping significance of our work.

Another way to look at the status of the study of religion within sociology is to ask how and whether religion is being *taught*—especially to undergraduates—in university departments of sociology. To get a very rough answer to that question, I looked at the on-line 1998–99 course listings from ten universities, all with high status as places to study sociology. The departments I surveyed included both public and private institutions and schools scattered throughout the regions of the country. Two of the ten had no courses on religion at all, nor any that mentioned religious topics in their course descriptions. Eight had at least one basic religion and society course. Of those eight, one had an additional course, two had two additional courses, and one had three, for a maximum of four courses on religion in any of these prestigious sociology departments. In several places, the description of the basic introduction to sociology course mentioned religion alongside the family, economy, stratification, and the like, as basic areas to be covered. But almost never was religion mentioned as a factor to be studied in more specialized courses on the family, social movements, organizations, political mobilization, race, gender, or any other aspect of society. That, of course, does not mean that professors do not touch on the significance of religion when teaching about other aspects of society. But it does mean that they do not generally list religion as a variable that is so fundamental to understanding their subject that it must be included in a basic description of the course.

And what about the study of religion in sociology graduate departments? Here my evidence is of a slightly different sort. In 1998, Stephen Warner and I conducted an informal on-line poll to discover how often sociology graduate students writing dissertations on religion-related topics were seeking advisors and readers outside their own departments, in most cases because their own department did not have the faculty resources necessary to support their work. We concluded that at any given time about two dozen Ph.D. students who are doing work in sociology of religion reach outside their own university to find at least one of their advisors. From the stories we heard, we think it is also a safe guess that a fair number of students who would like to write dissertations in sociology of religion are discouraged from doing so, either by active opposition from members of their department (we heard that reported from a couple of students) or because their department lacks a specialist on religion and discourages outside advisors.

None of these data-gathering exercises has been undertaken with the sort of comprehensive care that would be necessary to render a definitive verdict. Still, the picture they afford is that religion is a small but persistent presence in scholarly publishing in sociology. It is an even smaller, and not always surviving, presence in the curricula of sociology departments. The lingering relative absence of attention to religion in teaching and publishing in sociology reflects the current culture in the discipline, and it reflects the training and emphases of the last generation (or more) that has created that culture. When we look at what is being taught and published in the discipline as a whole, it would be easy to conclude that the study of religion is indeed marginalized and often excluded entirely from our professional efforts to understand today's society.

Deconstructing Disciplinary Myths: The Seeds of Change

Both the current situation and the theoretical heritage of sociology are shaped by the founding assumptions that linked modernization with secularization. Those founding assumptions have shaped the culture of the discipline, much as a founding myth shapes any culture.[16] Sociology's "myth of origin" makes sense of a great deal of what we see. But like all such stories, it makes most sense of the lives of those who are at the center of the culture they are seeking to explain, who occupy the dominant institutions and statuses of a society. Fundamentally, sociology's account of modernization has been a story about the intellectual elites, mostly white and mostly male, in Europe and the United States. It makes sense of the world they see and the life they lead, even if it could never be an adequate theory of social life here or anywhere else in the world. Because their own world was rationalized, specialized, and critical, the assumptions of the myth made perfect sense to the well-educated scholars who were seeking to develop a sociological theory of society.

This theory is, of course, utterly lacking as a description of much of the actual social world. Stephen Warner has pointed out many of the ways in which that old story—that old paradigm, in his words—no longer makes good sense of much of the data we encounter when we study religion.[17] It also fails to make sense because it is not—and probably never was—the story of everyone, either in Europe or in the United States.

The arguments about decline or "accommodation," for instance, only work if the thing to be explained is participation in existing "mainstream" institutions and adherence to official religious dogma. If we look beyond membership numbers in the establishment institutions to practices outside those institutions, we see a very different picture, one teeming with mystical phenomena and ritual practices.[18] Likewise, if we look beyond efforts to reconcile the grand theories of theologians with the grand theories of scientists, we encounter the common sense and experience of everyday life, where "rational" and "nonrational" explanations exist in a complex mix that would defy secularization assumptions.[19]

Over the last two decades the disjunction between the social world and the theories designed to explain it has reached crisis proportions in part because the people in the field are no longer exclusively the inhabitants of the old "center." As new cohorts of women, people of color, and researchers from outside the "Western" sphere have entered the field, critical, bottom-up theorizing, and data gathering have begun to overtake the old paradigm and open up the possibilities for new questions to be asked and new phenomena to be examined.[20]

The lively health of several associations of sociologists of religion, and the active participation of large groups of younger scholars, suggest that the field may indeed be changing. The Society for the Scientific Study of Religion and the Religious Research Association are interdisciplinary, but have majorities of sociologists. Both organizations publish moderately selective journals and host a joint meeting each fall that attracts 500 or more participants and presenters. Articles from the *Journal for the Scientific Study of Religion* are now the eighth most frequently cited among journal articles in sociology. The Association for the Sociology of Religion has been meeting in tandem with the American Sociological Association (ASA) meetings for fifty years and allows for the presentation of well over a hundred papers each year, many of them by graduate students and younger scholars. In addition, formed in 1994, the Religion Section in the ASA has brought a focus on religion directly into the larger professional body. The section has grown rapidly, with over four hundred members (a third of them students), at last count.

While the evidence from existing mainstream sociology journals and the curricula of major departments makes clear that much of the old culture is still in place, the evidence of lively interest in the study of religion among younger scholars offers a hint of different stories in the making. The old culture and its dominant myth of secularization are being dislodged, in part, by the diversity of persons who now occupy the field.

At least three major cultural events have challenged that old myth, as well. One is the growing global consciousness of our discipline and the erosion of development models that expected every society on earth to go through the same stages of change that Europe had experienced. As we have seen that societies from Iran to Indonesia and from Brazil to Bangladesh are moving in their own ways toward full participation in global markets and culture, we are also noticing that religion does not seem to be disappearing or retreating to the margins.

But we did not have to go halfway around the world to notice that religion did not seem to want to die. The rise of the new Christian Right in this country made abundantly clear that religious ideas and institutions have ample political, economic, and cultural power. Similarly, the appearance of a variety of new religious movements, many of them appealing to the very intellectual elites who were supposed to be immune from religion, created additional doubt about the adequacy of secularization as an account of our society's history and future.

Throughout this essay, I have returned to the ways in which our conceptual schemes have failed us and a new "paradigm" is emerging. It is a paradigm based on the decentering of modernism and secularization as the discipline's primary interpretive frame.[21] Modernist frames assumed functional differentiation, individualism, and rationalism as "the way things are." Modernist frames looked for a clear line between rational, this-worldly, action and action guided by any other form of wisdom. Modernist frames looked for the individualized "meaning system" that would be carved out of differentiation and pluralism. Today those frames are being dismantled, and we are seeing a fundamental shift in perspective that is allowing sociologists to see what they could not see before. New persons entering the field, new events that do not fit the old frameworks, and a new questioning of basic modernist presuppositions are combining to create new opportunities for the study of religion in sociology.

So where is this shift beginning to be evident? Where have we seen progress in sociology's ability to explain the obvious persistence of religious ideas and organizations?

- Attention to the experiences of these previously marginalized groups is one of the ways in which the study of religion is being revived and re-framed.[22] When the subject is women, life in the southern hemisphere, immigrants, and so on, the role of religion is often unavoidable.
- There have also been significant changes in the study of voluntary organizations. There is now a much more widespread recognition that when one speaks of the voluntary sector, one simply must include religious organizations and religious motivations.[23] Particularly as the political climate has turned attention to the role of churches in the delivery of social services, sociologists are paying more attention to religious organizations as a field of study.
- Similarly, there is a growing recognition that religious ideas, rituals, and organizations are important players in many social movements.[24] If one wishes to understand the dynamics of movement mobilization, atten-

tion to these religious dimensions is essential. At long last people are noticing that the role of religion in the civil rights movement, for instance, went beyond the fact that Martin Luther King happened to be a preacher.[25]

- Curiously, the study of organizations of all kinds has taken what some describe as a "cultural" turn.[26] As a result, scholars are paying attention to the ways in which every organization has its myths and rituals.[27] Some have even gone so far as to describe the governing assumptions of some organizational sectors in terms of a salvation myth.[28] Unfortunately, despite this talk about religion among organization theorists, the theorists often ignore the work of students of religion on just these phenomena.

- In the realm of sociology's general theories, feminist and other radical critiques have created a space for the nonrational.[29] While many of these critiques see religious power and symbols as oppressive, they nevertheless know that they must take such elements seriously.

- Changes in our research technologies have helped, as well. During the last decade, many of the major survey-research organizations have consulted with sociologists of religion and added questions on religion to the data bases that still form the bedrock on which so much of our sociological knowledge is built. With data to analyze, we can anticipate more published results in the future.

- At the same time, there has also been increasing skepticism about survey research and the presumably universal theories built from it. In a turn from the universal to the particular, case studies of human association have gained some currency. And where better to find people gathering than in religious groups?

The jury is still out. It is still possible that sociology's younger scholars and all those who are bringing new perspectives into the discipline may yet be forced to conform to the old culture. But it seems that the tide may be turning. Those younger scholars are both determined that the study of religion is essential to an understanding of society and determined that they will study religion from squarely within the mainstream of the field. They are determined to remain in the conceptual and methodological conversation of the discipline, determined to be both borrowers and lenders in that exchange. It is a conversation that promises to change the very myths that have shaped the field, and only as those myths are eroded will we as workers in the field be able to fulfill the promise of our science. Sociology will never be able to claim its birthright as a discipline until it takes off its Enlightenment blinders to pay attention to all the elements of the society it is supposed to be explaining.

Notes

This is a revised version of a paper presented at the conference on "Religion and Higher Education" at the University of Notre Dame, March 1999. Portions of this essay have also been published in *Christian Scholars Review* as "Christian Scholarship in Sociology: Twentieth-Century Trends and Twenty-First Century Opportunities," 24 (2000): 685–94.

1. Max Weber, *The Protestant Ethic and the Spirit of Capitalism*, trans. Talcott Parsons (Boston: Beacon, 1905 [1958]).

2. Kenneth Thompson, ed., *August Comte: The Foundation of Sociology* (London: Nelson, 1976).

3. Karl Marx, "Contribution to a Critique of Hegel's Philosophy of Right," in *Karl Marx: Early Writings*, ed. T. B. Bottomore (New York: McGraw-Hill, 1963 [1844]), 43–59.

4. See especially Max Weber, *The Sociology of Religion* (Boston: Beacon, 1922); and Max Weber, "The Social Psychology of the World Religions," in *From Max Weber: Essays in Sociology*, ed. H. H. Gerth and C. Wright Mills (New York: Oxford University Press, 1977).

5. Max Weber, *The Theory of Social and Economic Organization*, trans. A. M. Henderson and Talcott Parsons (New York: Free Press, 1947).

6. Emile Durkheim, *The Elementary Forms of the Religious Life*, trans. Joseph Ward Swain (New York: Free Press, 1915).

7. Emile Durkheim, "Individualism and the Intellectuals," in *Durkheim on Religion*, ed. W. S. F. Pickering (London: Routledge and Kegan Paul, 1975).

8. Talcott Parsons, "Religion and Modern Industrial Society," in *Religion, Culture, and Society*, ed. Louis Schneider (New York: Wiley, 1964), 273–98.

9. N. J. Demerath, III, *Social Class in American Protestantism* (Chicago: Rand McNally, 1965).

10. Among the recent studies to give attention to education's effects are Wade Clark Roof and William McKinney, *American Mainline Religion* (New Brunswick: Rutgers University Press, 1987); and Robert Wuthnow, *The Restructuring of American Religion* (Princeton: Princeton University Press, 1988).

11. See especially Wade Clark Roof, *A Generation of Seekers* (San Francisco: HarperSanFrancisco, 1993); and chapter 3 in Dean R. Hoge, Benton Johnson, and Donald A. Luidens, *Vanishing Boundaries: The Religion of Mainline Protestant Baby Boomers* (Louisville: Westminster/John Knox, 1994).

12. Reported in Roof and McKinney, *American Mainline Religion*, 57.

13. Phillip E. Hammond, *Religion and Personal Autonomy: The Third Disestablishment in America* (Columbia, S.C.: University of South Carolina Press, 1992).

14. See also Penny Long Marler and David A. Roozen, "From Church Tradition to Consumer Choice: The Gallup Surveys of the Unchurched American," in *Church and Denominational Growth*, ed. David A. Roozen and C. Kirk Hadaway (Nashville: Abingdon, 1993), 253–77.

15. Author's unpublished research.

16. For a similar argument, see Jeffrey Hadden, "Toward Desacralizing Secularization Theory," *Social Forces* 65 (1987): 587–611.

17. R. Stephen Warner, "Work in Progress Toward a New Paradigm for the Sociological Study of Religion in the United States," *American Journal of Sociology* 98, no. 5 (March 1993): 1044–93.

18. See, for instance, Daniele Hervieu-Leger, "Present-Day Emotional Renewals: The End of Secularization or the End of Religion?" in *A Future for Religion*, ed. William H. Swator, Jr. (Newbury Park, Calif.: Sage, 1993), 129–48. That such religious experiences are not irrelevant to the rest of life can be seen in the work of Richard L. Wood, "Religious Culture and Political Action," *Sociological Theory* 17, no. 3 (November 1999): 307–32; and Timothy J. Nelson, "The Church and the Street: Race, Class, and Congregation," in *Contemporary American Religion*, ed. Penny Edgell Becker and Nancy L. Eiesland (Walnut Creek, Calif.: AltaMira Press, 1997), 169–90.

19. An excellent example of history's turn to everyday religion is David Hall, ed., *Lived Religion in America* (Princeton: Princeton University Press, 1997).

20. See, for example, the essays by young scholars in Penny Edgell Becker and Nancy L. Eiesland, eds., *Contemporary American Religion: An Ethnographic Reader* (Walnut Creek, Calif.: AltaMira Press, 1997).

21. Here I draw on work I have elaborated in Nancy T. Ammerman, "Organized Religion in a Voluntaristic Society," *Sociology of Religion* 58, no. 2 (Summer 1997).

22. See, for example, R. Stephen Warner and Judith Wittner, eds., *Gatherings in Diaspora* (Philadelphia: Temple University Press, 1998). Renewed attention to African-American churches is also bearing theoretical fruit, as in Mary Pattillo-McCoy, "Church Culture as a Strategy of Action in the Black Community," *American Sociological Review* 63 (December 1998): 767–84.

23. Wuthnow's work has been critical in this turn. For example, see Robert Wuthnow, *Acts of Compassion: Caring for Others and Helping Ourselves* (Princeton:

Princeton University Press, 1991). But see also N. J. Demerath, III, Peter Dobkin Hall, Terry Schmitt, and Rhys H. Williams, eds., *Sacred Companies: Organizational Aspects of Religion and Religious Aspects of Organizations* (New York: Oxford University Press, 1998).

24. Christian S. Smith, ed., *Disruptive Religion: The Force of Faith in Social Movement Activism* (New York: Routledge, 1996).

25. Among the best studies is Aldon D. Morris, *The Origins of the Civil Rights Movement: Black Communities Organizing for Change* (New York: Free Press, 1984).

26. Paul J. DiMaggio, "The Relevance of Organization Theory to the Study of Religion," in Schmitt and Williams, *Sacred Companies;* and Roger Friedland and Robert R. Alford, "Bringing Society Back In: Symbols, Practices, and Institutional Contradictions," in *The New Institutionalism in Organizational Analysis*, ed. Walter Powell and Paul DiMaggio (Chicago: University of Chicago Press, 1991), 232–63.

27. John W. Meyer and Brian Rowan, "Institutionalized Organizations: Formal Structure as Myth and Ceremony," in *The New Institutionalism in Organizational Analysis*, 41–62.

28. Jeffrey Alexander, "The Promise of a Cultural Sociology: Technological Discourse and the Sacred and Profane Information Machine," in *Theory of Culture*, ed. Richard Munch and Neil J. Smelser (Berkeley: University of California Press, 1992), 293–323.

29. Dorothy Smith, "A Sociology for Women," in *The Prism of Sex: Essays in the Sociology of Knowledge*, ed. J. Sherman and E. Beck (Madison: University of Wisconsin Press, 1979), 135–87.

What We Make of a Diminished Thing

Religion and Literary Scholarship

ROGER LUNDIN

"The question that he frames in all but words," writes Robert Frost of the oven bird, "Is what to make of a diminished thing." With that question, Frost no doubt had in mind any number of judgments that one might make about the modern world. He was not averse, after all, to making both acerbic and avuncular comments about the grand themes of history, literature, and life. He was by nature an opinionated man, and when, especially in his later years, the American public turned to their Yankee poetic sage for wisdom, Frost was usually only too happy to deliver himself of a judgment.

In the final lines of "The Oven Bird," Frost was weighing in on a serious matter, one that had vexed American literature and literary scholarship for almost a century. It is the question of the proper imaginative response to the stark contours of a naturalistic view of the world. What do poetry and fiction, and the derivative task of criticism, have to do with a disenchanted world, one in which we encounter what Wallace Stevens calls "The Plain Sense of Things"? "It is difficult even to choose the adjective/ For this blank cold, this sadness without cause./ The great structure has become a minor house./ No turban walks across the lessened floors."[1]

In *God and the American Writer*, Alfred Kazin takes the measure of what he calls the "strange minds" that have produced American literature over the past century and a half. What these minds have discovered in that time, Kazin claims, is a universe bereft of benevolent presence and devoid of definitive purpose.[2] They have had to struggle within the void of unconscious nature and have had to assert the reality of the human imagination over against an always indifferent, occasionally hostile world. At first, in writers such as Emily Dickinson and Herman Melville, the shock of this discovery was palpable. "Those—dying then, / Knew where they went—" wrote Dickinson in 1882. "They went to God's Right Hand— / That Hand is amputated now / And God cannot be found—/ The abdication of Belief / Makes the Behavior small—."[3] In a number of later authors—from the bracingly affirmative William James to the positively eupeptic Richard Rorty—loss has been turned into gain. Having emerged from the monism and idealism of their Puritan past, American novelists, poets, and literary theorists of the past 150 years have moved inexorably into a pluralistic and pragmatic American present. In that present, Rorty claims, we have seen established "the autonomy and supremacy of . . . literary culture." In the nineteenth century, he explains, "there were philosophers who argued that nothing exists but ideas." In the late twentieth century, "there are people who write as if there were nothing but texts." And to Rorty, this represents progress.[4]

Naturalism and the Birth of Literary Studies

Over this period during which theistic idealism gave way to naturalistic pragmatism, the academic study of literature in America was born, developed, and flourished. Gerald Graff notes that "strictly speaking, there were no 'academic literary studies' in America or anywhere else until language and literature departments were formed in the last quarter of the nineteenth century."[5] Like other sectors of the university, English departments at the end of the nineteenth century were stocked with academic professionals whom Graff calls "investigators." "The prototype of the new professional," he writes, "was the German university professor in his lecture room or seminar, a man who supposedly transcended morality and ideology in his disinterested search for truth."[6]

Providing the philosophical impetus for this "new professional" and his "disinterested search for truth" was the naturalist consensus that emerged in the latter decades of the nineteenth century. Forged out of elements of Darwinian theory, post-Kantian philosophy, and the forces of urbanization and industrialization, this consensus represented a late development in a process stretching back at least several hundred years.[7] Max Weber speaks of this unfolding historical phenomenon as the "disenchantment of the world" and Charles Taylor has described it as the modern abandonment of belief in an "ontic logos."[8] In so naming this development, Taylor is referring to the loss of belief in the essentially worded *nature* of nature, the conviction that behind and beneath visible phenomena lurks a purposeful divine intelligence. From the seventeenth century on, he argues, we have "[come] to grasp this world as a mechanism" and to doubt that it is "the embodiment of meaningful order which can define the good for us." This move Taylor calls a "neutralizing [of] the cosmos" or "following Weber, [a] disenchanting [of] the world."[9]

It is of disenchantment of this sort that Frost writes in "The Oven Bird." "There is a singer everyone has heard," he begins, "Loud, a midsummer and a mid-wood bird, / Who makes the solid tree trunks sound again." This North American warbler is unlike other birds, for he sings in the middle of the day and the heat of the summer, at a time when other birds have the sense to be silent. He sings of diminishment and decline, echoing "that other fall we name the fall."

> He says that leaves are old and that for flowers
> Mid-summer is to spring as one to ten.
> He says the early petal-fall is past
> When pear and cherry bloom went down in showers
> On sunny days a moment overcast;
> And comes that other fall we name the fall.
> He says the highway dust is over all.
> The bird would cease and be as other birds
> But that he knows in singing not to sing.
> The question that he frames in all but words
> Is what to make of a diminished thing[10]

The oven bird had been described by naturalist John Burroughs, in a book that Frost knew, as "a very prosy, tiresome, unmelodious singer." But occasionally this utterly ordinary bird "is suddenly transformed for a brief moment into a lyric poet of great power." It shoots up from its perch, and from a vantage point high above the treetops, it "bursts into an ecstasy of song, rapid, ringing, lyrical; . . . brief but thrilling; emphatic but musical."[11] It is easy to see why Frost took this bird, with its "brief but thrilling . . . ecstasy of song," to be the emblem of the poet in a disenchanted world.

Frost wrote this poem in the early or mid-1910s, less than a century after his New England forebear Ralph Waldo Emerson had praised nature as an ever-voluble source of revelation. Confronted with both rationalism and materialism, which threatened to render nature silent and the human spirit lifeless, Emerson promoted a view of nature as a ceaselessly chattering counterpart to humanity. "In the tranquil landscape," he enthused in *Nature*, "and especially in the distant line of the horizon, man beholds somewhat as beautiful as his own nature." The "fields and woods" can "minister" to the human spirit, because they suggest "an occult relation between man and the vegetable. I am not alone and unacknowledged."[12] He saw, as one observer explains, the "naturalist's encounter with facts as a sort of automatic conjugation."[13] For Emerson and his cohort, nature never stopped talking, and everything it said was a revelation of the divine.[14]

For Emerson, this celebration of nature went hand in hand with the creation of a new, unique national literature. The American experience entailed, among other things, a freedom to confront nature and to elaborate human experience without the meddlesome influences of tradition and society. The supremely free American would be the Christ-like poet, one who would counter the effects of the fall. "For, as it is dislocation and detachment from the life of God, that makes things ugly, the poet, who re-attaches things to nature and the Whole—re-attaching even artificial things, and violations of nature, to nature, by a deeper insight—disposes very easily of the most disagreeable facts."[15] According to Emerson, the poet traces more distinctly—and describes more creatively—the myriad threads that tether the human spirit to the natural world: "He shall see, that nature is the opposite of the soul, answering to it part for part. One is seal, and one is print. Its beauty is the beauty of his own mind."[16]

Emerson offered his breezy maxims in the late 1830s and early 1840s, only two decades before Darwin published *The Origin of Species*. For the Concord sage's successors—for Dickinson, Edith Wharton, Stephen Crane, Frost, and others—nature was to turn suddenly and eerily silent. Within two decades of the close of the Civil War, a centuries-long tradition of reading nature as a revelatory text simply vanished.[17]

Yet as Richard Rorty describes it, the transformation that took hold dramatically at the end of the nineteenth century had actually begun a hundred years before. "About two hundred years ago, the idea that truth was made rather than found began to take hold of the imagination of Europe," he observes. In Rorty's telescoped history, the nineteenth century emerges as the period in which men and women realized for the first time that the world outside ourselves has nothing to say. "The suggestion that truth, as well as the world, is out there is a legacy of an age in which the world was seen as the creation of a being who had a language of his own." But since we no longer believe in such a being who is the source of language, Rorty avers, it makes no sense to argue that the world has anything to tell us: "the world does not speak. Only we do. The world can, once we have programmed ourselves with a language, cause us to hold beliefs. But it cannot propose a language for us to speak. Only other human beings can do that." This is a fully disenchanted world.[18]

Like a number of other late-nineteenth-century fiction writers, Stephen Crane knew this emerging naturalistic world well. "When it occurs to a man that nature does not regard him as important, and that she feels she would not maim the universe by disposing of him," he wrote in 1897, "he at first wishes to throw bricks at the temple, and he hates deeply the fact that there are no bricks and no temples." Nature has no concern for the survival or needs of the men who are stranded in "The Open Boat." In Crane's words, the man who faces extinction "desire[s] to confront [in nature] a personification and indulge in pleas, bowed to one knee, and with hands supplicant, saying: 'Yes, but I love myself.' A high cold star on a winter's night is the word he feels that she says to him," Crane concludes. "Thereafter he knows the pathos of his condition."[19]

Crane's stark naturalism, with its evocation of the pathos of the human condition, anticipated many developments in twentieth-century literature and theology, from the marble stoicism of Ernest Hemingway's prose, to the fatalistic ironies of Franz Kafka's fictive worlds, to the radical bankruptcy of natural theology as envisioned in Karl Barth's theology of crisis. In literary modernism, naturalism encouraged specifically the glorification of irony and paradox. It prized literature as a form of verbal protest against the steely coldness of the diminished world. Modernist art sought neither to re-present the world nor to change it; instead, it created an alternative to the sorry state of historical affairs and ordinary life. "A poem should be equal to:/ Not true," explained Archibald MacLeish in "Ars Poetica":

For all the history of grief
An empty doorway and a maple leaf.

For love
The leaning grasses and two lights above the sea—

A poem should not mean
But be.[20]

Or as W. H. Auden famously put it, in his tribute to Yeats:

Mad Ireland hurt you into poetry.
Now Ireland has her madness and her weather still,
For poetry makes nothing happen: it survives
In the valley of its making where executives
Would never want to tamper.[21]

Modernist Aesthetics

According to the high modernists, art could make out of diminished things objects whose very uselessness made them valuable. As Frank Kermode put the matter in an influential book of high modernist criticism, poetry and fiction speak to "a need in the moment of existence to belong, to be related to a beginning and to an end." They offer us "models of the world" whose purpose is to "make tolerable one's moments between beginning and end." Poetic fictions would be dangerous, if they were to become blueprints for human practices and the social order. Instead, they remain harmless fantasies that fill a great human need. "Our poverty—to borrow that rich concept from Wallace Stevens—is great enough, in a world which is not our own," Kermode concludes.[22]

As might be expected, the glorification of poetry's power "to make nothing happen," as well as the celebration of the practical uselessness of poetic fictions, created certain dilemmas for those who promoted the study of literature as a systematic academic endeavor. In an age beset by cataclysmic social and economic changes, to say nothing of global warfare, why should one bother with a self-confessed ephemeral activity?

Why should we spend material, financial, and intellectual resources on practices with no apparent consequences?

To answer such questions, Western literary scholars and artists largely attempted to elaborate theories promoting the rigorous study of supposedly frivolous forms. From the early decades of the twentieth century through the 1960s, various versions of the modernist paradigm governed literary study, and under the influence of that paradigm the scholarly examination of literature became a quasi-scientific cataloguing of the mysteries of pleasure. Building upon Coleridge's classic distinction—"A poem is that species of composition, which is opposed to works of science, by proposing for its *immediate* object pleasure, not truth"—the modernists largely conceded the didactic and rhetorical functions of language to other discourses and kept for imaginative literature the possibilities of pleasure.[23] In the Coleridgian tradition, those possibilities were many, to be sure, and the comforts of sophisticated pleasure were great. But in modernism, they became almost entirely the pleasures of self-conscious isolation.

For literary scholarship in the first six or seven decades of the twentieth century the Coleridgian model significantly shaped the relationship of religious belief to literary study. It allowed many who championed modernism to remain deeply religious and determined to separate their faith from their academic study.[24] Whether it was Cleanth Brooks with his New Critical science of explication, Northrop Frye with his taxonomy of archetypal patterns, or Douglas Bush with his Renaissance Christian humanism, the dominant critical schools of the early and mid-twentieth century—with the possible exception of the Marxism which flourished in the 1930s—separated questions of fact from those of value. They promoted the study of literature as a rigorous enterprise free of direct religious influence yet mysteriously destined to reach religious conclusions.

The work of Northrop Frye is representative on this score. An ordained minister in the United Church of Canada, he had wide critical influence in the 1950s and 60s. His *Anatomy of Criticism* presented itself as nothing less than an exhaustive scientific survey of the pleasurable productions of the human imagination. Above all else, Frye wanted literary criticism to be as scientific and exhaustive as possible. Of course, for him, the products of the human imagination ultimately had little or nothing to do with the world as it is or as it might become. After all, the study of that world belongs to the physical and social sciences and is not the subject of literature and its realms of desire.

In *The Educated Imagination*, Frye asks us to imagine ourselves as having been set down on a desert island. As you gaze out upon your island world and think of how you would like it to be, in Frye's words, "you soon realize that there's a difference between the world you're living in and the world you want to live in. The world you want to live in is a human world, not an objective one; it's not an environment but a home; it's not the world you see but the world you build out of what you see." This is the area of what Frye terms the "applied arts and sciences," and it occupies a ground between the inhuman world of nature and the completely human world of imagination.

In the world of the imagination, Frye asserts, "anything goes that's imaginatively possible, but nothing really happens. If it did happen, it would move out of the world of imagination into the world of action."[25] The world of art is a stubbornly timeless realm, and the study of it must become a science like all other sciences. Literary criticism should analyze and catalogue the phenomena of poems and plays with the same stringent standards of objectivity used to study the natural world. Frye "wanted to make literary criticism more like science—even, if possible, like math—and in order to legitimate that transformation, he famously asserted that 'the theory of literature is as primary a humanistic and liberal pursuit as its practice.'"[26] And what Frye wanted that science to study and catalogue were the workings of desire. For Frye, according to Frank Lentricchia, "desire is the deepest human center of governance, the intersubjective force which impels all activity of expression, all civilizing humanization and ordering of an indifferent and stupid nature."[27]

The Nietzschean Alternative

Frye's work represented one way—a way often chosen in the first seven decades of the twentieth century—for literary scholarship to make its peace with the naturalistic world. But there was another direction for the naturalistic legacy of the nineteenth century to take, and it was Nietzsche who showed the way. For him, the "disenchantment of the world"—what one of his translators calls the "dedeification of nature"—did not signal the need for an aesthetic retreat. Instead, the more diminished the reality that faced the artist, the greater the opportunity that reality afforded him. "The total character of the world," Nietzsche claims, "is in all eternity chaos— . . . a lack of order, arrangement, form, beauty, wisdom, and whatever other names there are for our aesthetic anthropomorphisms." Beauty and wisdom are purely human creations, and the universe has "no wish to become" anything other than what it is, which is a sphere in which "none of our aesthetic and moral judgments apply."[28]

"Nature, artistically considered, is no model," he argued in *Twilight of the Idols*. "Nature is *chance*. To study 'from nature' seems to me a bad sign: it betrays subjection, weakness, fatalism—this lying in the dust before *petty facts* is unworthy of a *complete* artist." Instead of stoic resignation, it is frenzied intoxication to which the Nietzschean artist is called. And the "essence of intoxication," he asserts in a sobering passage, "is the feeling of plenitude and increased energy. From out of this feeling one gives to things, one *compels* them to take, one rapes them—one calls this procedure *idealizing*."[29]

Nietzsche pushed "the affirmation of freedom," in Charles Taylor's words, "to its most uncompromising expression." Under the banner of the will to power, "the authoritative horizons of life, Christian and humanist," are cast off as impediments to this will. Yet Nietzsche knew that an unbridled "will to power" held its own dangers. So, he sought a "reconciliation between man's will and the course of the world," which he found in his idea of the eternal recurrence. Through this opaque doctrine, Nietzsche believed that he had found a way of defining the truly heroic life as one in which a person would will to relive eternally everything that had ever occurred to him or her.[30]

The legacy Nietzsche bequeathed to later generations thus combined a view of radical freedom with an understanding of inhuman fatalism. In a Nietzschean spirit, for the past three decades, literary theory has argued, in the main, against the disinterested study of nature and spirit and for the aggressive reappropriation of nature by spirit. In many quarters, literary theory has presented itself as an agent called to reform the given world by bringing it in line with certain, often unspecified, ideals. Yet at the same time, that theory has often represented the human subject as little more than a cipher, a product of inhuman forces beyond its comprehension, let alone its control. Hubert Dreyfus and Paul Rabinow point to these contradictory tendencies in an influential study of Foucault. At one moment, they accurately represent Foucault as a prophet who holds that "the task of the genealogist is to destroy the primacy of origins, of unchanging truths. He seeks to destroy the doctrine of development and progress." Yet immediately after this, they describe Foucault's genealogist as one who, having finished destroying "ideal significations and original truths," then turns his attention "to the play of wills." But what the free and "destructive" critic finds there is nothing but "subjugation, domination, and combat. . . . Instead of origins, hidden meanings, or explicit intentionality, Foucault the genealogist finds force relations working themselves out. . . . There is no subject, either individual or collective, moving history."[31]

The Nietzschean ascendancy, promoted by the likes of Foucault and Jacques Derrida, began around 1968, which Tzvetan Todorov identifies as the pivotal year of contemporary American literary studies.[32] The events of that year—the Tet offensive in Vietnam, the assassinations of Martin Luther King and Robert Kennedy, the protests and riots in Paris, in May, and Chicago, in August—were cataclysmic and seemed to portend a revolutionary change of some kind. The universities, of course, were not spared the tumult but indeed themselves became centers of disruption. English departments were singled out for scorn by some, seen as centers of privilege and bastions of an oppressive status quo. Henry Nash Smith, for example, felt the wrath of the reformers firsthand. A major scholar of early American literature, Smith served as the Modern Language Association president in the late 1960s. In that role, at the annual MLA convention, he had to respond to pointed charges about the immorality of conventional literary scholarship. One of his former students later reported that protesting faculty members and graduate students told Smith that "because 'objective' scholarship, criticism, and teaching failed to question the existing social and economic orders, they therefore represented nothing more than an immoral neutrality."[33] The attack on such "immoral neutrality" soon became a centerpiece of several of what were becoming the ascendant theoretical schemes.

The theoretical justification for these attacks was already at hand in Nietzsche's theories of language and power. In the 1966 paper that launched Jacques Derrida's North American career, the French philosopher traced structuralism's "decentering" of discourse to "the Nietzschean critique of metaphysics, the critique of the concepts of Being and truth, for which were substituted the concepts of play, interpretation, and sign

(sign without present truth)".[34] At the close of "Structure, Sign, and Play in the Discourse of the Human Sciences," Derrida spoke of modernism's "saddened, *negative*, nostalgic, guilty" lament for the absent origin and opposed to it what he called "the Nietzschean *affirmation*, that is the joyous affirmation of a world of signs without fault, without truth, and without origin which is offered to an active interpretation."[35]

Such a Nietzschean affirmation of a world of signs without fault fits well with liberal individualism's notions about the malleability of relationships and identities once considered fixed and firm. If the self is a social construct, writes James Miller in his recent intellectual biography of Michel Foucault, "one implication seems obvious: human beings as such lack any unchangeable rule, statute, or norm." That being the case, the human body presents itself to us a kind of text, as do the cultural practices and ethical standards that have constrained it through history. For Foucault, in Miller's words, all beliefs are nothing more than "a host of historically contingent rules, statutes, and norms, defined by customs, practices, and institutions every human being must grow up within."[36]

In an influential essay—"Nietzsche, Genealogy, History"—Foucault elaborates this Nietzschean understanding of selfhood and history. He questions all efforts to situate events, which are inherently singular, into "an ideal continuity—as a teleological movement or a natural process." Instead, Foucault holds, an event is nothing more than "a usurpation of power, the appropriation of a vocabulary turned against those who had once used it." A true historical sense discovers in history neither a providential pattern nor a secular story of moral or aesthetic development; instead, to have an accurate historical sense is to recognize that we merely exist "among countless lost events, without a landmark or a point of reference." Cut off from any search for transcendent truth and divorced from any theory of meaningful human development, knowledge becomes for Foucault an agent of our "enslavement" to violence. The absence of ends in human life means that knowledge must serve the purposes of constituting the self, even if that entails ultimate self-destruction. "Where religions once demanded the sacrifice of bodies," he concludes, "knowledge now calls for experimentation on ourselves, calls us to the sacrifice of the subject of knowledge."[37]

Foucault, in short, construes human life as an unceasing effort to turn the quest for knowledge into a process of self-creation and self-inscription. To know is to learn how to write the text of one's own body and life and to efface the writing that others—institutions and individuals, past and present—have done upon them. For Foucault, such activity follows in the heroic Nietzschean tradition of radical willfulness. In likening the idea of textuality to the idea of self- and world-formation, Nietzsche showed a way out of the impasses of aesthetic modernism and its passivity. With the theory of eternal recurrence, he sought to resolve both aesthetic and psychological dilemmas at once: "To redeem those who lived in the past and to recreate all 'it was' into a 'thus I willed it'—that alone should I call redemption."[38]

Nietzsche's language of redemption shows how contemporary literary theory has cleared a space for faith in scholarly life and cultural discourse, but the faith it has sanctioned is perhaps the most extreme form of Protestantism imaginable. It is a version of faith in which the locus of divine activity is not to be discovered in nature, sacrament, or scripture, nor in any realm beyond the world; instead, it is to be found entirely within the will and its fathomless, abysmal regions. "Nothing is at last sacred but the integrity of our own mind," Emerson asserted in "Self-Reliance." In literary theory in recent decades, what the Nietzschean emphasis has done is to strip Emerson's insight of its metaphysical pretensions by dismissing its claims to a connection between the self, on the one hand, and nature and God, on the other. It has wedded a stringent naturalism to the prophetic tradition's iconoclasm. It has done so, in good measure, by asserting that all claims to truth are forms of idolatry. H. Richard Niebuhr once defined radical monotheism as the form of religious faith which "dethrones all absolutes short of the principle of being itself." Contemporary American literary scholarship often appears to be a radical monotheism without the being.[39]

Suspicion and Restoration

Another way of describing the faith informing much recent literary scholarship would be to speak of its status as a "hermeneutics of suspicion." It was Paul Ricoeur's *Freud and Philosophy* that made this phrase current three decades ago. With this designation, Ricoeur sought to identify a set of complex assumptions that had surfaced in the work of Marx,

Nietzsche, and Freud in the second half of the nineteenth century. The "intention they had in common," he explains, was "the decision to look upon the whole of consciousness primarily as 'false' consciousness." Descartes had trained us to doubt everything but human consciousness. "Since Marx, Nietzsche, and Freud, this too has become doubtful. After the doubt about things, we have started to doubt consciousness."[40]

To suspicion's necessary work of demystification, Ricoeur opposed what he took to be the equally important view of hermeneutics "as the manifestation and restoration of meaning addressed to me."[41] But in contemporary literary studies, his call for a hermeneutics of restoration represents a lonely voice, for the idea of interpretation as the "restoration of meaning addressed" to us has all but vanished from theoretical discourse. Instead, the last several decades have witnessed what Foucault has championed as genealogical critique. This is critique whose goal is to trace linguistic and cultural signs *back* to their source in some region of biological or psychological compulsion. To use Ricoeur's term, Foucault argues that "what is addressed to us" must be suspected and exposed for what it is, an arbitrary interpretation imposed upon the flux of human life. Only then, after such exposure and suspicion, can the liberated work of self-construction begin. "If interpretation is the violent or surreptitious appropriation of a system of rules, which in itself has no essential meaning, in order to impose a direction, to bend it to a new will, to force its participation in a different game," Foucault argues, "then the development of humanity is a series of interpretations."[42]

In making this case, Foucault builds upon an argument laid out by Nietzsche in an 1873 fragment, "On Truth and Lie in an Extra-Moral Sense." There Nietzsche set it as his purpose to describe "how wretched, how shadowy and flighty, how aimless and arbitrary, the human intellect appears in nature." There is a desperate pathos about language and the human condition, "for this intellect has no further mission that would lead beyond human life." Its purpose is to hold "the most unfortunate, most delicate, most evanescent beings" for a minute in existence. And it does so by "shrouding the eyes and senses of man in a blinding fog," thus deceiving him about his wretchedness by giving him "the most flattering evaluation of knowledge itself." The universal effect of that knowledge is deception, and the tool of deception is language. A word is nothing but "the image of a nerve stimulus in sounds." At the same time, "the 'thing in itself' " or "pure truth" is "quite incomprehensible to the creators of language and not at all worth aiming for. One designates only the relations of things to man." Language conceals rather than reveals, for "truths are illusions about which one has forgotten that this is what they are."[43]

With its understanding of the subtle and potentially devastating relationships of language, deception, and power—and with its understanding of the situated nature of all discourse—contemporary literary theory might plausibly be seen as a revival of Augustinian insights about language and human finitude. For example, one can imagine most contemporary theorists agreeing with Paul Ricoeur's Augustinian claim about the primacy of language and the impossibility of a completely unsituated, unbiased human understanding: " 'the symbol gives rise to the thought.' . . . The illusion is not in looking for a point of departure, but in looking for it without presuppositions. There is no philosophy without presuppositions."[44] Or to put it another way, there is no scholarship without some form of faith at its foundation.

Yet the distance between Augustine and contemporary literary theory is dramatic. In puzzling over the mystery of the Trinity, Augustine wrote, "faith seeks, understanding finds. This is why the prophet says, 'Unless you believe, you will not understand.' " For the inheritors of Nietzschean critique, the formula varies slightly but significantly: "Unless you suspect, you will not understand." The presupposition of radical doubt has replaced that of belief, and understanding has come to be seen as the inevitable product of suspicion, the one mode of interpretation most likely to yield hermeneutical certainty. In describing the "hermeneutics of suspicion," Ricoeur had attempted to balance Nietzsche with Augustine in the interpretive enterprise: "Hermeneutics seems to me to be animated by this double motivation: willingness to suspect, willingness to listen; vow of rigor, vow of obedience." The Nietzschean tradition embraces naturalism as the ground of its "vow of rigor" but demonstrates little interest in the countervailing "vow of obedience."[45]

A singular need of modern literary study is for faith-based scholarship to articulate what a "vow of obedience" and "hermeneutics of restoration" would look like in contemporary form; the challenge is to incorporate the hermeneutics of suspicion within a reconstituted hermeneutics of restoration. To have validity, a faith-based criticism will need to forsake efforts to reject the recent past in the name of a lost, pristine antiquity, whether that past be the advent of Cartesianism, the rise of the Enlightenment, or the appearance of the hermeneutics of suspicion. While speaking of the need to recuperate forgotten or neglected resources—Ricoeur puts it that "beyond the desert of criticism, we wish to be called again"—the contemporary Christian critic of literature must also acknowledge the futility of efforts at naïve restoration. There is, the eighteenth-century German aphorist G. C. Lichtenburg once observed, "a great difference between believing something *still* and believing it *again*."

To understand what it might mean for contemporary literary scholarship to "believe again," we might return to our earlier discussion of American naturalism and the silence of nature in Crane's "The Open Boat." We recall that when the main character is tempted to cry out on nature, he realizes that he is not likely to receive a response of any kind. "A high cold star on a winter's night is the word he feels that she says to him. Thereafter he knows the pathos of his condition." Here Crane offers what might be called the naturalistic base line for modern literature and humanistic study. The irreducible givens of life are the products of biological and chemical processes ruled by laws indifferent to human moral standards and spiritual longings.

In its mild form, this naturalism surfaces in the opinions of one interlocutor in an Oscar Wilde dialogue, "The Priority of Art." Wilde's "Vivian" points out to her conversational companion that while "one touch of Nature may make the whole world kin, . . . two touches of Nature will destroy any work of Art. If, on the other hand, we regard Nature as the collection of phenomena external to man, people only discover in her what they bring to her." She offers the example of Wordsworth, who "was never a lake poet. He found in stones the sermons he had already hidden there."[46] In Wilde's hands, the pathos of nature is turned into an occasion for a happy discovery of poetic power and the delights of language.

In its more stringent versions, this naturalism emerges in Nietzsche's attack upon nature in *Twilight of the Idols*. And in both its mild and more hostile versions, this naturalistic view assumes that consciousness and language are curious epiphenomena that reveal a great deal about human need but show us nothing about the structure of things or the ends for which those things were created. That is to say that the only givens in human life are those of genealogy and origins, for their realities are wired into the nature of things; questions of teleology and eschatology are solely matters of human aspiration and point to nothing beyond the pale of nature.[47] To be wise is to acknowledge this state of affairs, and it is in this sense that Crane speaks of the human condition as a *pathetic* state.

But there is another way to think of pathos. The pathos to which Crane refers is closely related to eleos and phobos, Aristotle's terms for the emotions aroused in the cathartic experience of tragedy. As Gadamer points out, the standard translation of eleos and phobos—as pity and terror—does not do justice to the Greek original; eleos is a mixture of fear and mercy, while phobos is a fright that borders on panic. Each is a pathos, a powerful emotion charged with an unmistakably religious significance. "What a man has to learn through suffering is not this or that particular thing," he writes in *Truth and Method*, "but insight into the limitations of humanity, into the absoluteness of the barrier that separates man from the divine. It is ultimately a religious insight—the kind of insight that gave birth to Greek tragedy." Given this religious insight, Gadamer concludes that all "experience is experience of human finitude." The truly experienced person is one who knows that he or she is master neither of time nor of the future. In all its pathos, experience drives us to "acknowledge the real. The genuine result of experience, then—as of all desire to know—is to know what is."[48]

When considered theologically, "to know what is" is to see in the givenness of things something more than materials and occasions for the accident of consciousness to work upon. To be certain, to view *givenness* in this latter fashion is one element of our encounter with reality, for art is the product of the workings of consciousness upon the elements of human experience and the things of this world. The genealogy of the human subject—its origins in complex realities of biological development, sexual desire, and psychological need—cannot be denied. But at the same time, human consciousness is summoned beyond itself by the claims of the ideal and the call of the sacred.

A contemporary Christian literary criticism needs to articulate the nature and possibilities of such claims and such a call. It can most effectively do so by developing interpretive practices that are polyphonic and dialogical rather than monistic and monological. These are terms most often associated with the work of Mikhail Bakhtin, who drew significantly from the fiction of Fyodor Dostoevsky, *The Brothers Karamazov* in particular, to develop his dialogical understanding of fiction and truth. Bakhtin praised Dostoevsky's willingness to give extraordinary ideological and emotional latitude to characters with whom he clearly disagreed, such as Ivan Karamazov. Dostoevsky did so, according to Bakhtin, because he believed that truth emerged only through the play of divergent voices. "Truth," he wrote in his book on Dostoevsky, "is not born nor is it to be found inside the head of an individual person, it is born *between people* collectively searching for truth, in the process of their dialogic interaction."[49]

Particularly in his early work, Bakhtin drew explicit connections between the person of Christ and the nature of interpretation. His model for human understanding was one in which the different strands of dialogue move towards a genuine polyphonic unity whose model is Christ. It was Jesus, after all, who managed to enter fully into the world without losing his divine attributes and otherness. As such, he offers the pattern for an encounter with otherness in which we can understand identity as a matter of *both* sameness and difference. For Bakhtin, the ultimate dialogic experience is "a *conversation* with Christ. 'The word as something personal. Christ as Truth. I put the question to him.' "[50]

Where Bakhtin stresses the dialogical encounter with the other in his theological understanding of literary study, Ricoeur focuses more directly upon the internal dynamics of dialogue.[51] His theological understanding of literary study and interpretation, that is, is rooted in his anthropology. For Ricoeur, the "conflict of interpretations" has to do with the multiple modalities of the self, and in the lead essay of his book by that name, he details the three distinct kinds of interpretation that correspond with the different modes of human selfhood.

The hermeneutics of suspicion is grounded in what Ricoeur terms the "archaeology of the subject," by which he means the manifold origins of the human subject in the unconscious forces of desire. "It is in deciphering the tricks of desire," writes Ricoeur, "that the desire at the root of meaning and reflection is discovered." The *cogito*, the free-standing agent of Cartesian self-consciousness, must look "behind itself" to discover, "through the work of interpretation, something like [the] *archaeology of the subject.*" That *cogito* must suspect its own self-consciousness and seek its origins, as well as its destiny, outside itself. The "archaeology of the subject" confirms that "language is deeply rooted in desire, in the instinctual impulses of life." That being the case, one of the duties of interpretation is to trace symbols and stories back to their origins in the encounter of the subconscious with the natural world.[52]

Ricoeur understands, however, that a hermeneutics of suspicion that stands alone is but one more form of monological discourse. To become dialogical, suspicion needs to be augmented by the elements of a genuine hermeneutics of restoration, which Ricoeur locates in both a teleology of the subject and an eschatology of the sacred. A teleology, or hermeneutics of the spirit, he argues, shifts the "origin of sense, so that it is no longer behind the subject but in front of it." Where the archaeology of the subject discovers meaning in what precedes the subject and the texts it interprets or produces, a teleology of the subject allows "each figure [to] find its meaning, not in what precedes but in what follows."[53] It recognizes that identity has to do not just with origins, as naturalism would have it, but also with destinies, as the Abrahamic faiths have held for several millennia.

According to Ricoeur, there is in human understanding a ceaseless dialectic of the different archaeological, teleological, and eschatological forces that emerge in the play of language and culture. The conflicting hermeneutical frameworks in this dialectic all point "to the ontological roots of comprehension." Each also "in its own way affirms the dependence of the self upon existence"—its "dependence on desire glimpsed in an archaeology of the subject, its dependence on the spirit glimpsed in its teleology, its dependence on the sacred glimpsed in its eschatology." Because these separate ways of understanding depend upon one another in a dialogical relationship, rival interpretive schemes need not be seen as "mere 'language games,' " for each element—archaeological, teleological, and eschatological—is necessary to the larger framework of understanding.[54]

In drawing upon theological resources to understand interpretation and the nature of literary study, such figures as Gadamer, Ricoeur, and Bakhtin are acknowledging the poverty of naturalistic schemes of human understanding. To a significant extent, the confusion evidenced in the theories of language and selfhood that dominate contemporary literary scholarship can be traced to the attempt of romanticism, as exemplified in the case of Emerson, to ground spiritual and moral values in the transcendent self. In the wake of naturalism's dismantling of that self, efforts to continue in this vein have taken on an increasingly desperate air. To some observers, such efforts appear doomed, because they attempt to dis-

cover in either aesthetic detachment or Nietzschean willfulness a sufficient foundation for moral, spiritual, and cultural life. In coming years,
faith-based literary scholarship will need to follow the example of Bakhtin,
Ricoeur, and Gadamer and seek to recuperate resources that naturalism
has suppressed, neglected, or forgotten.

In a poem addressed to his senses, "Precious Five," W. H. Auden issues
commands to each of the five senses —"Be patient, be modest, be civil,
look, and praise"—and he implores them to "be happy" and do as they
"are told." In a passage that seems to allude to Stephen Crane's desperate
cry to the heavens, Auden tells his senses that if he were "To face the sky
and roar / In anger and despair / At what is going on," the response he
would get would be

> That singular command
> I do not understand,
> *Bless what there is for being,*
> Which has to be obeyed, for
> What else am I made for,
> Agreeing or disagreeing?[55]

To a literary culture trained to think of its art as a strained response to
diminished things, the call to "bless what there is for being" may make
little sense. Yet here again it is Frost who has gauged more accurately the
spiritual and emotional state of the modern subject. "He thought he kept
the universe alone," begins another of his poems on the subject of diminished things,

> For all the voice in answer he could wake
> Was but the mocking echo of his own
> From some tree-hidden cliff across the lake.
> Some morning from the boulder-broken beach
> He would cry out on life, that what it wants
> Is not its own love back in copy speech,
> But counter-love, original response.[56]

Those who seek, in literature and life, "counter-love, original response"
long for something more than what Walter Ong has called the "curiously

silent, nonrhetorical universe" bequeathed to us by naturalism.[57] And so it is that to those who sense the barrenness of naturalistic theories of language and the self, Auden's command to "bless what there is for being" may take on the character of a promise, just as Gadamer's claim that tragedy makes us "acknowledge the real" and " know what is" may serve as a most remarkable comfort indeed.

Notes

I revised and expanded this essay while serving as a fellow at the Erasmus Institute at the University of Notre Dame. For their helpful criticism, I would like to thank the participants in the fellows' seminar at the institute, particularly James Turner, Gary Gutting, Wesley Kort, and Bill Donahue. Mark Noll also gave an early draft of this essay a close reading and offered astute suggestions.

1, Stevens, "The Plain Sense of Things," in *The Palm at the End of the Mind: Selected Poems and a Play*, ed. Holly Stevens (New York: Vintage, 1972), 383.

2. Kazin, *God and the American Writer* (New York: Alfred A. Knopf, 1997), 3–23.

3. Poem #1581, in *The Poems of Emily Dickinson*, ed. R. W. Franklin (Cambridge: The Belknap Press of Harvard University Press, 1999), 582.

4. Rorty, *Consequences of Pragmatism* (Minneapolis: University of Minnesota Press, 1982), 139.

5. Graff, *Professing Literature: An Institutional History* (Chicago: University of Chicago Press, 1987), 1. For the emergence of the humanities in American universities, see an excellent new study, Jon H. Roberts and James Turner, *The Sacred and the Secular University* (Princeton: Princeton University Press, 2000).

6. Graff, *Professing Literature*, 62.

7. In a laudatory essay written in 1909, John Dewey cites Darwin as the most important source of naturalism. The 1859 publication of *The Origin of Species* "marked an epoch." It overturned teleological "conceptions that had reigned in the philosophy of nature and knowledge for two thousand years" and replaced them with genetic explanations. *The Influence of Darwin on Philosophy and Other Essays* (1910; Amherst, N.Y.: Prometheus Books, 1997), 1, 9.

For the modern naturalist consensus, see, among many other studies, Reinhold Niebuhr, *The Nature and Destiny of Man*, vol. 1: *Human Nature* (New York: Scribner's, 1941), 18–22; Charles Taylor, *Sources of the Self: The Making of the Modern Identity* (Cambridge: Harvard University Press, 1989), 337–51; and Steven C. Rockefeller, *John Dewey: Religious Faith and Democratic Humanism* (New York: Columbia University Press, 1991), 453–55.

One of the most compelling accounts of the aesthetic and spiritual impact of naturalism—upon a particular kind of temperament, to be sure—is contained in Henry Adams's famous account of "The Dynamo and the Virgin": "Historians undertake to arrange sequences,—called stories, or histories,—assuming in silence a relation of cause and effect. These assumptions, hidden in the depths of dusty libraries, have been astounding, but commonly unconscious and childlike; so much so, that if any captious critic were to drag them to light, historians would probably reply, with one voice, that they had never supposed themselves required to know what they were talking about . . . [Adams] insisted on a relation of sequence, and if he could not reach it by one method, he would try as many methods as science knew. Satisfied that the sequence of men led to nothing and that the sequence of their society could lead no further, while the mere sequence of time was artificial, and the sequence of thought was chaos, he turned at last to the sequence of force; and thus it happened that, after ten year's pursuit, he found himself lying in the Gallery of Machines at the Great Exposition of 1900, with his historical neck broken by the sudden irruption of force totally new." *The Education of Henry Adams*, in *Novels, Mont St. Michel, The Education*, ed. Ernest Samuels and Jane N. Samuels (New York: Library of America, 1983), 1068–69.

8. Taylor, *Sources of the Self*, 186–92.

9. Ibid., 149, 148. There is, of course, another story that can be told about the history of "disenchantment." Elsewhere Taylor argues that are generally "two kinds of theories" meant to explain secularization. "One makes the decline in personal belief the motor, and explains the secularization of public space as a consequence of it; the other reverses the relation, and sees the changing place of religion in social life as the crucial factor, and the retreat of individual belief as flowing from it." Taylor, Foreword to Gauchet, *The Disenchantment of the World: A Political History of Religion*, trans. Oscar Burge (Princeton: Princeton University Press, 1997), ix. Taylor notes that the former explanation "has given an important role to the rise of science," while the latter view, which has gained in importance in the twentieth century, sees religion more "as the way we experience or belong to the larger social whole." Foreword, x.

10. Frost, "The Oven Bird," in *Collected Poems, Prose and Plays*, ed. Richard Poirier and Mark Richardson (New York: Library of America, 1995), 116.

11. Burroughs, *Ways of Nature* (Boston: Houghton Mifflin, 1905), 41. Frost knew the writings of Burroughs well; his set of Burroughs's complete works is housed in the Fales collection at New York University. The connection to Burroughs is instructive, because it provides yet another link of Frost to Emerson. Lawrence Buell explains that for both John Muir and Burroughs, "Emerson was the first American literary star to fill their firmaments. . . . Burroughs, or so he claimed, turned from Emersonian essays to nature writing in order to establish

his individuality from the master." *The Environmental Imagination: Thoreau, Nature Writing, and the Formation of American Culture* (Cambridge: The Belknap Press of Harvard University Press, 1995), 322.

12. Emerson, *Nature*, in *Essays and Lectures*, ed. Joel Porte (New York: Library of America, 1983), 10, 11.

13. Lee Rust Brown, *The Emerson Museum: Practical Romanticism and the Pursuit of the Whole* (Cambridge: Harvard University Press, 1997), 60.

14. John Irwin has made a convincing argument for the centrality of Jean-François Champollion for the writers of antebellum America. His deciphering of the Rosetta stone in the 1820s served for them as a symbol of the potential of the poet to unlock the meanings of nature's hieroglyphics; his accomplishment was significant enough to merit mention in many of the greatest works of the period, from Thoreau's *Walden*, to Poe's *Eureka*, to Melville's *Moby Dick*. Irwin, *American Hieroglyphics: The Symbol of the Egyptian Hieroglyphics in the American Renaissance* (New Haven: Yale University Press, 1980), 3–11.

For Emerson, the hieroglyph became a central symbol of poetry and its divine power. *Nature* asserts that "Every man's condition is a solution in hieroglyphic to those inquiries he would put." And throughout that work, he says the same of nature: "The moral law lies at the centre of nature and radiates to the circumference. It is the pith and marrow of every substance, every relation, and every process. All things with which we deal, preach to us. What is a farm but a mute gospel?" *Nature*, 7, 29.

15. "The Poet," in *Essays and Lectures*, 455.

16. "The American Scholar," in *Essays and Lectures*, 56. At times, Emerson questioned sharply his Transcendental scheme and its many assumptions about nature and the self. Perhaps nowhere did he do so as forcefully as in the 1844 essay "Experience": "It is very unhappy, but too late to be helped, the discovery we have made, that we exist. That discovery is called the Fall of Man. Ever afterwards, we suspect our instruments. We have learned that we do not see directly, but mediately, and that we have no means of correcting these colored and distorting lenses which we are, or of computing the amount of their errors. Perhaps these subject-lenses have a creative power; perhaps there are no objects. Once we lived in what we saw; now, the rapaciousness of this new power, which threatens to absorb all things, engages us. Nature, art, persons, letters, religions,—objects, successively tumble in, and God is but one of its ideas. Nature and literature are subjective phenomena; every evil and every good thing is a shadow which we cast." "Experience," in *Essays and Lectures*, 487.

17. For understanding the New England Puritans' practice of reading nature as a spiritual book, there are many valuable studies of the practice of typology. Perhaps the most cogent and creative of them all remains Sacvan Bercovitch's

The Puritan Origins of the American Self (New Haven: Yale University Press, 1975). See also Perry Miller, *Errand into the Wilderness* (Cambridge: The Belknap Press of Harvard University Press, 1956) and Miller, *Nature's Nation* (Cambridge: The Belknap Press of Harvard University Press, 1967).

This Puritan habit of mind was rooted, of course, in the history of the trope of the "Book of Nature." See Ernst Robert Curtius, *European Literature and the Latin Middle Ages*, trans. Willard R. Trask (Princeton: Princeton University Press, 1991), 402–26, and Basil Willey, *The Seventeenth Century Background: Studies in the Thought of the Age in Relation to Poetry and Religion* (New York: Columbia University Press, n.d.), 24–40.

18. Richard Rorty, *Contingency, Irony, and Solidarity* (Cambridge: Cambridge University Press, 1989), 5, 6. Only a quarter century after Emerson offered his cheerful assessment of the volubility of nature, Emily Dickinson took a different view of things:

> The Veins of other Flowers
> The Scarlet Flowers are
> Till Nature leisure has for Terms
> As "Branch," and "Jugular."
>
> We pass, and she abides.
> We conjugate Her Skill
> While She creates and federates
> Without a syllable—[#798]

Darwin deepened within Dickinson suspicions she already had about Romantic claims for a spirit in nature. Where Emerson centered the linguistic act in the union of self with nature—"All facts in natural history taken by themselves have no value, but are barren, like a single sex. But marry it to human history, and it is full of life."—Dickinson viewed language as a human reality to which nature remained oblivious and impervious. "We conjugate," while "She creates and federates / Without a syllable."

19. Stephen Crane, "The Open Boat," in *Prose and Poetry*, ed. J. C. Levenson (New York: Library of America, 1984), 902. A pathos like Crane's is also strongly indicated in the work of his contemporary, the philosopher William James. In *Pragmatism*, James concludes of experience that "truth grows up inside of all the finite experiences. They lean on each other, but the whole of them, if such a whole there be, leans on nothing. All 'homes' are in finite experience; finite experience as such is homeless. Nothing outside of the flux secures the issue of it." *Writings 1902–1910*, ed. Bruce Kuklick (New York: Library of America, 1987), 601.

20. MacLeish, "Ars Poetica," in *Western Wind: An Introduction to Poetry*, 2d ed., ed. John Frederick Nims (New York: Random House, 1983), 529–30. Two of the most cogent treatments of the relationship of naturalism to literary theory remain M. H. Abrams, *The Mirror and the Lamp: Romantic Theory and the Critical Tradition* (New York: Oxford University Press, 1953), and Frank Lentricchia, *After the New Criticism* (Chicago: University of Chicago Press, 1980). Abrams is particularly instructive on what we might call the early history of naturalism, its antecedents in Newtonian physics and early modern rationalism, while Lentricchia addresses more specifically the twentieth-century engagement of creative writers and literary theorists with a fully developed naturalistic view of the world.

21. Auden, "In Memory of W. B. Yeats," *Collected Poems*, ed. Edward Mendelson (New York: Random House, 1976), 197.

22. Kermode, *The Sense of an Ending: Studies in the Theory of Fiction* (London: Oxford University Press, 1967), 4.

23. Coleridge, *Biographia Literaria,* ed. James Engell and W. Jackson Bate (Princeton: Princeton University Press, 1983), 2:13.

For a telling analysis of the relationship between modernist poetics and the academic study of literature, see Gail McDonald, *Learning to be Modern: Pound, Eliot, and the American University* (Oxford: Clarendon Press, 1993). In addition, for an important reminder of the materially grounded nature of the modernist poetic enterprise, see Lawrence Rainey, *Institutions of Modernism: Literary Elites and Public Culture* (New Haven: Yale University Press, 1998).

Of the many different forms that the relationship between stark naturalism and aesthetic modernism took, one of the most intriguing emerges in the memoirs of veterans of World War I and World War II. Paul Fussell has written the classic study of the effect of WWI on English literature, *The Great War and Modern Memory* (New York: Oxford University Press, 1975). Fussell's account of his own WWII experience illustrates the close connection between stringent naturalism and aestheticism: "The boredom, misery, and pain aside, what better preparation than a war for a lifetime devoted to the study of people and the language they're enmeshed in? The intensity of my new opposition to meaninglessness and vagueness, and ultimately dissolution, was perhaps one source of my later passionate concern with 'form' in art and expression." Of the host of veterans who went on to become distinguished teachers of literature, Fussell writes, "[They were] aiming at the teaching of English literature to a generation unbrutalized by war. We all hoped, secretly, if not openly, that our efforts would help restore subtlety, civility, and decency after their wartime disappearance. This seemed almost a religious act, demanding from its devotees their complete emotional and spiritual commitment. The world was now to be saved from its folly, brutality, and coarseness of conscience by the techniques of close reading and disciplined explication." *Doing Battle: The Making of a Skeptic* (Boston: Little, Brown, 1996), 177, 184–85. See also Alvin Kernan, *Crossing the Line: A Bluejacket's World War II Odyssey* (1994; Bluejacket Books, 1997), 146–49.

24. For a considerable minority, of course, including Fussell and Kernan, aestheticism offered a means of dispensing entirely with Christian practice and profession. But as the above citation from Fussell demonstrates, even those in the agnostic minority tended to speak of literature in salvific terms and reverential tones.

25. Northrop Frye, *The Educated Imagination* (Bloomington: Indiana University Press, 1964), 16–17, 19, 22.

26. Caleb Crain, "The Shock of the Old," *Lingua Franca*, 9.2 (March 1999): 36.

27. Lentricchia, *After the New Criticism*, 15.

28. Nietzsche, *The Gay Science,* trans. Walter Kaufmann (New York: Vintage, 1974), 168.

29. Nietzsche, *Twilight of the Idols/The Anti-Christ*, trans. R. J. Hollingdale (London: Penguin, 1990), 82, 83.

30. Taylor, *Hegel* (New York: Cambridge University Press, 1975), 563.

31. Dreyfus and Rabinow, *Michel Foucault: Beyond Structuralism and Hermeneutics*, 2d ed. (Chicago: University of Chicago Press, 1983), 108–9. It is on this point of contradiction—between the genealogist's sense of himself as a perceptive destroyer and his reading of history as a scene of vast forces that create the idea of subject—that the most telling critiques of Foucault and the poststructuralist project have been offered. Alasdair MacIntrye has presented a particularly incisive analysis. See *Three Rival Versions of Moral Enquiry: Encyclopaedia, Genealogy, and Tradition* (Notre Dame: University of Notre Dame Press, 1990), 196–215. "The genealogist has up till now characteristically been one who writes *against,* who exposes, who subverts, who interrupts and disrupts. But what has in consequence very rarely, if at all, attracted explicit genealogical scrutiny is the extent to which the genealogical stance is dependent for its concepts and its modes of argument, for its theses and its style, upon a set of contrasts between it and that which it aspires to overcome—the extent, that is, to which it is inherently derivative from and even parasitic upon its antagonisms and those towards whom they are directed, drawing its necessary sustenance from that which it professes to have discarded" (215).

32. Todorov, *Literature and Its Theorists: A Personal View of Twentieth-Century Criticism*, trans. Catherine Porter (Ithaca: Cornell University Press, 1987), 182–91.

33. Richard Bridgman, "The American Studies of Henry Nash Smith," *The American Scholar* 56.2 (Spring 1987): 268. For a firsthand account of the battles in the English departments over the last forty years, including the dramatic shift

from aesthetic to epistemological and political concerns, see Kernan's memoir, *In Plato's Cave* (New Haven: Yale University Press, 1999).

34. Jacques Derrida, *Writing and Difference,* trans. Alan Bass (Chicago: University of Chicago Press, 1978), 280.

35. Ibid., 292.

36. Miller, *The Passion of Michel Foucault* (New York: Simon and Schuster, 1993), 69.

37. Foucault, "Nietzsche, Genealogy, History," in *The Foucault Reader*, ed. Paul Rabinow (New York: Pantheon, 1984), 88, 96.

Charles Taylor sees in Derridean deconstruction a "Nietzschean background" but also "a contemporary liberationist attempt." For Taylor, the "liberating intent" in Derrida is undercut by the latter's refusal to "affirm any good." Foucault, on the other hand, sought to affirm a good of a kind, especially in the final years of his life. "In his very last interviews," writes Taylor, "he espoused the ideal of the aesthetic construction of the self as a work of art. There is a deep problem here because of the difficulty of detaching a notion of the aesthetic from the other strands in modern thought that Foucault still wanted to repudiate. But what is striking again is the kind of unrestrained, utterly self-related freedom that this ideal entails." *Sources of the Self,* 488, 489.

38. Nietzsche, *Thus Spoke Zarathustra: Second Part,* in *The Portable Nietzsche*, trans. and ed. Walter Kaufmann (New York: Penguin, 1976), 251.

39. *Essays and Lectures,* 261. Niebuhr, *Radical Monotheism and Western Culture* (New York: Harper, 1970), 37.

For a sympathetic reading of the Nietzschean tradition's iconoclasm, see Merold Westphal, *Suspicion and Faith: The Religious Uses of Modern Atheism* (Grand Rapids: Eerdmans, 1993).

Hans Jonas has made a convincing connection between the radically contingent universe envisioned in Blaise Pascal's radical monotheism and the deified psychology of Nietzscheanism: "Gone is the *cosmos* with whose immanent *logos* my own can feel kinship, gone the order of the whole in which man has his place. That place appears now as a sheer and brute accident."

"The *deus absconditus*, of whom nothing but will and power can be predicated, leaves behind as his legacy, upon leaving the scene, *the homo absconditus*, a concept of man characterized solely by will and power—the will for power, and the will to will. For such a will even indifferent nature is more an occasion for its exercise than a true object." *The Gnostic Religion: The Message of the Alien God and the Beginnings of Christianity* 2d ed. (Boston: Beacon Press, 1963), 323, 324–25.

40. Paul Ricoeur, *Freud and Philosophy: An Essay on Interpretation,* trans. Denis Savage (New Haven: Yale University Press, 1970), 33.

41. Ibid., 27.

42. Foucault, "Nietzsche, Genealogy, History," 86. Alasdair MacIntyre situates Foucault's genealogical critique within its self-confessed Nietzschean setting: "Nietzsche, as a genealogist, takes there to be a multiplicity of perspectives within each of which truth-from-a-point-of-view may be asserted, but no truth-as-such, an empty notion, about *the* world, an equally empty notion. . . . The conduct of life requires a rupture, a breaking down of . . . idols, and a breaking up of fixed patterns, so that something radically new will emerge." *Three Rival Versions*, 42–43.

43. Nietzsche, "On Truth and Lie in an Extra-Moral Sense," in *The Portable Nietzsche*, 42–43, 45, 47.

44. Ricoeur, *The Symbolism of Evil*, trans. Emerson Buchanan (Boston: Beacon Press, 1967), 348.

45. Ricoeur, *Freud and Philosophy*, 27. At the conclusion of his discussion of the "double vow," Ricoeur observes that "it may be that extreme iconoclasm belongs to the restoration of meaning." The Nietzschean critique is inclined to see that iconoclasm not as a stage in the course of the unfolding of meaning but as the end and sum of meaning.

46. Wilde, "The Priority of Art," in *The Modern Tradition*, ed. Richard Ellmann and Charles Feidelson, Jr. (New York: Oxford University Press, 1965), 19.

47. There is a sense in which even naturalism must assume a teleology of some kind, because it must consider its own emergence to be a sign of favorable development. In an essay on John Dewey, Rorty concedes that "teleological thinking is inevitable, but Dewey offers us a relativist and materialist version of teleology rather than an absolute and idealist one." There is such a thing as "moral progress," Rorty claims, and to say that it "occurs is to say that later societies are more complex, more developed, more articulate, and above all more flexible than their predecessors. It is to say that later societies have more varied and interesting needs than earlier ones, just as squirrels have more varied and interesting needs than amoebas." *Truth and Progress: Philosophical Papers*, vol. 3 (New York: Cambridge University Press, 1998), 305, 304.

48. Gadamer, *Truth and Method*, 2d rev. ed., trans. Joel Weinsheimer and Donald G. Marshall (New York: Crossroad, 1989), 357. To be certain, Gadamer's insight about the nature of tragedy does not require a theistic explanation. Joel Weinsheimer, for example, interprets Gadamer's meditations on tragic limitations as a sign of the supremacy of history rather than as proof of providence: "Being experienced is the consciousness of finitude. It is the understanding that something exceeds understanding, a consciousness of history and one's own historicality. This conscious openness to experience is what Gadamer means by hermeneutic consciousness." *Gadamer's Hermeneutics: A Reading of* Truth and Method (New Haven: Yale University Press, 1985), 205.

49. Bakhtin, *Problems of Dostoevsky's Poetics,* ed. and trans. Caryl Emerson (Minneapolis: University of Minnesota Press, 1984), 110.

50. Gary Saul Morson and Caryl Emerson, *Mikhail Bakhtin: Creation of a Prosaics* (Stanford: Stanford University Press, 1990), 62.

Though they worked completely independently of each other, Bakhtin and Gadamer were in agreement on many points in their understanding of interpretation. Like Bakhtin, Gadamer drew heavily upon theology—in his case, German Lutheranism—in developing his theory of interpretation. For Gadamer, it was the Lutheran emphasis upon the self-emptying quality of the Incarnation that particularly informed his view of hermeneutical application. Just as texts open themselves to multiple interpretations and uses, so did God in Jesus Christ sacrificially offer himself to mankind. The fact that interpretation always involves application—receiving is also using—no more endangers the identity of the text than God's revelation of himself in Christ threatens or diminishes his eternal and unchangeable nature. Paul Althaus writes, in explaining Luther's theology of the cross, "God shows that he is God precisely in the fact that he is mighty in weakness, glorious in lowliness, living and life-giving in death." *The Theology of Martin Luther,* trans. Robert C. Schultz (Philadelphia: Fortress Press, 1966), 34.

51. In his later work, Ricoeur examines more explicitly and thoroughly the theme of otherness. In his groundbreaking early work on hermeneutics, however, he focused his concerns around selfhood and its internal dynamics. For the turn to "otherness" in his later work, see Paul Ricoeur, *Oneself as Another,* trans. Kathleen Blamey (Chicago: University of Chicago Press, 1992).

52. Ricoeur, "Existence and Hermeneutics," trans. Kathleen McLaughlin, in *The Conflict of Interpretations,* ed. Don Ihde (Evanston: Northwestern University Press, 1974), 21, 20.

53. Ibid., 21.

54. Ibid., 22–24.

55. Auden, *Collected Poems,* ed. Edward Mendelson (New York: Random House, 1976), 449, 450.

56. Frost, "The Most of It," in *Collected Poems, Prose, and Plays,* 307.

57. Ong, *Ramus, Method, and the Decay of Dialogue* (1958; Cambridge: Harvard University Press, 1983), 318.

9 | Historical Theology Today and Tomorrow

BRIAN E. DALEY, S.J.

The most honest way to begin any survey of scholarship such as this is to show one's own hand right from the start. So I have to tell you: although I answer to the name of patristic scholar, I think of myself primarily not as a historian but as a theologian. That word, of course, itself calls for further explanation, and I have to confess that my notion of what theology is is probably rather old-fashioned (or at least classical): theology, as I understand it, is what people of religious faith do to integrate that faith into their intelligent awareness of the world around them—faith seeking understanding, in Anselm's phrase; faith reverently but seriously examined, by all the available strategies of rational reflection. And faith, for Jews and Christians at least, is always fundamentally historical, in that it is rooted in the life and worship of a community whose history is a memory of being chosen and carried and saved from destruction by God; faith is the acceptance of a message whose credibility lies in its continuing connection with crucial, revelatory events of the past. As a Catholic, too, I assume that our way of being connected with those events is always more than just the affirmation of some normative textual witness, such as the Bible, on its own; it includes the whole tradition of interpretation and lived observance that sets the very conditions in which the message is proclaimed and the Bible is read. Faith lives from the tradition of preaching and theological interpretation, just as theology is always oriented towards preaching and grounded on the historically lived experience of faith.

All of which makes it seem obvious, to me at least, that *Christian* theology (which is all I can really speak about, and all that I am sure fits this description of what theology is) can never be properly done without a clear and conscious awareness of its own history. St. Gregory of Nazianzus describes theology as "philosophizing about God," and the phrase is

117

certainly apt; theology has always used the mental disciplines and categories of the best contemporary philosophies of its age, and needs to remain involved in the analysis of human experience and language at its most general and logically rigorous levels, if it is to understand the full human implications of faith. But while philosophy can be, and often is, done—for good or ill—without much conscious attention being paid to the historical growth of the philosophical tradition or to the cultural and historical context of the philosophical vocabulary, the same cannot be done by theology without the risk of seriously failing at its central task The God about whom theology "philosophizes" is a God whom we can only speak and think about because he has worked and spoken in our history; and our only way of coming to know him is through the historical chain of witness, of worship and preaching and philosophical reflection, of the community of faith—the community in which the Christian Scriptures have been formed and recognized as canonical, and in which the main norms for interpreting Scripture have been forged in the course of the centuries.

My own special area of study is the growth of Christian doctrine and theological reflection in the early church—the first eight centuries, more or less, of Christianity. It is common in the United States today to refer to this kind of academic enterprise as "historical theology," a term mainly meant to distinguish the kind of thing I and my medievalist or Reformation colleagues do from "systematic theology." I have never been convinced that this distinction is particularly helpful, either as description or prescription; it seems to me, for the reasons I have just sketched out, that *genuine* Christian theology must always be both historical *and* systematic: consciously aware of the tradition of intelligent faith and its scriptural and liturgical roots, and consciously trying to ask the "So what?" question for today's believer—to ask how some particular aspect of the preached tradition can make sense, in the whole context of what we understand about ourselves and our world. Systematic theology, as it is usually done in America today, really means *modern* theology, as opposed to a theology that takes extensive account of earlier sources. But I would strenuously contend that the study of the actual religious content of ancient or medieval Christian texts can be just as much a theological enterprise as the study of the theologians most *à la mode*. One can read the dialogues of Plato, for example, as a witness to classical Athenian language and culture, or as examples of philosophical arguments to be examined and judged in the same way we do contemporary arguments, or as works that can only really be understood in the context of their own culture but which still have something urgent and valuable to say to us in ours. In the same way, theological works from other ages can either be seen as items of evidence for cultural and social history, as footnotes or foils to modern theological argument, or as works whose religious content is to be taken seriously in its own right, even though that content cannot be fully understood if the reader is unaware of the social and human shape of the world in which it was written. This last way of understanding early Christian theology is the rubric under which I attempt to study it myself.

This rather long introduction is really meant to give a sense of my own academic starting-point, and perhaps of my own prejudices and interests, as I try to summarize briefly what I see as the present condition and future prospects for the historical study of religion, and especially for my branch of it: patristic theology. To understand where patristic studies seem presently to be going, it is important, first of all, to reflect on what it has left behind; in some ways, I think that could be described as a declericalizing, even a dechurching of the history of theology. From the eighteenth until perhaps the last quarter of the twentieth century, most of the interest in the study of ancient or medieval Christian theology was focused on what the Germans call *Dogmengeschichte*: the history of the formation of the major, officially recognized doctrines that define the contours of the churches and set up the rules for ecclesial communion. Whether it was the Catholic histories of doctrine, from the labors of Louis Le Nain de Tillemont in eighteenth-century France to those of Jules Lebreton and Aloys Grillmeier in our own, or the Protestant surveys reaching their zenith in the works of historians like Adolf von Harnack and Friedrich Loofs at the turn of the present century and finding an admirable exemplar in the 1960s in Jaroslav Pelikan's five-volume survey, *The Christian Tradition*, the underlying agenda of most classical studies of the field has been to clarify the development of church-dividing and church-identifying issues: controversies, arguments, important councils and conciliar formulas, and the work of great theological figures like Athanasius and Augustine and Luther, who have defined the shape of the major denominations' confessions of faith through the centuries. Just as the aim of much political history through the middle decades of this century might be seen as basically aimed at telling the story of the evolution of modern nation-states in terms that would, as far as possible, affirm the value of contemporary institutions, so historical theology tended above all to explain the background of why Lutherans or Anglicans or Catholics believe and worship as they do.

The focus of this kind of historical study began showing signs of change perhaps as early as the 1950s, when a kind of revisionist spirit began to seep into the study of early Christianity. A number of mainstream Catholic and Protestant scholars began questioning the validity of some of the labels of orthodoxy traditionally attached to certain controversial figures: the Antiochene school of biblical interpretation and theology, long considered either heretical or dangerously close to it because of its strong emphasis on the strict distinction between the divinity and the humanity of Christ, became a popular object of sympathetic treatment and seemed curiously modern in its stress on the autonomy and integrity of the created, historical order. In the wake of this rediscovery, scholars from the 1950s through the late 1970s began writing monographs to show that most of the major heretics of the scholastic handbooks had often been grossly maligned by the Church authorities that condemned them: that Origen was a faithful churchman as well as a theologian and exegete of extraordinary precocity, that Pelagius was not really a Pelagian, that Nestorius was not really a Nestorian, and that Arius was simply a pastoral leader who wanted to present Jesus as an example of spiritual growth. Along with this tendency towards a loosening of dogmatic categories, liberal Protestant scholars—starting with Walter Bauer in the late 1930s—began questioning the validity of the classical assumption that Christian orthodoxy represents the linear intellectual development of core teachings and ideas implicitly present in the New Testament writings and the original apostolic preaching. Bauer's hypothesis, which remained influential in North America long after it had been largely forgotten in Europe, and which eventually found a kind of new life in more recent deconstructive approaches to Christian literature, was that the earliest forms of Christian faith, as found in different ancient centers of civilization, differed much more widely and more substantially than we now suspect; that much of what later came to be thought heretical (such as so-called "Gnostic" Christianity) was often as representative of primitive Christian belief as orthodoxy was, and that the very distinction between heresy and orthodoxy in the early Church was based more on the self-interest of bishops, intent on shoring up their own power, than on the inherent authenticity or inauthenticity of the doctrines under discussion.

In the 1980s, historical research on early and medieval Christianity revealed signs of a more radical shift of interest: a clear loss of interest in the development of Christianity's doctrines and "big ideas," and a new fascination with the life and concerns of ordinary Christians. Inspired, no doubt, by a wider change of focus throughout historical studies, and led by the work of the French *annales* school, scholars of the early Church began to make ever greater use of the questions and methods of social history to identify what the religious experience and faith of all classes and groups of Christians may have been in earlier centuries, especially on questions that are of burning concern in the modern West: studies began to appear of the treatment of the poor in the early Church, of class and racial tensions, of the role of women and children in Christian society. The strictly theological concerns of early Christian writers ceded priority of place, in many patristic and medieval journals, to studies of early Christian ideas on clothing and food, or to ancient practices surrounding childbirth and dying. Ascetical practices, pilgrimage, the cult—and even the theft—of relics, sexual behavior, and anything concerning the ancient understanding and treatment of the body had now clearly replaced the ancient dogmatic controversies as the "hot topics" of early and medieval Christian research, the subjects to cut one's scholarly teeth on.

To some degree, this change of focus clearly meant new freedom of movement for a discipline that had tended to be locked in by denominational concerns. Familiar sources could be approached again with new questions, and sources that had seldom been looked at—hagiographical materials, lesser chronicles, nonliterary documents such as papyri and inscriptions—could now be looked at as major sources for the life of whole sectors of ancient Christian society that had previously been ignored. Yet like all academic changes of fashion, this new wave of interest had its negative aspects: scholarship could fairly easily be used as the vehicle for advancing the political aspirations of self-proclaimed minorities seeking greater social influence; a certain antiintellectual and antitheological animus often showed itself, sometimes justified by the thinly veiled suggestion that serious theological argument is, in any case, the preserve of an educated male elite; and much of what came to be published as fresh and original scholarship seemed deliberately intended to shock its more traditional readers and titillate its more curious ones. The bizarre, the naughty, the funky—articles, for example, on nocturnal emissions in the Desert Fathers, or transvestism in early Byzantine monasticism—came to be more and more the order of the day, and gave at times a certain air of frivolity to the academic study of Christian origins.

This "turn from doctrine" that I have been describing also brought some serious new emphases, however, that could be termed genuinely theological in their own right.

1. The first of these, evident also since the late 1970s and early 1980s, has been a strong new emphasis on recovering the texts and practices of early and medieval Christian *spirituality*. Saying this, of course, may still leave many people puzzled, since "spirituality" is a word with many possible meanings—not all of them very Christian or very theological. My point is simply that as interest seems to have waned, in the last twenty-five or thirty years, in the development of classical doctrine and in the give-and-take of theological argument in early and medieval Christianity, it has certainly grown, to a degree unprecedented since perhaps the late sixteenth century, in early and medieval Christian approaches to prayer, mystical experience, ascetical practice, and union with God. Peter Brown's famous article, "The Rise and Function of the Holy Man in Late Antiquity," in the *Journal of Roman Studies* of 1971, set the tone for a revival of interest in ancient ideas of holiness that at times has approached the intensity of a craze. Bernard McGinn's history of Western Christian mysticism, which has now reached the year 1350 at the end of the third volume, offers a learned and balanced survey of one major strand in the development of the Christian experience of God. A number of new series—notably the Paulist Press's *Classics of Western Spirituality*—now flourish, making available classics of the Christian spiritual tradition previously unavailable to modern readers, usually with informative introductory essays and thorough annotations. And there are more popular essays, too, attempting to claim many of these classics for the self-help or new-age audience. I just put down an attractively published little volume, which I found at a religious bookstore, in which the author attempts to interpret various passages from *Sayings of the Desert Fathers* as embodying a kind of Jungian take on Zen Buddhism! All of this, clearly, can have an affinity with the search for ancient exotica that I mentioned before—for

new, offbeat, colorful approaches to what sometimes seems a forbiddingly remote part of the Christian tradition; but it seems, too, to represent the general thirst many commentators have observed in the post-Vietnam generation of the West to find an experience of God, or at least of some version of transcendence, that is practically accessible to anyone who wants it, and that is not necessarily bound to the intellectual and institutional strictures of a worshipping community.

2. A second new area of interest in early and medieval Christian writings, now growing very fast among young scholars in the field, is the study of early Christian biblical interpretation. From our own doctoral applicants and present students at Notre Dame, at least, I can say that this seems to be the most flourishing "growth industry" of patristic and medieval theological studies at the present time. One practical reason, clearly, is that much of this field is yet unploughed. Although many of the fathers and medieval monastic and scholastic authors left behind vast commentaries and sets of homilies on biblical books, relatively few of these have been critically edited or translated, and fewer still have been seriously studied for their exegetical or theological content. The assumption has been, for the last four centuries or so, that they represent an approach to Scripture that has little to say to a modern reader: arbitrarily allegorical, primitive in their lack of textual expertise and historical consciousness, fanciful rather than scientific. Now, in a time of postmodern awareness that texts are, and must be, read from as many interpretive viewpoints as there are readers, and that legitimacy of interpretation is much more difficult to identify than we used to think twenty years ago, patristic and medieval approaches to biblical texts offer a rich field for reflection on what those texts might mean precisely as "holy Scripture": as the foundational texts of a community of faith, within a continuous if constantly varying tradition of perspective and application. These earlier approaches to exegesis also seem to many younger scholars today to suggest at least working examples of ways we might ourselves read biblical texts intelligently as engaged believers, without introducing a break between the "original" meaning of the authors or redactors—recoverable, one hopes, through the historical researches of the dispassionate scholar—and their meaning within the longer tradition of Christian reception and response. While early or medieval Christian attempts at explaining the meaning of a passage may still often strike us as foreign or far-fetched, they at least open up

our exegetical imagination to wider possibilities of what might be involved in reading the Bible in faith.

In recent centuries, as I have said, little scholarly work has been done on ancient or medieval biblical commentary. Apart from a thoughtful and suggestive new book by Frances Young, most of the recent secondary surveys and monographs on early Christian exegesis are fairly sketchy; the first volume of Henri de Lubac's influential *Exegese medievale*, originally published in 1959, appeared in a fine English translation last year, and we can only hope that the series will be continued. I am myself involved in one of two large-scale projects under way to make a representative sampling of patristic biblical interpretation available in the form of full-length commentaries on books of the Bible; a sampling constructed entirely from passages from ancient preachers and commentators, carefully selected for their theological and spiritual interest, and freshly translated for the contemporary reader. If the present crop of doctoral theses are a clue to future scholarship, we should be seeing a substantial number of serious new studies of early Christian biblical interpretation in the next decade.

3. Related to this interest in biblical exegesis are various contemporary lines of research on the earlier Christian tradition that one might call theological, although not doctrinal in the classical sense. A number of works have appeared in recent years on the hermeneutics and methodological presuppositions of ancient and medieval biblical interpretation: Karen Jo Torjesen's important work on Origen's exegesis is a good example. David Dawson's widely read study, *Allegorical Readers and Cultural Revision in Ancient Alexandria*, attempts to set ancient pagan, Jewish, and Christian allegorical interpretation in the perspective of contemporary cultural theory, a project he plans to expand into a wider reflection on the methodological and theological implications of the figural reading of texts, as seen through the theories of ancient and modern authors. Harry Gamble's *Books and Readers in the Early Church* offers rich information on the *realia* of ancient writing and reading, while Brian Stock's *Augustine the Reader* studies Augustine's particular habits of interpretation. Other scholars have begun to take a serious interest in the history of early and medieval Christian preaching: Hughes Oliphant Old has already published three fresh and readable volumes of what promises to be a comprehensive study of this neglected subject. Others, including Averil Cameron, Peter

Brown, and Thomas Schmitz, are studying the distinctive character and role of rhetoric in early Christianity and the secular society that surrounded it. Along with works on preaching, a number of new dissertations and monographs on the "care of souls" in the early church have been inspired by Pierre Hadot's attractive and persuasive study of the more "pastoral" and "spiritual" side of late antique philosophy, which appeared in English under the title *Philosophy as a Way of Life*. In all of these varied lines of research, the one common factor seems to be that contemporary researchers on early Christianity appear, in general, to be far less interested than their forebears two or three decades ago in the formation of classical doctrine and theological ideas—all of which they tend simply to assume as known—and far more interested in the *way* the Christian Bible and the wider Christian kerygma was imagined, interpreted, communicated, and applied. Even the most recent large-scale history of Christian theology to begin appearing in English—the new Italian series now being published by Liturgical Press, with a massive and impressive first volume on the patristic period by Angelo di Berardino and Basil Studer—is not so much a history of doctrine as a history of theological method, and of the very conception of the theological task itself. Thematic content, for the moment at least, seems to have yielded place to form and praxis.

Part of our task, as I understand it, is to consider not only "present positions" in the historical approach to religion, but also "future prospects." Like most of us schooled in history, I am less confident in making long-term predictions than I am in observing past changes; but I suspect that many of the features of the present landscape will set the scene for work in historical theology for the next few decades. Translations of patristic and medieval theological works into modern languages will surely play an increasing role in publication in the field, and will consume, I suspect, a larger part of the scholarly energy of those who command ancient Christian languages, if only because such scholars are now a vanishing breed within the wider academic population. If the rest of the church and the world is to have access to the traditions of early and medieval Christianity in the future at all, they will need to have it via modern translations. This is now true for classic works in Latin and Greek that many a parish minister or priest, a hundred years ago, might have been able to consult in Migne's *Patrologia*, and it is still more true of the vast corpus of valuable spiritual and theological works in Syriac, Coptic, Armenian, and other early Christian languages, most of which have never been translated at all. To say that translation is bound to play a larger part in the historical study of early and medieval Christianity is not, in my view, to suggest that the scholarly community is likely to be deprived of more valuable research; on the contrary: translation is the ultimate work of interpretation, and lies at the foundation of all other interpretive study. It will mean, however, that greater recognition will have to be given by the academic establishment to the value of translation—and also to the editing of texts—as an original scholarly enterprise, and as a contribution to knowledge.

In the area of historical theology, my own principal area of interest, I do detect small but unmistakable signs, in new publications and in the interests and questions of the young scholars I talk to, that a revival of interest in the explicitly theological thinking of ancient and medieval Christianity may be in the making. If such a revival should materialize, it will probably center on the great themes of Christian preaching and worship and theological reflection—the reality of God and God's relation to the world, the person of Christ, the central reality of redemption and grace, the nature of Christian hope—as well as on the hermeneutical presuppositions and linguistic practices of ancient theologians and preachers. But it will probably not be couched in such explicitly confessional terms, or with such a confident sense of the unfolding process of the development of Christian doctrine, as was the *Dogmengeschichte* of the nineteenth and early twentieth centuries.

Just the other day I was having lunch with an extraordinarily bright and perceptive young doctoral student in our department here at Notre Dame, who is studying patristic theology and who has a strong interest in modern philosophy and hermeneutics. I asked him if he had any ideas yet, towards the end of his first year, of what he might want to work on for his dissertation. He looked up at me, hesitated a moment as if embarrassed by the simplicity of his thought, and said: "God!" "I've come to realize this year," he continued, "that the most fascinating thing about early Christian theologians is really the sense they have of the reality of God: what they felt we can say about divine being, how we become aware of our relationship to him and how that relationship grows, how God is present in the world. . . . I'm not sure yet," he added, "of what author's approach to God I want to study, or how I can limit and focus this into a manageable topic, but that's where I want to do my work." And I found myself saying to him in my head: Right on! This kind of thing may seem like it's been done before, but it sounds like it might come out looking entirely new, at your hands. And what else is there, after all, that would be so much worth the effort? Fascinating as Byzantine monastic transvestism may have been to us for a while, our study is *theology*, and *God* is what it's really all about.

Institutions and Sacraments

The Catholic Tradition and Political Science

CLARKE E. COCHRAN

Scholars are no different from other humans; they never leave home. Despite how far they travel geographically, intellectually, or professionally, their formative experiences stay with them, entering research in myriad ways, from robust expression to strong rejection, in subtleties of style or in fundamental themes. When religious faith is central to these experiences, their presence raises special challenges.

Catholic at birth and ordained a Catholic deacon in mid-academic career at a public university, I have always drawn upon the Catholic tradition in my research and publication as a political scientist, at the beginning in highly implicit ways, lately quite explicitly. In this chapter I reflect on how I see the relationship between the faith of my home and my scholarship in a university and a discipline far from home.

Until recently my research did not focus directly on the Catholic tradition, but that faith always helped to form my approach to basic research questions. My publications involved standard political philosophy questions (freedom, justice, authority, community) and appeared in standard political science journals. To the extent that my research concentrated directly on religion, my arguments pointed political science to relationships between religion and politics that prior research had neglected, and they probed the irreducible and creative tensions inherent in such relationships. Political science needed to take religion more seriously as an actor in liberal democracy. These were matters that in principle political scientists from any religious or philosophical background could wrestle with. To use the vocabulary that emerged in the Lilly Seminar, my scholarship was and is "universal," but grounded "perspectivally." My research represents both scholarship grounded in religion and scholarship about religion.

In the last few years, particularly the academic year 1998–99 spent as a senior research fellow of the Erasmus Institute at the University of Notre

Dame, my interests turned directly toward Catholic principles and Catholic institutions. One can go only so far with research on "religion in general" before one confronts specific religions in all their particularity. Yet as with all my research, I aim to discover and communicate truths that could form part of the political science mainstream. It has been difficult to adjust my research to the Catholic tradition explicitly, to attend directly to what I had been dwelling in tacitly. I sometimes tried to imagine the experience of a fish suddenly asked to study water. I have found it difficult to write about Catholicism, to find the proper voice of faith and political science.

Yet, as I reflect on my recent scholarship, it seems that by attending to Catholic faith and its intellectual traditions more transparently I have discovered political phenomena involving central Catholic concerns, but that also point beyond the Catholic world.

An Argument in Three Steps

I have begun to outline an argument in three large steps. The first starts from the fact that Catholics build highly structured institutions, but they do so in recent decades in the context of a Catholic institutional identity crisis, one familiar in higher education and in parish life. I am particularly interested in the ways this crisis appears in health care institutions and to a lesser degree in social service institutions like Catholic charities. These institutions today experience a crisis of identity rooted in all the familiar challenges to the Catholic church in the modern world. But in health care and social service agencies the crises also involve fundamental changes in institutional life; for example, a changing clientele. The people now served in Catholic hospitals, nursing homes, or clinics are different from those who would have come at their founding thirty, fifty, or one hundred years ago. Moreover, these institutions are now highly professionalized and secularized, imbued with the norms, procedures, and rules of medicine, social work, and other professions. Finally, government policies affecting health care and social service institutions have changed dramatically in the last decade, and these institutions struggle with how to respond while maintaining a distinctive Catholic identity. Thus the first of the three steps is to try to think about the meaning of Catholic institutions and the challenges that health care and social service institutions face.

The second step examines the tradition of Catholic social teaching as it has evolved over the last hundred years in familiar categories: the common good, stewardship, subsidiarity, the dignity of the human person, and so forth. It seems to me on reflection that valuable as this tradition has been,[1] its categories are not sufficient to understand the challenges that health care and social service institutions face, nor are they sufficient to navigate politically the essential tensions that exist on the border between Catholic institutions and public life. Therefore, we have an institutional crisis and a tradition of social thought with a certain richness but one which is inadequate to significant dimensions of the challenge.

My third claim, then, is that the sacramental perspective in the Catholic tradition facilitates understanding the dynamics on this uneasy border between religious institutions and public life. By the sacramental tradition I mean the notion that the grace of God and the human experience of transformation meet in signs, symbols, and rituals that mediate the encounter. Sacraments are privileged moments of meeting God; they transform the self. Catholic sacramental theology clearly makes this assertion regarding the classic seven sacraments. I argue that sacramentality pervades Catholic thinking and institutions beyond baptism, Eucharist, and the other sacraments. The sacramental perspective calls Catholic health care institutions better to represent Christ to the sick, but also better to represent Christ to the culture at large. The sacramental perspective helps the church to see the face of Christ in the sick and the injured, especially to see the face of Christ in those pushed aside as market and government busily rearrange the furniture of the health care system.

From these three points I hope to derive a theoretical argument about the political significance of sacramental theology, which I briefly summarize here.[2] A sacramental approach to Catholic social theory will have two aspects: *iconic* and *indwelling.* The *iconic* dimension refers to the ways in which persons and institutions of the church are to image Christ, to be icons of Christ. Iconic sacramentality evokes the church as sacrament, a distinctive witness to the reality of Christ's redemption in human lives. "In the fullest sense of the word, a sacrament is the pledge of Christ's availability to a particular individual; the tangible pledge of his willingness to enter upon an encounter."[3] Iconic sacramentality summons institutions (particularly those, like hospitals, that have secular counterparts) to configure themselves to Christ in such a way that they appear as Christ, that

Christ is visible and personal in them, in ways not possible for non-Catholic (or at least non-Christian) institutions. Iconic sacramentality would characterize both their particular ministries of service and their entry into the political arena; indeed, the former would ground the latter.

The *indwelling* dimension requires that Catholics see in the mundane things of the world, in ordinary people and daily human activities, signs of the presence of Christ. In Gerard Manley Hopkins's image, "The world is charged with the grandeur of God,/It will flame out, like shining from shook foil. . . ." In this regard, the gestures of ordinary medical care, undertaken in totally secular settings and without religious motivation are sacramental too, if the human soul perceives a touch of divinity (without any requirement that it be translated directly into Catholic or any other faith vocabulary). This form of sacramentality is most pertinent to Catholic social theory, however, when it awakens Christians to see Christ in the most "un-Christ-like" persons—outcasts, addicts, prisoners, and so forth—the people of Matthew 25:31–46.[4]

The iconic and the indwelling dimensions are conceptually separable but are really two movements of a single reality. The iconic directly points to the reality of the mystery of God (present, for example, in real water, real bread, and real oil transformed in sacred rituals); the indwelling acknowledges the presence of God in everything *real* (apart from overtly sacred times, spaces, and actions).

Iconic as Representation

Catholic hospitals, nursing homes, and hospices have a mission within history to cure the injured, care for the aged, and comfort the dying; but they also witness to eschatological meaning beyond cure, care, and comfort. This witness makes them icons of Christ and justifies them as specifically Christian institutions. Representation of Christ occurs, not in mission statements, lectures, or exhortations, but in the daily work of nurses, aides, social workers, administrators, physicians, and pastoral staff, whose actions are transparent to the divine, though often quite imperfectly.[5]

Thus far, representation has little specifically political content. Indeed, most of its implications point to the internal structure of Catholic institutions themselves, without overt regard for their political consequences. If church institutions imitate Christ, then like Christ and the woman with the hemorrhage or like the puzzled saved in Matthew 25:31–46 ("Lord, when did we see thee hungry and feed thee . . . ?"), it will not know whom it touched. It will witness to unknown people with unknown results.[6] Taken to heart, this iconic vision urges self-criticism by Catholic institutions, which will want to know to what degree they are or are not living up to the challenge to represent Christ to the world. Taken seriously, it suggests specific reforms in Catholic health care delivery.[7] But when and how does iconic sacramentality become political?

There is one simple and important sense in which representative church institutions are political. Representation is public, and the political is a subset of the public. Moreover, that which is public will often be drawn, willingly or unwillingly, into the political orbit. Sacramental witness links public and private life, through individual heroic actions (for example, of health care workers) that become public knowledge, or through public institutional decisions (for example, to refuse to perform certain procedures or to keep open at great cost an unprofitable but crucial service to the uninsured poor). What Lisa Sowle Cahill says of the contribution of religious traditions to bioethics is true also of their public witness: "The relevance of religion to bioethics does not lie primarily in any distinct or specific contribution to the process of moral argumentation, nor in lifting up 'religious' behaviors defensible only on faith, revelation, or church authority. Rather, it depends on the formation of socially radical communities that challenge dominant values and patterns of social relationship, not by withdrawing from the larger society, or by speaking to it from outside, but by participating in it in challenging and even subversive ways."[8]

Therefore, Catholic institutions that work to become (however imperfectly) iconic representations of Christ thereby become public and political. This is particularly clear for health care institutions that, because of the ways in which health care policy and Catholic institutions evolved, have long-standing and deep connections to the world of politics through licensure, health and safety regulation, Medicare and Medicaid funding, and a wide variety of other public programs. As with dance partners, when one changes steps, the other reacts. Therefore, if Catholic health care institutions, responding to a call distinctively to witness Christ, change their organization, practices, or ministry locations, then government programs will have to reply.

Sacramental Indwelling—The Impulse of Solidarity

The iconic aspect of sacramentality remains close to the theology of ecclesial sacraments in that both depend upon official representatives of the church—the priest in the sacrament of baptism, for example; Catholic hospitals in health care. The indwelling aspect moves away from the distinctively ecclesial. Rather than God's presence discovered in the extraordinary actions of the church and its ministers, God appears in the ordinary. As Stephen Schloesser puts it, "Sacramentality binds us to seeing the finite world as the bearer of the infinite. Or put another way perhaps more importantly: Sacramentality regards the singular with a nearly-infinite significance."[9]

Though sacramentality always refers to mutual encounter between God and humanity, the representational aspect is asymmetrical: God acts; humans respond. Institutions witness Christ; persons and public react. Indwelling sacramentality, however, is more symmetrical, each adapting to the other. In the Incarnation, God empties God of fullness, taking on human materiality. Sacramentally God adapts to human ways, including the ordinary needs of life.[10] From the other side, humans perceive God's operation in common occurrences. Scriptural examples are the canticles of Hannah and of Mary (1 Sam 2:1–10; Luke 1:46–55), in which typical historical reversals of fortune become signs of God's favor. Sometimes these meanings are taken literally, the idea that God has a "plan" for each person's life. The Catholic sacramental perspective, however, is not literal but rather a "seeing through" or "into" genuinely *human* actions and choices that nonetheless reveal to sacramental sight signs of God's justice and mercy, within which human action occurs and to which it refers.

Taking the case of health care, one might say that iconic sacramentality reveals God in the "successful"; that is, when a Catholic hospital's actions make clear God's desire for healing and wholeness. The indwelling aspect of sacramentality, however, can discern God's presence even more mysteriously in the nonhealing inseparable from medicine and prosaic human experience. Iconicity moves to transcend or transform death, evil, and violence; indwelling does not blink from dirt, horror, and failure, but sees God at work there too.[11]

Although sacramental theologians of the 1970s and 1980s often referred to the dynamic and transforming character of sacraments, they had little to say, except in passing, about justice, poverty, or social theory generally. Yet Catholic sacramental vision, seeing the divine in worldly things (what doctors and nurses do by daily tending wounds and imparting hope), establishes a way of connecting politics and eternity without a dogmatizing ideology. In other words, Catholic political action springing from this kind of sight does not depend primarily upon principles that too often become distorted into ideological slogans—freedom, justice, equality, class consciousness—but upon seeing and responding to God in the person of those needing health care and requiring someone to help them get it, politically if necessary. Sacramental political thinking does not deny the significance of justice, freedom, and dignity for Catholic social theory, but it binds them to the institutional life of the church. The politics that issues from this response to the other may indeed call upon the common good, equality, and subsidiarity (for example), but it is not ultimately founded upon them but upon sacramental encounter.

There are two connected movements that constitute indwelling sacramental politics; each expresses the solidarity foundational to this vision. The first movement is toward those social groups whose wounded humanity reveals the presence of Christ; the second movement is from that humanity toward political advocacy to advance the human dignity of these groups and, thereby, to advance the common good of the entire community.

Relevance to Mainstream Political Science?

Perhaps this argument might be thought interesting but really part of the internal business of the Catholic tradition, that is, as merely perspectival. But it is more than that. As I worked through these ideas as a political scientist, they suggested fundamental limitations of contemporary political science. If this is so, then thinking about institutions in a Catholic way contributes to the discipline. The most obvious limitation is political science's insensibility to the role that Catholic (and other religious) institutions play in political and public life. Discussing church-state controversies, for example, political scientists, and constitutional lawyers as well, most often consider schools and funding for private elementary and secondary education, but seldom address the billions of government dollars that flow into Catholic hospitals, nursing homes, charities, and service agencies every year. It is important to bring this phenomenon to the surface, to ask what is going on, and to consider implications of the daily relationship between big government and big religious institutions, a relationship both financial and political.

Beyond this obvious point, however, there is a more significant theoretical point. It now seems to me that the representational life of institutions, the way institutions mediate meaning, has been neglected in political science generally. Institutions are important in their own right and their internal life has an import. Yet political science tends to treat institutions simply as convenient collections of individuals transmitting desires or interests to the political system.[12] We fail to attend to the meaning of the institution itself. But institutions are not simply utilitarian, not simply means to ends set by autonomous individuals or by powerful groups or classes, though obviously institutions do have utilitarian purposes. All institutions of any depth, not Catholic health care or religious institutions alone, are icons or sacramental witnesses of something more fundamental. They witness to ideas, beliefs, relationships, and loyalties. They sustain commitments in those who belong, and they initiate new members into a particular culture. Moreover, institutions create realities that stem from these fundamental commitments. They communicate and shape cultural, political, and religious meaning. They are places of transforming encounter. Disneyland is more than a mere place for children's entertainment. A Catholic, Jewish, or Baptist hospital is more than a location for the practice of modern medicine. It is an icon of distinctive meaning. If such institutions are only places for the practice of medicine, they have become shells, filled with meaning by medical culture, a source different from their founding identity.

If the argument just sketched rings true, there are two implications. One is for Catholic faith itself. I hope to persuade Catholic social theorists that there are important gaps in their theory and that these gaps are reparable with materials from the larger tradition itself. Specifically, the tradition is not sufficiently aware of the role of Catholic institutions directly involved with politics and government. Nor has it focused sufficient attention on the resources that sacramental theology brings to Catholic social theory and Catholic social institutions. Second, I want to persuade political science and political theory that there is an important contribution that a Catholic sacramental perspective can make to under-standing institutions on the public-private border.

Broader Implications

My attempt to be both universal, in the sense of speaking to the larger dis-cipline, and at the same time particular, rooted and grounded in the Catholic tradition, suggests that the dichotomy itself is inadequate and flawed. One must be both universal and perspectival. All political science research is, I believe, both "objective" and "subjective," concerned with both "facts" and "values." In short, the familiar social science dichotomies that have divided political scientists between empiricists and normative theorists are false and misleading. I incline towards Michael Polanyi's con-cept of personal knowledge, in which all knowing—scientific or moral or religious—depends upon indwelling.[13] In what Polanyi calls "tacit know-ing" we attend *from* fundamental assumptions to which we are personally committed (for example, a discipline's methodology or set of theories) in order to attend *to* something else (a particular problem within the disci-pline or a particular feature of the world). Knowledge is "personal," not objective or subjective. Analogously, we might attend from a religious tra-dition, Catholic sacramentality, in order to attend to a more general theo-retical problem in social life; in the present case, the political meaning of institutions. This attending from in order to attend to is done with the intent of discovering and warranting universal knowledge.

Catholic intellectual traditions, despite their diversity, commonly appeal to the potentially universal convincing force of human reason; indeed, the gift of faith, too, is universal, in the sense of being open to all persons. *Truth* is the aim of both reason and revelation. As Nicholas Wolterstorff describes John Paul II's position in the 1998 encyclical letter *Fides et Ratio:* Faith "enables reason to exercise its powers within realms to which it would otherwise have no access whatsoever."[14] So Catholic claims are uni-versal but clearly also grounded in a particular Christian perspective on human nature, reason, and the effects of sin, as well as on a tradition of institution-building grounded in a sacramental view of the relation be-tween humanity and divinity. The universal claim is inseparable from the particular community making the claim.

There will be no way to "prove" (on a scientific or quasi-scientific model) assertions about politics and policy made by scholars working within the Catholic tradition, just as there is no way to prove theological claims made from within the tradition. Such assertions, however, have valid warrants, intersubjectivity, and legitimate convincing power if they meet standards of truth that transcend particular traditions of inquiry. Polanyi sketches at least five such standards.[15]

- Intimations of fruitfulness; that is, an indeterminate range of intrinsically interesting new problems and questions open for investigation when the relevant claim is made and accepted by a community of inquirers;
- knowledge claims that are made with "universal intent";
- knowledge claims that manifest exactitude or precision;
- formulation of claims that manifest "intellectual beauty"; and
- "adherence to a society respecting truth"; that is, openness to communication to and with others (a criterion that meshes with Richard Bernstein's "engaged fallibilistic pluralism," a motif of the Lilly Seminar that he introduces in his essay in this volume).

Institutional Implications

Religious Institutions of Higher Education

If all institutions are iconic, as sacramental political theory claims, then religiously affiliated colleges and universities will communicate (willy-nilly) a particular ethos. This ethos will be partly congruous and partly incongruous with the traditions in which the institutions operate. If this is so, then each college or university should self-consciously attend to the messages communicated by its way of embodying the tradition. Three forms of attention suggest themselves, forms that must be adapted to the wide variety of institutional settings in religious higher education.

1. A Catholic, Protestant, or Jewish institution might foster special places for reflection on the institution's tradition and its implications for curriculum and internal community life. Such places can be either

disciplinary (for example, Catholic social thought as an explicit component of a department of political science) or multidisciplinary (for example, a center of Jewish Studies).

2. There should be space for persons in every discipline to think about
the tradition's bearing on the methods and substance of the disciplines.
Ways of indwelling a tradition and attending from it to the discipline's research and teaching issues will differ from discipline to discipline. The
Mennonite tradition affects literature differently than sociology does. Faculty retreats, sabbatical programs, and seminars are ways to foster reflection on these effects.

3. Straightforward expressions of the founding traditions are also vital,
such as worship services, departments of theology and biblical studies, and
programs of community service grounded in explicit expression of the
institution's understanding of faith and social action. These will consciously
try to form student character.

Secular Institutions of Higher Education

Secular institutions are as iconic as their religious counterparts, though
their visage represents other and undoubtedly multiple traditions of
knowing. The face of such institutions is more difficult to read than that
of their religious counterparts. Secular institutions should welcome the
different ways that individual faculty will explore their disciplines and the
disciplines' problems. That is, internal pluralism is an appropriate commitment. In the absence of this commitment, secular institutions can be
as rigidly conformist as religious ones. Wise secular institutions will also
facilitate engagement among traditional ways of knowing and welcome
faculty and students who engage religious traditions as part of the mix.
Pluralism without interaction is merely academic cold war. Institutionally-
sponsored retreats, ceremonies, and service commitments will, however,
have appropriate secular flavors different from their counterparts in religious institutions.

Implications for the Disciplines

The implications of the institutional and sacramental perspective, of
course, vary by discipline. Every discipline has its regional and national and

international organizations. These include members from both religious and secular institutions. Therefore, one of their missions is to foster dialogue across methodological and substantive boundaries when these bear upon religious commitments. Let me use political science as an example.

I belong to two organizations that foster such dialogue. The Religion and Politics Section of the American Political Science Association assembles around the traditional substantive questions of political science (power, attitude formation, voting behavior, representation, freedom, authority, and justice) as they are encountered in the influence of religious institutions, attitudes, and principles upon courts, legislatures, executives, political parties, interest groups, media, and the larger political culture (and vice versa). Its members come from religious and secular institutions; they are believers and unbelievers of a wide variety, united only by their teaching and research focus on the manifestations of religion in politics. They represent the traditional subfields of political science—comparative politics, international politics, American politics, political theory, and methodology. The section's meetings concentrate on the craft of political science and on research problems basic to the discipline as a whole. Its meetings, however, foster appreciation for the variety of members' religious, philosophical, and methodological perspectives. At the same time, it has advanced political science's understanding of the interaction of religion and politics; that is, it is a clear example of engaged fallibilistic pluralism.

The second organization is Christians in Political Science, an "affiliated group" of the American Political Science Association. There is the same diversity of research and teaching interests and diversity of secular and religious institutions as in the Religion and Politics Section (indeed, the memberships have considerable overlap), but the unity is one of faith. All members are committed Christians, primarily evangelical, but also Catholics and mainline Protestants. The organization's special focus is on how Christian faith illumines research problems, confronts familiar assumptions, or presents challenges to teaching in both secular and religious settings.

These organizations, and their legitimacy within institutional political science, have been places where different traditions of knowing encounter each other and clarify, test, critique, and correct each other's truth claims.

Within this disciplinary exchange, the Catholic voice will insist on the importance of religious institutions as legitimate centers of representation, political advocacy, and reflection on political principles. It will refuse to let institutions be regarded simply as epiphenomena. The Catholic voice will help to keep alive a humanist tradition in a social science overly fascinated by quasi-scientific methods. It will insist on the legitimacy of the explanatory power of religious experience.[16] Since mainstream political science neglects Christian tradition generally and Catholic tradition particularly, rigorous research grounded in that tradition will have a strangeness that can startle at least some political scientists out of complacent assumptions, methods, and assertions.[17] Political science has traveled rather far from its home in political philosophy; the Catholic tradition of institutional sacramentality reminds the discipline of its still-living roots.

Notes

1. Valuable to Catholics and to non-Catholic political actors and scholars; for example, note the recent influence of Catholic just-war thinking.

2. More extended statements may be found in Clarke E. Cochran, "Institutional Identity; Sacramental Potential: Catholic Healthcare at Century's End," *Christian Bioethics* 5 (April 1999): 26–43; "Sacrament and Solidarity: Catholic Social Thought and Healthcare Policy Reform," *Journal of Church and State* 41 (Summer 1999): 475–98; and "Taking Ecclesiology Seriously: Catholicism, Religious Institutions, and Healthcare Policy," in Thomas W. Heilke and Ashley Woodiwiss, eds., *The Re-Enchantment of Political Science: Christian Scholars Engage Their Discipline* (Lanham, MD: Lexington Books, 2001): 169–92.

3. E. Schillebeeckx, O.P., *Christ the Sacrament of the Encounter with God* (New York: Sheed and Ward, 1963), 80.

4. Finding a term that works here is difficult, and "indwelling" is not fully satisfactory. Other terms, however, have too much theoretical or rhetorical baggage.

5. Richard A. McCormick, *Health and Medicine in the Catholic Tradition: Tradition in Transition* (New York: Crossroad, 1984), 32–43.

6. Hans Urs Von Balthasar, *Razing the Bastions: On the Church in This Age*, trans. Brian McNeil, C.R.V. (San Francisco: Ignatius Press, 1993), 66–68.

7. Cochran, "Institutional Identity."

8. Lisa Sowle Cahill, "Can Theology Have a Role in 'Public' Bioethical Discourse?" *Hastings Center Report* 20 (Special Supplement, July/August 1990), 12.

9. Stephen Schloesser, S.J., " 'Holy the Firm': Irony, Hope, and the Catholic Imagination," Presentation for the Catholic Imagination Project (Creighton University: November 10, 1997), 1–2.

10. Michael J. Baxter, C.S.C., "Reintroducing Virgil Michel: Towards a Counter-Tradition of Catholic Social Ethics in the United States," *Communio* 24 (Fall 1997): 515.

11. I am indebted to Stephen Schloesser for this insight.

12. Even valuable and insightful works, such as Allen D. Hertzke's *Representing God in Washington: The Role of Religious Lobbies in the American Polity* (Knoxville: University of Tennessee Press, 1988), attend almost exclusively to this sense of representation.

13. Michael Polyani, *Personal Knowledge: Toward a Post-Critical Philosophy* (New York: Harper Torchbooks, 1964), and *The Tacit Dimension* (Garden City, N.Y.: Anchor Books, 1967).

14. Nicholas Wolterstorff, "Special Section: *Fides et Ratio/Faith & Reason*," *Books & Culture* (July/August, 1999): p. 29.

15. Polanyi, *Personal Knowledge*.

16. See the remarks of Alan Wolfe, Monika Hellwig, and Nancy Ammerman in the "Report of the Sixth (and Final) Meeting of the Lilly Seminar on Religion and Higher Education," Inn by the Sea, Cape Elizabeth, Maine, October 1–3, 1999, pp. 2–3, and 8.

17. See the remarks of James Turner in the "Report of the Fifth Meeting of the Lilly Seminar on Religion and Higher Education," Fuller Theological Seminary, Pasadena, California, May 14–15, 1999, p. 14.

11 | Selving Faith

Feminist Theory and Feminist Theology Rethink the Self

SERENE JONES

In this brief essay, based on my presentation at the Lilly Seminar meeting in Pasadena in May 1999, I would like to discuss how my grounding in the Christian tradition has influenced the work I do in feminist studies and legal theory. I am presently finishing a book on the relationship between feminist political and literary theory and classical Christian theology. At the Lilly conference at Notre Dame in March, I presented an overview of the book as a whole. Here I want to talk in more detail about just one of its sections—the section where I lay out a feminist theological account of "the self" which is grounded in the Reformed doctrines of justification and sanctification but which also draws on recent work in poststructuralist feminist theory and psychoanalytic trauma theory.

Before I launch into this topic, let me say a few things about how I understand my work as a theologian. It is common to describe the task of a theologian as that of articulating the language of the Christian faith in terms accessible to the present day. As this definition suggests, the task of the theologian is to stand within the rich and deeply varied traditions of Christianity and attempt to speak its truths in a language that present-day folks not only understand but "believe into." This task involves, of course, engaging in an ongoing critique of the tradition because, as the tradition is brought into conversation with the present, its own limits and gaps are exposed.

As a traditionally trained theologian, I have engaged wholeheartedly in this task during the eight years I have been teaching in a divinity school. In particular, I have tried to bring the tradition into conversation with feminist concerns. Not surprisingly, when I do this, I often find myself in conflict with those places where the tradition rather stubbornly refuses to budge in its insistence on the inferior status of women and its preference for patriarchal relations of power. When I come to these places, I deploy the common theological strategy of using the tradition against itself. I point to those places in the tradition where it is clear that divine grace equally embraces men and women and that God wills that relations of justice and peace mark all our social interactions. Using these normative claims from the tradition, I selectively trim away those places where the tradition seems to undermine its own emancipatory impulses.

What I have just described is the approach feminist theologians typically take to the task of theological reflection—one which I heartily embrace. However, let me add to this another set of insights. The longer I engage in this strange activity of wandering around in a tradition of stories and doctrines that claim to tell us "the truth" about the world, the more I am convinced that theologians are also called to do the *exact opposite* of what I have just described. Instead of taking faith's language and putting it through a kind of meat grinder that makes it palatable to modern tastes, I increasingly find myself wanting to challenge modern tastes with the strangeness of the tradition's coarse and messy language. To use Hans Frei's famous image, I see myself trying to pull our world into the strange world of scripture. In our present-day, consumerist, capitalist culture, this strategy seems to me, at times, to be even more subversive than the above-mentioned accommodationist strategy, particularly when the tradition is allowed to echo through our daily affairs with strange-sounding normative themes like community, justice, and love.

Having said this by way of introduction, let me shift to the main topic of my talk and show you one example of how I address present-day feminists' concerns about the nature of the self by using seemingly strange, old-fashioned terms like "justification" and "sanctification."

I begin with a comment about what are for me two central themes in feminist theory's reflections on the nature of the self.

Like most feminist theorists working in the academy today, I have been strongly influenced by poststructuralist, feminist accounts of "identity." These accounts attempt to lay bare the gender assumptions that shape western understandings of the "self." I have been especially convinced by de Beauvoir's famous statement that "one is not born woman, one becomes one," that "biology is not destiny." I even like the much maligned argument of Judy Butler that "gender" is a cultural code which functions like a dramatic script which we perform and which also performs us. I particularly appreciate the way this material on gender construction relentlessly pounds away at the precious "gender essentials" that Western thought, in various forms, has posited in its descriptions of the self. As a feminist, I have found this dismantling of gender essentials liberating. Not only does it reveal how deeply sexist cultural patterns cut into our understanding of male and female, masculine and feminine, but it also reminds us that changing these patterns is an arduous process because, in most cases, they appear to us as natural truths. For both these reasons, I applaud feminist poststructuralists' "de-centering of the subject"—its so-called "fracturing of the self." I might add as well that, as a theologian, I think this insight is loaded with theological significance.

However, my appreciation for this deconstructive form of feminism is tempered by another set of feminist insights. As with most feminists, I began my sojourn into the territory of feminism through a series of very practical political engagements. In college, I began working with women who were survivors of domestic violence, sexual abuse, rape, and incest. Unfortunately, as you are all no doubt aware, this is not a small group of people. I can hardly teach a class on feminism at Yale without a number of women coming forward to name their experience of these kinds of harms. And those that speak are usually the healthier ones. When I teach, I can look out and see others as well—haunted women—anorexic, afraid to speak, women whose bodies bear the marks of a trauma that continues to silence them. As a theologian, I believe that if the gospel is to be heard in the present day, it must surely speak to them as well.

My understanding of the psychic dimensions of this reality has been expanded in recent years by a growing body of literature dealing with "trauma." This literature has taken as its subject three groups of trauma survivors: veterans of World War I, holocaust survivors, and incest survivors. What it describes in painful detail is how violence has the capacity to strip the self of the basic mental mechanisms that hold it together. It describes how, when a person is traumatized, their structures of meaning shatter as their nervous system quite literally inverts its synaptic patterns; when this happens, the self is "undone" in such a way that not only ordered speech but also memory itself dissolves. Psychic borders, emotional boundaries, linguistic edges—all of these things that normally function like the skin which holds the self together—are profoundly compromised. According to this material, violence has the power to quite literally "de-stabilize the subject" by traumatically "fracturing the self," and what is needed for healing is not further fracturing but rather narrative gestures that can serve to knit the self back together, gestures of embrace and closure, gestures that author agency anew.

When I take this literature on trauma and place it next to deconstructive accounts of gender essentialism I just described, it's not hard to see that they stand in basic conflict. Set side-by-side, one can see that what is considered by poststructuralists to be a deconstructive act that liberates the self is considered by the trauma theorists to be an act that reperforms the very violence that it seeks to resist. Or put in other terms, on the one side we find a group of theorists who imagine that decentering the subject is the way *out* of the gender prison, while on the other side we find a group of theorists who describe that decentering as itself the prison from which we need to escape. In this context, the question becomes: what does one do with this seeming conflict between these equally important feminist insights into the nature of the self? What is a feminist to do?

Against the backdrop of these two comments on the nature of the self, let me turn to the field of theology and begin with a few autobiographical comments. I was raised in the mainstream, Reformed Protestant denomination, the Christian Church, Disciples of Christ, and I am the daughter of a theologian and a psychotherapist who, for most of their lives, have been both political activists and rather traditional Christians. In this context, "having faith" meant not only holding particular kinds of beliefs about God and the world, it also meant engaging in a series of practices which formed a way of life—practices like hymn singing, extending hospitality to the poor and the stranger, taking seriously a day of Sabbath rest, celebrating and honoring the beauty of the human body, caring for the sick and being present to the dying. In this rich mix of beliefs and practices (and all the messiness that goes with them), I developed an understanding of the "self" that, I believe, intuitively drew me both to the poststructuralist literature and to the trauma theory, for both resonated deeply with the practical wisdom of my faith.

My recent work in the field of Reformed Christian theology has also confirmed for me that there are deep resonances between this material and not just Christian practices but also the actual doctrines that make up the core of this Protestant tradition. In particular, I have found embedded in the doctrinal logic of "justification" and "sanctification" sources for thinking about the relation between feminist poststructuralism and trauma theory. To these two doctrines, I now turn.

At the heart of the Reformed account of the Christian religion is the claim that faith is a gift bestowed by God upon the believer. As such, faith is radically contingent upon divine initiative—divine grace. Since the days of Calvin, Reformed theologians have devoted themselves to delineating exactly how this grace comes to rest upon us. Out of this conversation have arisen two now classical accounts of the economy of grace: justification and sanctification. It is said that when God comes to the believer through the power of the spirit and faith is sparked, God's grace *justifies* and *sanctifies* the sinner. Further, when this justification and sanctification occur, only then does the full self emerge from its bondage to sin and begin to flourish. As such, justification and sanctification are considered person-constituting moments: they define the space within which the self comes into being (is born) and then unfolds into covenant history. And it further asserts that apart from this grace, we are dead—albeit the living dead.

These two economies of grace are quite different. The best known, of course, is the economy of justification made famous through the work of Martin Luther. To describe how a believer is "justified" by God, Luther tells a three-part story that unfolds as a courtroom drama. First we meet a sinner who is desperate and exhausted because she has been trying to live according to the Law that God has set before her—to flourish—and yet try as she might, she is unable to do so. In fact, the harder she tries, the more she realizes how inadequate she is to the task. And this repeated failure has kindled in her a great fear. She recognizes that she is held in a prison-house of sin and thereby destined to eternal alienation from God. As a sinner rightly condemned by the Law, she thus comes before God, afraid and helpless.

The story, however, takes a rather unexpected turn in the second scene. Instead of announcing the deserved verdict of "guilty," the Divine Judge says to the person caught in sin, in an act of totally unmerited generosity, "I forgive you and promise you life eternal." The sinner is thus "justified" by this divine verdict. In the third scene, the sinner is given the chance to actually hear this verdict publicly proclaimed, perhaps in a sermon, perhaps in the sacraments. Whatever the occasion, when she fully comprehends this good news, she responds in faith and, in that moment, she experiences her freedom for the first time. She is free, not because she is sinless, but simply because God has decided to forgive her. She then goes into the world filled with gratitude to God for the gift of her freedom while knowing all along that she remains a sinner. To use Luther's language, she knows she is now defined by an alien righteousness which has been imputed to her through an unmerited act of divine grace. Her life as a justified believer in Christ thus unfolds in this wondrous but messy tension—a life marked as *simul iustus et peccator*—simultaneously saintly and sin-filled.

It strikes me that this is powerful description of, among other things, the way in which God's divine judgment falls on the lives of women and men whose realities are circumscribed by the dominant logic of the restrictive gender roles depicted by feminist poststructuralists. Like sin, the discourse of gender permeates all aspects of our lived reality, and try as we might, it often seems impossible to escape its grasp, for it resides in the very marrow of the language we speak. By sheer force of will, one cannot leave behind this constitutive discourse of selfhood, this prison-house of sin. And yet, it is within this context that God's grace breaks in upon us from the outside, as it were, and judges us harshly for our failure while simultaneously authoring for us a new script of responsive agency into which the self can become and hence be sanctified. In God's act of justifying forgiveness the self is undone or deconstructed by a grace which, on the one hand, judges the false strictures we use to define ourselves while, on the other hand, giving back to us a reborn self that is authorized to reach into the future for the sanctifying grace which awaits it. Thus, according to the logic of justification, to become a person of faith requires being radically deconstructed in order to be broken free from sin and thereby opened to life with God.

But this drama of justifying grace alone is not enough. The Reformed tradition has refused to stop here in its account of the self and offers us yet another account of how divine grace comes to rest upon us: the drama of God's sanctifying grace. According to John Calvin, the Reformer who developed a hearty doctrine of sanctification as a complement to Luther's account of justification, the sanctification/regeneration of the believer occurs as an ongoing process and not as a momentary decision of God. Persons are sanctified when the grace of God comes to rest upon them with such pervasive power that it begins to actually reshape the material contours of their living. In this drama, grace is described as forming us—as creating, defining, enveloping, structuring the life of the believer. In this way, sanctifying grace brings narrative coherence to our identity as we are conformed to the life of Christ. And for Calvin, this process happens in community; it happens in the church, which he describes as a "Mother" who gives birth to us and nurtures us as we grow into adulthood and cares for us until we leave her, in our dying, so that we might rest eternally in the embrace of God. Note that whereas in justification the grace of forgiveness remains forever alien to us, the grace of sanctification quite literally takes up its home in our bodies and our actions and materially transforms the conditions of our existence.

For me, this account of a sanctifying grace which envelops and holds us speaks powerfully to the situation of women who, by virtue of the sins of the world around them, have been stripped of psychic form. For the person who is formless and scattered, this grace rests upon her, not as a de-constructive gesture, but as an enclosing gesture. As the self is wrapped in this grace, healing occurs as narrative coherence is spun around her. I par-ticularly like the image of grace in this second form, as a Divine love which "adorns" women by placing on them garments of righteousness wherein they are permitted to flourish. I should add as well that once the garments of righteousness work their healing power, the self of faith will again be deconstructed by justifying grace, but this time the deconstructive force of the undoing has as its is aim freedom and the authoring of agency—both of which remain constitutive elements of what the self becomes in faith.

Let me conclude with three brief comments.

First, this drama of grace in its dual unfolding—its undoing us and re-making us—is beautifully captured by a poetic image used by the French feminist theorist Luce Irigaray. She describes how "woman" has for cen-turies now worn psychic and physical clothes designed according to man's desire. What she needs now in order to truly flourish, Irigaray contends, are clothes of her own choosing; she needs to be adorned in garments that flow with a grace which revels in her individuality, her particularity. This glorious raiment, Irigaray adds, functions like an envelope that en-closes and defines her. To this image of envelopment, however, Irigaray also adds the reminder that the purpose of an envelope is to allow its con-tents to travel towards the other—envelopment for the sake of agency.

Second, I realize that in this brief discussion I have left a number of very important questions unaddressed. One of the issues is the status of the person who is not a "person-of-faith" in this account of identity. How does this undoing and enveloping grace operate in relation to her? This is certainly a question that should be treated more fully, but it has not been my focus in this presentation.

Third, I began my biographical comments with the statement that it is not only Christian doctrines but a whole Christian way of life, comprising multiple practices, that grounds my Christian feminist work. So central are these practices, I believe, that I could easily write this same paper, using not the doctrinal formulations of justification and sanctification as my starting point, but rather using Christian practices which embody these two kinds of grace. If I were to write such a paper, I would focus first on practices that embody justification—practices in which the self and the community perform acts of opening up towards the other—practices of hospitality wherein the border between self and other is blurred and agency is forever posited anew through the power of forgiveness. I would then focus on another set of sanctifying practices, practices in which the integrity of personhood is honored, practices of enclosure and envelopment—the adorning practices of ordination in its varied forms.

Let me state this even more clearly. In addition to teaching at Yale Divinity School, I frequently teach graduate seminars in the Women's Studies Program and at the Yale Law School, both of which capitalize on my ongoing interest in feminist theory and legal theory while also allowing me to be explicit about my own grounding in distinctly Christian theological traditions. In a typical class session—let's say one in which we are doing a poststructuralist analysis of gender and self—I find myself responding to the material in one of several ways. Sometimes, I find the material pushing me to ask questions that challenge my theology—in a good way. When this happens, I am productively provoked to do some theological rearranging and rethinking. Sometimes, I find the material saying, in another language, things quite similar to things I want to say as a theologian. In this case, I translate from one to the other. Sometimes, I find myself saying to material, no, it can't be that way. I see it differently from the perspective of my tradition. In this last scenario, the insights I bring from the tradition sometimes have the potential to reflexively challenge theory to change its ways. Sometimes, however, such a shift appears impossible and the two simply stand at odds.

Religious Concerns in Scholarship

Engaged Fallibilism in Practice

RICHARD J. BERNSTEIN

Participating in the Lilly Seminar on Religion and Higher Education has provided an opportunity to reflect on complex issues concerning scholarship and religion. In this paper I want to sketch—in bold strokes—my vision of a democratic society as engaged fallibilistic pluralism. This will serve to set the context for a more personal discussion of the origins and purpose of two of my recent books: *Hannah Arendt and the Jewish Question*, and *Freud and the Legacy of Moses*. In particular I will reflect on how certain questions or concerns stemming from my religious background have influenced some of my scholarly work as a philosopher.

I

The ideal of a democratic society that I want to defend is an engaged fallibilistic pluralism. This is an ideal that is not only appropriate to guide the development of a democratic society but is also appropriate for the scholarly activities that take place in the university. For understanding this ideal each of the three terms is essential and each qualifies the others. First, engaged fallibilistic pluralism must be sharply distinguished from a variety of other doctrines that pass under the name of "pluralism."[1] There is "fragmenting pluralism," in which centrifugal forces are so strong that we are able only to communicate with persons who share our own biases and prejudices; "flabby pluralism," which indulges in superficial, glib poaching; "polemical pluralism," an ideological weapon employed to advance one's own view while ignoring the claims of others; "defensive pluralism," a form of tokenism in which we play lip service to others "doing their own thing" but are already convinced that there is nothing important to be learned from them; and there is "paternalistic pluralism," which pretends to be tolerant of what we consider less enlightened and inferior. One could add many other varieties to this list.

An engaged fallibilistic pluralism has nothing to do with skepticism, relativism, or nihilism—and it does not entail or slide into these positions. I categorically reject what Karl Popper once called the "myth of the framework" whereby we falsely assume that we are so locked up in our own frameworks, languages, and forms of life that we cannot even communicate with those who are in different frameworks. An engaged pluralism is wary of the talk of incommensurability because the appeal to incommensurability frequently turns out to be an excuse for a practical (moral) failure to try to understand what is radically different, rather than some sort of insuperable theoretical or epistemological barrier.

The significance of "fallibilistic" pluralism lies in its rejection of all forms of fundamentalism that appeal to absolute certainty—whether they be religious or secular. Secular fundamentalism can be just as misplaced or misguided as religious fundamentalism. Positively stated, an engaged fallibilistic pluralism requires the cultivation of a set of virtues and practices: a willingness to listen to others and to resist the temptation to impose one's own favored categories, standards, and prejudgments; an imaginative heurmeneutical sensitivity directed toward understanding what confronts us as radically different; a willingness to defend our beliefs and claims when challenged; the courage to give up our most cherished beliefs when they are seriously called into question.

The term "engaged" is perhaps most important because it implies real encounter, a serious effort to understand what is other and different. Such an engaged pluralism (and remember I am sketching an ideal) requires trust and respect—even when there is a sharp agonistic disagreement. Such pluralism thrives on conflict; it doesn't seek to eliminate conflict but is committed to the belief that conflicts can be adjudicated, if not always reconciled, in a reasonable and discursive manner. John Courtney Murray once epitomized this type of pluralism when he defined a community as a group of individuals "locked in argument." The ideal that I am sketching—when it is spelled out—has some strong consequences.

1. The presumed neutral ideal of bracketing all prejudgments or prejudices in our lives and inquiries is neither possible nor desirable. Philosophers

as different as Gadamer, Peirce, James, and Popper have all argued in support of this thesis that some prejudgments are unavoidable. Furthermore, we are always already shaped by the multiple traditions to which we belong. As Gadamer eloquently says, we belong to traditions before they belong to us. The vital question that we confront is how to distinguish productive and enabling prejudgments and traditions from those that are distortive and unwarranted. This is not something that can be determined once and for all by a priori fiat. Rather it is a fragile and temporary achievement, one that emerges in and through our critical encounters with different and opposing perspectives. This is why Pierce places so much emphasis on the appeal to a critical community of inquirers—a notion that is extended by Josiah Royce's ideal of a community of interpreters.

2. Although our beliefs, commitments and prejudgments are rooted in the traditions that have shaped us, we cannot avoid making validity claims that transcend local and particular contexts. Willy-nilly we are always making claims that we take to be true or valid for anyone. If we did not have this capacity, we would never be able to communicate. This is what I take to be the heart of the Habermasian claim that communication itself presupposes the ability to make and to seek to warrant universal validity claims. Of course, this does not mean that we always know how to warrant such claims.

3. I have already indicated that engaged fallibilistic pluralism is wary about appeals to incommensurability. Let me indicate why, i.e., what lies behind this caution. The fascination (which sometimes seems to be an obsession) with talk about incommensurability, self-enclosed forms of life, language games, frameworks, conceptual schemes, etc. has become very fashionable in the twentieth century. This sort of talk tends to reinforce what Wittgenstein in his *Philosophical Investigations* calls a "picture" that holds us captive. According to this seductive picture, these forms of life are understood to be something like self-enclosed monads which are windowless in the sense that once we are locked into one of these monads, we cannot really communicate with the outside. Now this is a picture that has contaminated discourses ranging from the philosophy of science to multiculturalism. And if I may be dogmatic for the moment, I am convinced that it is based on a false understanding of the nature of language, understanding, and inquiry. Living languages and living traditions are sufficiently porous and open so that one can always reach beyond them and

seek to understand and communicate with what is genuinely other and different. This does not mean we can achieve some sort of perfect understanding, but neither does it mean that we must forever remain "outside" what we are seeking to understand and interpret. It is a perverse irony that Wittgenstein, who did so much to explode the very idea of self-contained and self-enclosed incommensurable forms of life, is frequently cited as the source for this misleading picture.

4. Although I have characterized engaged fallibilistic pluralism as an orientation from which one is prepared to defend one's beliefs, convictions, prejudgments, and commitments with the best possible reasons that one can give, I also want to affirm that there are no fixed permanent neutral criteria for determining what constitutes good reasons—or what has been called "the force of the better argument." In serious debates many of our sharpest disagreements are about what are to count as good reasons. This is especially prominent today in the fierce debates about what sorts of reasons are appropriate for "public reason." Here too we must be wary of two false extremes: thinking that there are always some overarching neutral criteria to which we can appeal to adjudicate our differences; and thinking that if such a metaframework is lacking then "anything goes." If we recall the virtues and practices that I cited earlier as conditions for an engaged fallibilistic pluralism, then we should not have any anxiety about acknowledging that determining what ought to constitute good reasons is itself rationally contestable and open to debate.

What do these reflections have to do with the questions concerning scholarship grounded in religion? My direct answer is: Everything! But let me explain. In light of my comments about prejudgments and traditions above, it should be clear that some of us have been profoundly shaped by religious traditions. These are constitutive of our very being-in-the-world. In many areas of scholarship they do not (and ought not) play any role in inquiry. Whether one is religious or not is irrelevant to the validity claims that one makes as a mathematician or a physicist, although even here one's religious background and training may well have something to do with one's motivation or one's interpretation of what one is doing qua physicist or mathematician. But in other areas of scholarship, especially in the fields of the humanities and the social sciences, our religious convictions may have a profound influence on what scholarly questions we ask and how we deal with them.

On the basis of what I said earlier about prejudgments and traditions, I see no good reason to exclude—at least for some persons—scholarship that is oriented by their religious convictions and questions. Of course there are many ways in which scholarship can be oriented by religion, and some are clearly objectionable—for example, when such an orientation becomes an excuse for disregarding accepted standards for evaluating evidence. But we should realize that in some cases, an individual's religious convictions and questions can be productive and enabling. In my ideal society and ideal university there should be an opportunity, and even the encouragement, for such scholarship. Someone who takes his or her own religious convictions and questions seriously may well approach different areas of inquiry with a hermeneutical sensitivity that is lacking in others.

II

I would like to illustrate some of the general principles that I have stated with reference to my own recent books: *Hannah Arendt and the Jewish Question* and *Freud and the Legacy of Moses*.[2] It seems appropriate to tell the story of how I came to write them. Several years ago I received an invitation that surprised me. I was invited to give a series of lectures at a major university on a Jewish theme—lectures that would be published. Although at that time I had written on a variety of philosophic thinkers and themes, I had never written anything that dealt explicitly with Jewish issues. The person who invited me to lecture knew this. He explained that the purpose of the lecture series was to provide an opportunity for scholars to think about their Jewish background and heritage, to reflect about its significance for their scholarly work. I was unable to accept this invitation, but there was a phrase in his letter that I was unable to forget: "to write the one 'Jewish' book that you always wanted to write." That phrase struck a resonant chord. I realized that there was a "Jewish" book that I wanted to write. I wanted to explore how a number of twentieth-century thinkers, who had made significant contributions to culture, confronted their own Jewishness and Jewish heritage. My idea was to explore these questions for a range of thinkers—from those who were professed atheists like Freud to those for whom Judaism was central for their thinking, like Levinas. Writing for me has always been a personal quest and source of self-discovery.

Frankly, I wanted to explore how others—especially thinkers central for my work—dealt with questions that I was asking myself.

I decided to begin with a chapter on Hannah Arendt. I had written about Arendt's political thinking, and I had the good fortune to know her during the last few years of her life. I had a superficial acquaintance with some of her early Jewish and Zionist writings, but like many others I thought these were marginal to her "important" work dealing with politics, philosophy, history, and totalitarianism. But the more closely I examined those writings and her personal and intellectual development, as well as her extensive correspondence with her friends and teachers, the I more I realized just how central her struggle with the Jewish question had been in her intellectual formation. Arendt had been brought up in a secular home where the word "Jew" was scarcely mentioned. During most of her youth (including her university years) she had little interest in history and politics—and no interest in Jewish history or religion. The truth is she was much more fascinated with Christian religious thinking then with Judaism. (She wrote her dissertation on St. Augustine.) But beginning in the 1920s when she started working on her biography of Rahel Varnhagen, the eighteenth-century Jewish woman who gathered many of Germany's intellectuals in her salon, Arendt herself was confronting questions about her own Jewish identity. Arendt's Jewish concerns were not parochial. They influenced her thinking about modernity, history, politics, action, the nature of totalitarianism, and evil. Increasingly, I felt that I was discovering a "new" Arendt, for I became convinced that Arendt's ongoing confrontation with Jewish and Zionist issues provided fresh insight into her thinking. I felt I could not do justice to the topic in a chapter. So my chapter on Arendt turned into a book.

Some of my friends (and best critics) have observed that my Arendt book is both passionate and moving. It certainly is a very personal book, not because I identified with Arendt's hypotheses and claims, but because I did identify with her probing *questions*. I want to emphasize two points about the writing of this book. My own Jewish background, and especially the questions I was posing to myself, enabled me to be sensitive to aspects of Arendt's life and thinking that had been neglected or passed over by many other scholars who had examined her work. In this respect, my own distinctive hermeneutical perspective provided an important perspective on Arendt. But in my study I advance many theses and claims that go beyond this perspective. I argue that it is a mistake to think her understanding of politics and action is exclusively (or even primarily) based on the Greek polis. I argue that her conception of the banality of evil is compatible with her reflections on radical evil. I argue that *one* source for her idea of republican councils is her thoughts about how Jews and Arabs might live together in Palestine. These and other claims are to be evaluated by considering the relevant reasons and evidence with which I support them. Such claims are fallible and open to public criticism. In this respect I endorse that Habermasian theme that validity claims must be validated by the appropriate scholarly evidence. I am not claiming—indeed I categorically reject—any suggestion that one's religious background and/or concerns are a source for a special epistemological insight. Submitting one's validity claims to public discussion and critique is perfectly compatible with the acknowledgment that religious concerns can provide a distinctive hermeneutical sensitivity.

My Freud book was originally supposed to be another "chapter," but it too turned into a monograph. It is very different from the Arendt study, but it originated and was motivated by similar concerns about Jewishness and Judaism. I have been reading and rereading Freud since the time I was a graduate student in the 1950s. I have long been fascinated by a short preface that Freud wrote in 1930 for the Hebrew translation of *Totem and Taboo*. In the preface Freud describes himself as someone who has not only abandoned the religion of his fathers but is estranged from all religion. He then poses the following question to himself: "Since you have abandoned all these common characteristics of your countrymen, what is there left to you that is Jewish?" And he replies, "a very great deal and probably its very essence." But Freud confesses that he cannot express this essence in words and doesn't give any further explanation of what he means. I wondered if Freud ever tried to answer this question. Quite independently, I was also intrigued by Freud's last published book, *Moses and Monotheism*. This is the book in which Freud makes the apparently outrageous claim that Moses was really an Egyptian priest or nobleman and the even more shocking claim that the Jews murdered Moses in the wilderness. Many critics, and even defenders of Freud, have dismissed *Moses and Monotheism* as the "folly" of an old man who was losing his creative powers. But I always felt that *Moses and Monotheism* was far more interesting and important than frequently acknowledged. Indeed I think—this is the thesis of my book *Freud and the Legacy of Moses*—that this is the place where Freud answers the question, what is the essence of (his) Jewishness. *Moses and Monotheism* is about the dynamic character of religious traditions—especially the Jewish tradition. Freud argues that there is a pattern of trauma, repression, latency, and the return of the repressed. He argues that the Jewish tradition is marked by *Fortschritt in der Geistigheit*—an "advance in intellectuality" or a "progress in spirituality." The legacy of the strict ethical monotheism of Moses is this intellectual and spiritual heritage, one which required and fostered instinctual renunciation and guilt. Nevertheless it is the character of the Jewish people that has enabled them to survive persecution and violent anti-Semitism. Freud, I argue, proudly identifies himself with this legacy of Moses.

Once again, I confess that I did not write this book as a disinterested observer. I was particularly fascinated by the way in which the mature Freud always insisted that he was an atheist but nevertheless proudly identified himself as a Jew. Unlike many of his contemporaries, Freud never sought to deny his Jewish heritage. In the final analysis, I do not think he gives an adequate account of religion, Judaism, and Jewishness. But I do think that Freud has taught us that any adequate account of the transmission of a religious tradition must deal with its unconscious dynamics as well as the conscious narratives and rituals for handing it down to future generations. I would insist on two points: the Gadamerian point that the questions I was pursuing in the study of Freud were certainly influenced by my own identification with the Jewish tradition; and the Habermasian thesis that the validity claims that I make about Freud, and especially my primary thesis about how to read *Moses and Monotheism*, are open to public critical discussion and should be judged by the adequacy of the evidence and reasons I employ to support my claims.

Consistent with my own pluralist convictions, I certainly do not want to suggest that the approaches that I have taken in my Arendt and Freud books are the *only* way in which one's religious background and the identification with a religious tradition can influence and shape one's scholarly pursuits. I think of it as *a* way, one that has been important for me. It illustrates the fruitful way in which my Jewish concerns have shaped my scholarly quest.

Notes

1. I have sought to articulate and defend this conception of democracy in greater detail in *Beyond Objectivism and Relativism* (Philadelphia: University of Pennsylvania Press, 1983), and in *The New Constellation* (Cambridge: MIT Press, 1991).

2. Richard J. Bernstein, *Hannah Arendt and the Jewish Question* (Cambridge: MIT Press, 1996); *Freud and the Legacy of Moses* (Cambridge: Cambridge University Press, 1998).

PART III | Religious Perspectives
& Teaching

Reflections on Practice

13 | Teaching History as a Christian

MARK A. NOLL

For my purpose, the general question—"Should teaching reflect the religious perspective of the teacher?"—must be translated into a more particular question: "How should teaching modern history— primarily the history of Christianity, primarily within recent European and North American societies—reflect my religious perspective?"[1] In this specific case, religious perspective is provided by the Christian convictions of traditional confessional Protestantism. With such a perspective added to latent historical curiosity, I am provided as a professor of history with a huge range of subjects of great intrinsic interest. The same perspective also provides manifold reasons for respecting the integrity of students and for encouraging them to function as intellectual agents ultimately responsible for their own learning. Being a Christian seems to lead naturally to curiosity about historical events related in some way to Christianity and to treatment of students with Christian charity.

Only on unusual occasions calling for more particular self-reflection does it seem necessary to tease more out of what usually remain background convictions. I am probably typical as a historian in that I do not think about higher-level questions of theory and practice as often as I do about questions related to plausible explanations for specific historical events and circumstances. Still, the foreground and the background are inevitably part of one totality, so it is useful to face questions like this from time to time. Historians and philosophers of history are not usually the same people, but asking historians to do a little philosophy or theology of history shouldn't hurt them, much.

In April 1994 Wheaton College's Institute for the Study of American Evangelicals hosted a consultation on the subject of "Religious Advocacy and the Writing of American History." As diversity now goes, the group that convened was relatively homogeneous. But even with participation limited to those who were willing to address the implications of traditional Christian belief for historical writing, it was still possible to hear from a number of viewpoints: Protestants of several varieties, Roman Catholics of several varieties, ex-Protestants and ex-Catholics still preoccupied with their birthright religious traditions, ex-Protestants and ex-Catholics now peacefully unconcerned about their former religions, and ex-Catholics who had returned at least partway to the church. But religious positioning was hardly the only operative variable, for this group of about twenty academics also numbered defenders of Enlightenment intellectual objectivity, advocates of pre-Enlightenment Christian practice, and supporters of a wide variety of post-Enlightenment postmodernist positions. Over the course of three days we heard from those who felt that postmodernism opened up spectacular opportunities for renewing Christianity, those who felt that postmodernism spelled the end for traditional Christianity, those who held that postmodern trends should be cautiously exploited in order to promote traditional Christianity, and those who kept asking, "just what do we mean by postmodernism?" Some held that the author's or teacher's voice was essential in any historical account of religion, some felt it was irrelevant, while the majority landed somewhere in between: yes, most said, the author's or teacher's voice cannot and should not be avoided, but, no, even with all proper deference to modern theory, history is still primarily about people and events in the past more than about those who write about people and events in the past. The book from the conference was edited by a believer and an unbeliever; it included enough authors writing from different angles—they included Catherine Albanese, Paul Boyer, Elizabeth Fox-Genovese, Eugene Genovese, George Marsden, Murray Murphey, Paul Ribuffo, Grant Wacker, and Leslie Woodcock-Tentler—to reveal the complexity of the subject.[2]

After attending this conference and then reading the book, I have been forced to ask whether an intellectual free-for-all, however stimulating, gets us anywhere. In our current situation, the author's or teacher's voice in the study of history is, variously, here and celebrated, here and regretted, absent and unmissed, absent and missed, as well as sort-of present and sort-of-welcomed. Making sense of this clash of current practices in such a way as to say something general and persuasive is more than I can do.

Reflecting on the current clash of opinion has, however, clarified my own sense of vocation as a Christian who writes and teaches about particular episodes, regions, and problems in the history of Christianity. In so doing, it has strengthened the connection in my mind between what as a Christian I believe and what as a historian I do. To be sure, I do not think that ruminating on my own activities as a historian constitutes much of an argument about the practice of other teachers. Nonetheless, contemporary self-consciousness about the historian's role in history-writing—and here I have been helped especially by the work of Philip Gleason, E. Harris Harbison, Bruce Kuklick, George Marsden, and David Novick—has been a great stimulus to self-understanding.[3]

Modest Epistemological Confidence

That self-understanding has led, first, to a firm belief that when I teach students in a history class, we are engaged in more than just projecting contemporary power relationships back onto the screen of the past. Put positively, increased confidence in the truthfulness of historic Christianity—in the religion defined by the Apostles' Creed, the Nicene Creed, and the Chalcedonian definition concerning the person of Christ—has almost completely freed my mind from skepticism about the human ability to understand something about the past. Historical study is not a game. The creeds affirm that God created the world, including the universe of human interactions; that God testified to the noetic capacities of humanity by becoming incarnate in human flesh; and that, by providing for human salvation through the person of Jesus Christ, God showed that people could discover at least partial truth about events and circumstances in the past as well as the present. Since these creedal realities define my faith, I have implicit confidence that, because of how God has configured the world, teaching about the past may actually uncover the truth about the past.

Or at least some of the truth some of the time in some circumstances, for the epistemological assurance provided by Christian belief is a confidence attended with much humility. The same creedal Christianity that banishes historical skepticism also administers a powerful check to blithe overconfidence in the capacities of historical knowledge. The same creeds that justify confidence in the human ability to discover truth through historical research also testify eloquently to human finitude, human fallenness, and human situatedness in particular cultures. For their part, each of these fundamental Christian beliefs reinforces a postmodern sense that history-writing must reflect local circumstances, can never be absolute or complete, and—most of all—can never offer any human the sort of factual or moral knowledge possessed by God alone. In short, historic Christianity offers a hopeful framework in which to pursue the truth about past situations but also an entirely realistic expectation about the partial character of the truth resulting from historical investigation.

So, one might query, does creedal Christianity produce only confusion about the possibility of historical knowledge? Does it merely take away with one hand what it offers in the other? Not at all, for if the heart of Christianity is the incarnation of God the Son, so the heart of historical knowledge is its duality between universal certainties and culturally specific particularities. Christianity as a religion features a striking convergence of the particular and the universal. The incarnation of Jesus Christ was a very particular event, circumscribed by the particular cultural circumstances of its day, and yet Christians have always held that this very particular event contains the most grandly universal meaning. This conjunction of thorough localism with militant universalism has been put best by missiologists who study the cross-cultural diffusion of Christianity— for example, the Scot Andrew Walls, the Englishman Leslie Newbigin, or, as in the following sentences, the Gambian Lamin Sanneh:

> The localization of Christianity is an essential part of the nature of the religion, and . . . without that concrete, historical grounding Christianity becomes nothing but a fragile, elusive abstraction, salt without its saltness. This is the problem which dogs all attempts at defining the core of the gospel as pure dogmatic system without regard to the concrete lives of men and women who call themselves Christian. And it is precisely the historical concreteness of Christianity which makes cross-cultural mutuality possible and meaningful. . . . World solidarity and national particularity are not necessarily in conflict. . . . The Christian perspective on this matter may help resolve enduring difficulties in the relationship between the universal and the particular, and hence between gospel and culture.[4]

Following these missiologists, it is possible for a Christian not to be surprised if historical work offers the most intimate combination of solidly-
grounded truth and completely contextualized construction.

The challenge to self-awareness in the contemporary academy turns
out to contribute to my understanding of classical Christian dogma. On
the one hand, that dogma provides reasons for considerable confidence in
the possibility of historical knowledge. On the other, specifically post-
Christian thinking helps show how often Christians have attempted to
exert political or ideological hegemony in ways that contradict the message of the cross standing at the heart of creedal Christianity.

By no means does adherence to traditional Christian faith solve all
metaphysical and practical problems in the writing or teaching of history.
Nonetheless, creedal Christianity does offer a platform for adjudicating
contemporary discussion of the relationship between scholars and their
scholarship. Being a Christian offers grounds for standing with intellectual traditionalists who contend for the security of knowledge, but also
reasons for going to all but the finish line with postmodernists who contend for the plasticity of knowledge.

The result has been to put myself at ease about the position from
which I give voice as an author and teacher. Over against grand aspirations for objective historical science, as also against traditional church historical practices of most ecclesiastical communities, I am content to be
considered a dangerous relativist. But over against the world of contemporary critical theory, I am equally content to be seen as a naive objec-
tivist. The combination of these positions offers considerable equipoise
for standing before a class to lecture, discussing assigned readings with
students, or wading into a pile of research papers.

Ideological Imperialism?

Traditional Christian faith, as I understand it, supports historical practice
in yet another way. That support is to provide an argument for why the
historical interpretations of nonbelievers are valuable for my own Christian purposes, though it is an argument bound to cause offense. Because I
believe that in Jesus Christ "all things came into being . . . and without
him not one thing came into being," (John 1:3, NRSV) and that Christ

"himself is before all things and in him all things hold together," (Col. 1:17, NRSV), I am moved also to believe that all effective writing and teaching about history is carried out under something roughly equivalent to Christian cosmological assumptions, even by historians who adhere to other religions or to no religion at all.

In my view, effective historical investigation reveals some aspects of the truth about past situations. Again in my view, the world and all its human possibilities have been made by God. Furthermore, as I see it, the human ability to know something about the past depends upon a series of epistemological relationships sustained by God. These convictions lead to the intellectually imperialistic conclusion that effective, responsible historical writing exists by the specific grace of the one true God, which is the Trinity named and worshiped by Christians.

I am troubled only slightly by the imperialistic implications of these convictions because of the self-denying ordinances that are built into the fabric of Christian belief itself. For instance, the traditional Christian assertion that the redeemed are rescued by God through grace, and not because they are smarter than other people, means (among other things) that Christians have much to learn about the past that can be taught only by those standing outside the believing community. Another self-denying ordinance is the Christian conviction that all people, believers and non-believers alike, are made in the image of God and retain an inherent potential for redemption. The bearing of this conviction on intellectual practice means that believing historians should never dismiss the labors of nonbelieving historians since those labors, like the historians themselves, retain an inherent dignity before God.

The current climate of critical self-scrutiny has proved an asset in helping me to relate the faith I profess much more self-consciously to the work I do. It has also given me a perspective from which to say something about the author's or teacher's voice.

The Voice of a Christian Historian

My opinion on the specific question of the teacher's voice must be somewhat ambiguous. Part of that ambiguity comes from disciplinary location. If an axis could be constructed between a historian as pure type and a religionist as pure type, I would be considerably closer to the historian's pole than to the religionist's pole. It seems to me that academics who define themselves as religionists are more inclined to theorizing in general, alongside whatever particular research they pursue, than are historians. In my experience, historians tend to read theory in order to sharpen their research, while at least some religionists read theory because they like it. My respect for the study of religion is in fact great, especially when the fruits of that study are presented in ordinary language and when they respect the irreducible character of religious experience. Yet contemporary debate over authorial stances seems to me most productive when it enables historians to ask fresh questions of the past and thereby to see more richly, complexly, and fully *"wie es eigentlich gewesen."* However much I learn from modern discussions about things in general, in my historical work I still am interested in how people "worshiped God"—not in how they "practiced religion"; how they sang hymns and celebrated the Eucharist— not in how they "engaged in ritual behavior"; or in how they read "the Bible" rather than "a sacred text."

For the question of a teacher's voice, the difference between studying something as a historian or studying it as a religionist is important, because the desire of religionists to explain persistent human patterns seems naturally to require more self-disclosure than does the effort to explore the particular connections involved in a particular historical situation.

At the same time, historians need to be as honest with themselves and their students as do religionists, and so I fully support the practice of scholars telling students something about where they are coming from. In 1976 Henry May spoke of the need for historians to "abandon the comforting pose of academic impartiality and declare their allegiances."[5] That requirement is even more pressing than when he wrote those words.

In addition, the question of the author's or teacher's voice depends also on the kind of writing or teaching attempted. Sometimes believing academics address their faith communities rather than the academy as a whole. Sometimes academics, including believing academics, speak more to change values, perceptions, assumptions, or commitments than to illuminate features of the physical or human worlds. Such self-conscious preaching demands a set of evaluative criteria different from that of more strictly academic communication. For directly adversarial purposes it seems only appropriate for the authorial voice to be more prominent than in more strictly academic writing. If I can cite my own case as the example I know best, I felt it only appropriate to speak forthrightly in the first person in a book admonishing my fellow evangelical Protestants to do a better job with intellectual life than I did in writing a general history of Christianity in North America. But I also felt it was necessary to say more about my convictions and intentions in that general survey, in order that readers might know what kind of book they were getting into, than in my monograph on Princeton College in the early republic. For that book I assumed that readers who made it through to the end would recognize some of the convictions with which I wrote, but I was more interested in drawing attention to a neglected group of influential Princetonians and to the problems with which they dealt than I was in promoting any particular view of my own.[6]

The situation is similar in teaching. Students need to know less of what I think when the chronology of Western industrial expansion is at issue. They deserve to know a little more about why I might structure an American history survey course around the expansion of the market. I should provide them still more about the deep structure of my beliefs when I am interpreting the human effects of American industrialization.

For the last case I should probably be prepared to say why I consider industrialization in the United States as both good and evil. As a Calvinist I believe that meaningful work is a gift from God to be pursued (within ethical boundaries) as one way of exercising the human stewardship over creation spoken of in Genesis 1:28. From this angle, the diversity of jobs created by industrialization and the opportunities for technological development offered by industrialization have been a good thing, especially when the formation of new industries liberated individuals and families from the mind-numbing and precariously productive routines of traditional agricultural toil. At the same time, since as a Christian I do not believe that humans live by bread (or prepackaged food or radios or suburban houses or any other material object) alone, I am apprehensive about the dehumanization often promoted by industrialization—first, in treating workers as cogs in machines, and, second, by encouraging whole populations to believe the lie that a person's life is worth the abundance of things he or she possesses. By no means should students be required to accept these judgments. But by trying to explain how I reason from an evaluative framework to the complexity of a multilevel individual case, I hope to train students in making such judgments themselves, while also opening them to the possibility that my evaluative framework is itself worthy of consideration.

Another ambiguity about addressing the question of the teacher's voice arises from what appears to me as misspent energy. Because I am convinced that what happened in the past and what happens outside my particular cultural location is just as real as what I experience, and because I think it is really possible to learn real things about those other situations, I am simply much less concerned with debate over what *can* and *should* be done historically than with what *is* being done historically. For general reading, thus, I am much more engaged by books like David Martin's account of pentecostals in South America, or Samuel Moffett's on the history of Christianity in Asia, or the several noble attempts that have recently been published to canvass the history of Christianity in Africa than I am by books—helpful, necessary, and appreciated though they are—about how humans construct reality. Similarly, for more particular work, I am almost entirely captivated by authors whose research illuminates the connections that actually existed, or may be plausibly argued on the basis of evidence to have existed, between Christianity and other social realities in the North Atlantic region during the age of revolution and economic takeoff rather than by any book, however superb, that attempts to describe in general terms how humans exist as religious, economic, and political beings. I do appreciate the chance to read about modern and postmodern debates in the *New York Review of Books* and to attend academic conferences, but the books I really want to read are done by historians writing on some aspect of the past.

Authors and teachers should not muffle their voices. Rather they should be as forthright and as openly self-critical as possible about defining that voice. But all of us should recognize that the question of the teacher's voice is itself framed by larger questions about teachers, voices, and the things teachers teach. For teaching by people who hold beliefs like mine—whether Christians or those practicing another religious or secular faith that provides a similar structure for viewing self and the world—one should expect to receive some sense from the teacher about how that voice relates to what is taught in class or written on the page. But students and readers should also expect, because of what the teacher believes, not to find that voice as interesting as what the voice is talking *about*.

A final issue for someone who holds Christian views like mine is the question of teaching alongside others who hold to Christianity differently or who do not hold to Christianity at all. My sense of the Christian faith encourages me to say that such intellectual pluralism is most welcome indeed, just so long as both the historical events studied and the meaning of studying historical events are as open to critical self-reflection and debate as possible. The only historians with whom I would find it hard to work or students whom it would be impossible to teach are nihilists, deductive dogmatists, or others who know the full truth about past events before they set out to study those events.

Notes

1. This paper began as remarks in November 1995 on a panel at the American Academy of Religion devoted to the subject, "The Author's Voice and the Study of North American Religions"; they were revised substantially for oral presentation at a September 1998 meeting of the Lilly Seminar on Religion and Higher Education devoted to exploring personal religious convictions in relation to teaching; and they have been once again substantially revised for this publication. Multiple revision cannot, however, mask the fragmentary, personal character of the piece; it remains an effort to explain to myself why I approach teaching history as I do more than a formal defense of a well-defined intellectual position.

2. Bruce Kuklick and D. G. Hart, eds., *Religious Advocacy and American History* (Grand Rapids: Eerdmans, 1997).

3. Gleason, *Keeping the Faith: American Catholicism, Past and Present* (Notre Dame: University of Notre Dame Press, 1987); Harbison, *Christianity and History* (Princeton: Princeton University Press, 1964); Kuklick, "The Mind of the Historian," *History and Theory* 8 (1969): 313–31; Kuklick, note on "Methods," in *Churchmen and Philosophers from Jonathan Edwards to John Dewey* (New Haven: Yale University Press, 1985), 301–3; Marsden, afterword on "History and Fundamentalism," in *Fundamentalism and American Culture . . . 1870–1925* (New York: Oxford University Press, 1980), 229–30; Marsden, "What Difference Does Christian Perspective Make?" in *History and the Christian Historian*, ed. Ronald A. Wells (Grand Rapids: Eerdmans, 1998), 11–22; Peter Novick, *That Noble Dream: The "Objectivity Question" and the American Historical Profession* (New York: Cambridge University Press, 1988); I offer somewhat more systematic assessment of contemporary ideas about history in "History Wars I–IV," *Books & Culture: A Christian Review*

(May/June 1999): 30–34; (July/August 1999): 22–25; (Sept./Oct. 1999): 38–41; (Nov./Dec. 1999): 42–44.

4. Sanneh, "Gospel and Culture: Ramifying Effects of Scriptural Translation," in *Bible Translation and the Spread of the Church: The Last 200 Years*, ed. Philip C. Stine (E. J. Brill, 1990), 10–11.

5. Henry F. May, *The Enlightenment in America* (New York: Oxford University Press, 1976), xvii.

6. Mark A. Noll, *The Scandal of the Evangelical Mind* (Grand Rapids: Eerdmans, 1994); *A History of Christianity in the United States and Canada* (Grand Rapids: Eerdmans, 1992); *Princeton and the Republic, 1768–1822* (Princeton: Princeton University Press, 1989).

14 | Questions of Teaching

DENIS DONOGHUE

Perhaps I should mention that I am a cradle Roman Catholic; born in Ireland to parents who were practicing Roman Catholics if not ardent in that faith. I grew up in the church and have never thought of leaving it. This has not complicated my life as a teacher, mainly because I don't feel that my duty in that regard is either confessional or pastoral. I will talk about my experience as a teacher of English, Irish, and American literature at New York University and, before that, at University College, Dublin, and Cambridge University. But it may be useful to speak to a text. If I were to teach a course in modem English poetry, I might include William Empson's "This Last Pain." It is a difficult poem, written at a time when many English poets, acting on T. S. Eliot's authority, thought that the best style for coping with modern problems would take the poems of Donne as its model; would try to develop ways of amalgamating disparate experience—to use Eliot's phrase in "The Metaphysical Poets" (1921). Here is the text of Empson's poem as it was published in the several editions of his *Collected Poems*, beginning in 1935. When it first appeared in *New Signatures* (1932) it did not have the fifth stanza:

> This last pain for the damned the Fathers found:
> "They knew the bliss with which they were not crowned."
>   Such, but on earth, let me foretell,
>   Is all, of heaven or of hell.
>
> Man, as the prying housemaid of the soul,
> May know her happiness by eye to hole:
>   He's safe; the key is lost; he knows
>   Door will not open, nor hole close.

"What is conceivable can happen too,"
Said Wittgenstein, who had not dreamt of you;
    But wisely; if we worked it long
    We should forget where it was wrong.

Those thorns are crowns which, woven into knots,
Crackle under and soon boil fool's pots;
    And no man's watching, wise and long,
    Would ever stare them into song.

Thorns burn to a consistent ash, like man;
A splendid cleanser for the frying-pan:
    And those who leap from pan to fire
    Should this brave opposite admire.

All those large dreams by which men long live well
Are magic-lanterned on the smoke of hell;
    This then is real, I have implied,
    A painted, small, transparent slide.

These the inventive can hand-paint at leisure,
Or most emporia would stock our measure;
    And feasting in their dappled shade
    We should forget how they were made.

Feign then what's by a decent tact believed
And act that state is only so conceived,
    And build an edifice of form
    For house where phantoms may keep warm.

Imagine, then, by miracle, with me,
(Ambiguous gifts, as what gods give must be)
    What could not possibly be there,
    And learn a style from a despair.[1]

Empson also added a few sentences of notes:

Her: the soul, the mistress; *he:* the housemaid. *But wisely:* "it is good practical advice, because though not every ideal that can be imagined can be
achieved, man can satisfy himself by pretending that he has achieved it
and forgetting that he hasn't." This touches Mr. Wittgenstein neither as
philosophical argument nor as personal remark. The idea of the poem
is that human nature can conceive divine states which it cannot attain;
Mr. Wittgenstein is relevant only because such feelings have produced
philosophies different from his. "As the crackling of thorns under a
pot, so is the laughter of a fool." A watched pot never boils, and if it
boiled would sing. The folly which has the courage to maintain careless
self-conceit is compared to the mock-regal crown of thorns. By the
second mention of hell I meant only Sheol, chaos. It was done somewhere by missionaries onto a pagan bonfire.[2]

I'll add a few notes of my own, mostly suggesting the gist of the lines,
and then try to acknowledge the fact that we are reading a poem, not an
essay in a journal of philosophy or theology.

We have a poem of nine stanzas, each four lines long, the first two lines
are rhyming pentameters, the second two rhyming octosyllabics. The
pentameters make a statement, the octosyllabics a comment on the statement.[3] Stanza 1: the first line alters the normal sequence of subject-verb-
object to emphasize the formality of the occasion, the pain and the
finality of it. The monosyllabic rhyme of "found" and "crowned" leaves
no room for doubt. "Found," because the Fathers of the Church were
nasty enough to go out of their way to search for the ultimate pain, being
content with nothing less. Line 2 introduces the governing motif of the
poem, the discrepancies in which people have to live, as here the rift between knowing bliss at a distance and not enjoying it. Further instances
of discrepancy include that between earth (which is all we have) and the
hell threatened, the heaven offered, both chimeras: the separation of body
and soul in stanza 2: the difference between conceiving something and
having it occur: in stanza 8 the feigning, the pretense of acting upon a
conception: the difference between an edifice of form and a house, corresponding to that between phantoms and real people: the discrepancy between apprehending what is there and imagining it: and finally the only
saving grace, not given but hard won, the possibility of learning a style
from a despair. The poem is a grim anthology of discrepancies.

Stanza 2: the housemaid sees the mistress's felicities by peering through the keyhole. Man is safe, even in servitude. At least his condition can't get any worse: door won't be opened, keyhole won't be closed. Discrepancy again, but man can put up with it. No need to be envious of the mistress's happiness, it is specious because without body. There may be good reasons for contemplating such states, but only gods could enjoy them. Stanza 3: what Wittgenstein said in the *Tractatus Logico-Philosophicus* (1921) was: "A thought contains the possibility of the situation of which it is a thought. What is thinkable is possible too."[4] He seems to have wanted to keep fictions not entirely apart from their possible consequences in action. Empson's "who had not dreamt of you" may refer to someone, a girl maybe, or even to any reader of this poem. "But wisely" seems to say: work your fictions for all they are worth, and gradually you will grow into them. But Empson, thirty years after writing the poem, was dismayed to be told by a reader that "This Last Pain" was "like Oscar Wilde saying that you ought to wear a mask and then you'll grow into the mask." Empson told Christopher Ricks:

> This seemed to me positively embarrassing. . . . I do feel it's writing, as it were, to a theory without my being quite sure what the theory comes to, or what it means or something. I felt rather doubtful whether it meant anything very sensible.[5]

The anonymous reader was close to the mark in his reference to Wilde and masks. The idea of assuming a mask, especially one that brought you to an extreme point of difference from your given self, was a common device at the end of the nineteenth and the beginning of the twentieth century. Yeats, following Wilde, was its most resourceful exponent. Empson in his later years decided against it on the grounds that it was embroiled in the theory of Symbolism and encouraged self-deception. He eventually thought that a poem should respect "the tradition of fair public debate."[6] Self-deception isn't involved in the present stanza, but stanza 4 considers the risk of it, particularly for Christians who identify themselves with Christ or at least try to imitate him. Christ's crown of thorns, woven into knots of belief, boils a fool's pots. In Ecclesiastes (vii.6): "For as the crackling of thorns under a pot, so is the laughter of the fool: this also is vanity." A watched pot never boils, as Empson's note says, and if it boiled would sing. "Song" seems to be his word for the heroic daring of living well, in the absence of good reasons for holding to any religious belief. In stanza 5 those who leap from pan to fire should also admire the "brave opposite" of returning to the grim ordinariness of the frying-pan. They should admire it precisely because they have chosen the other direction: other people have made a different but equally decent choice. In stanza 6 the painted slide is one's fiction, a poor thing but one's own and good enough to sustain a worthy life. According to stanza 7, the best device is to live by these fictions, which need not be elaborate; though the more lavish they are the more we can enjoy them and not analyze their origin too much. In stanza 8, "Feign then" is the most forthright imperative of the poem, corresponding in its openness to the "decent tact" that conducts itself in silence. "Act that state" goes back to Wittgenstein with another instance of discrepancy, a bold "as if." "Form" is good form, ordinary decency, but also feasible structures, including this poem as a composition inhabited by various phantoms. In the last stanza "Imagine, then" echoes "Feign then," both are secular and genetic miracles, the mind acting in the mode of its freedom, a gift not of God but of the gods. "A style" is a way of being in the world, but also an achievement of "song." "A despair" is, I suppose, a particular occasion of the universal predicament. But it may have a more pointed reference. In *Either/Or* Kierkegaard says that "when the age loses the tragic it gains despair."[7] In Greek tragedy, "even if the individual is moved freely, he still rested in the substantial categories of state, family, and destiny." These categories are not available to modern man, so he has to act on his own authority and take upon himself the guilt and despair of "not having acted otherwise than he has."[8]

It is commonly agreed that "This Last Pain" ponders a dilemma that Empson shared with many of his contemporaries and especially with his master, I. A. Richards. In *Principles of Literary Criticism* (1924) and *Science and Poetry* (1926) Richards took it for granted that religious belief was now impossible: the question was, how to live a good life in the absence of an explicit system of belief and practice. Also: how to write or read a work of literature, given that many statements in literature are untrue. "O, My Luve's like a red, red rose," Robert Burns claimed. He lied. Richards worried about the problem of science, poetry, and truth-telling. He often changed his mind about it, but in the books I've mentioned he maintained that it was still possible to make imaginative use of statements that were known to be untrue or at best unverifiable, provided you didn't delude yourself into thinking that they were indeed verifiable, as sound as the best science. You could make statements that would bear upon your attitudes and motives, whether they were scientifically sound or not. I think that my love is like a red, red rose in some respects: she's beautiful and she won't live or stay beautiful forever. But we would think poorly of Burns if he balanced his books so precisely: there is a time for hyperbole. Richards, like Empson, thought that the crucial thing was not to deceive yourself, even if your tribute to the girl went over the top. Empson held "that the prime intellectual difficulty of our age is that true beliefs may make it impossible to act rightly; that we cannot think without verbal fictions; that they must not be taken for true beliefs, and yet must be taken seriously; that it is essential to analyse beauty; essential to accept it unanalysed; essential to believe that the universe is deterministic; essential to act as if it was not."[9]

My own method of dealing with this problem is one for which I don't claim any originality: it asks not whether a statement in "This Last Pain" is true, false, or unverifiable but whether I could imagine someone quite sane and honorable making the statement and holding to it. Let us say that the implied speaker of the poem is an atheist: specifically, he doesn't believe in the Christian God, and he has settled for the authority of reason, common sense, and the prejudices of an Englishman of Tory sensibility. To read Empson's poem I have to try to imagine what it would be to think as the implied speaker of the poem thought. Put like that, I don't find it difficult to imagine such a person in such a state of mind. What must it be to be different? the poet Hopkins asked himself. Imagination is the capacity to conceive states of mind and being utterly different from one's own. Coleridge thought that such capacity was one proof of Shakespeare's genius: he could imagine experiences at the furthest remove from his own and find words to make them present. Imagination, in a writer, does not act apart from words or before them. D. W. Harding has argued, in *Experience into Words*, that a writer is distinguished by his bringing the language—English, French, or another—to bear upon the imagining at a notably early stage of the transaction. People who are not writers think and conceive and imagine, as best they can, and then look about for the words that best express what they mean. Writers don't allow any interval between their conceiving a situation and their discovering it among the words: if they cannot discover it among the words, they cannot have it at all.

I mention these matters now because they bring me at length to my theme, the difficulties I have met among the many pleasures of teaching literature. There are four main ones. The first is that most students assume that a language is transparent; that they can look straight through the words as through a clean window and see the real world outside, independent of the words. Language merely calls attention to an instance of reality that is to be found intact apart from the language. Students think that a language is merely a helpful instrument, the saw a carpenter uses to cut up the wood he has chosen: the wood is one thing, the saw another. No wonder they read a novel as if it easily resolved itself into the lore of politics, economics, or sociology in its vicinity. Or as if the language of a novel were the same as that of an editorial in *The New York Times*. It is nearly impossible to convince students that the theme of a poem and the situation implied by a novel exist only so far as they are at one with the language and inseparable from its particular ways on that occasion. You can't remove the language—the precisely adjudged words—from *Dubliners* and find Dublin awaiting your attention. Dublin is there, but not Joyce's Dublin. Joyce's Dublin does not exist apart from the multitude of his discoveries among the words and sentences of the English-Irish language he heard, spoke, and imagined. If you want to circumvent Joyce's particular ways with the language—his style or styles—your interest in his fictions is not a literary one: it is an interest that could be satisfied just as well by walking the streets of Dublin and keeping your eyes and ears open. To satisfy a literary interest in a work of literature, there is no alternative to the practice of literary criticism.

The second difficulty is that most students have no notion of literary form. Their culture has assured them that an interest in form is mere Formalism or Aestheticism, sign of an insipid, epicene disposition. Even if I were to quote Bakhtin, a critic of high standing in the profession, I would have difficulty gaining a hearing for this claim:

> What one still fails to understand, then, is the idea of a *formal enrichment* as distinct from "material" enrichment or enrichment in content. And yet this idea is the fundamental, the motive idea of cultural creation.

Cultural creation does not in the least strive to enrich the object with material immanent to that object. Rather, it transposes the object to another axiological plane, bestows the gift of *form* upon it, transmutes it formally.[10]

I have found it hard to persuade students that "This Last Pain" is a poem to the degree to which it articulates certain feelings—fears, despairs, resistances—or, better, brings them to the condition of form or, better still, performance. Richards sometimes compared a successful poem to the central nervous system in a healthy body: the system receives countless impulses and sensations and brings them to a high degree of order. If it didn't, the body would be overwhelmed by the excess and chaos of its sensory occurrences. Again Richards compared a poem to a telephone exchange receiving electronic messages, sorting them out, and sending them on their way. Deadlock is bad, balance is good. The comparisons are too behavioristic to convince, but no matter: they make the essential point about order and performance. A literary critic reading "This Last Pain" would be concerned to discover the active principle—active because it is a form of energy—which directs the poem from first word to last; how it begins with an assertion of earthly damnation, considers several images or figures as means of discovery—keyhole, thorns, ash, a projector's slide, edifice, style—finding the subject by finding the speaker's particular sense of it; and how it brings the sense of it to a feasible degree of clarity and poise. The consolatory power of a work of literature is real, because it lets us see that a mess of conflicting feelings can be brought to order, though not to heel. The poem becomes an experience in the reading as one enters upon the situation enacted in the words and sways to the tone of it as it changes from stanza to stanza, each stanza a new direction of energy, a desperate force of care. In that respect the poem is a human action, a graph or polygraph of feeling as one word discloses the possibility and the need of another. The desired end is poise, the feelings brought into equilibrium. A poem is, at its best—its most achieved—what Robert Frost called it, "a momentary stay against confusion." It is hard to ask students to think about this, to reflect that the form of the Empire State Building is only one kind of form; that there are forms wherever natural or human energy is productive, performative, as in a wave, a windhover fluttering, a caress, Mahler's *Das Lied von der Erde*.

The third difficulty follows from these two. Students insist on knowing what a poem means, and they think of meaning as something detachable from the poem. There must be a meaning and it must be discursive. They are skeptical if you say that a poem is an action and that to read the poem is to follow the action and take part in it. The meaning of the poem is the experience of reading it as an action. Every aspect of the action tells; especially what Richards and Empson called the tone of the poem, the quality the best poems have of acknowledging every constituent of the situation, the issues, their degree of seriousness, the movement from one mood of it into another, and—not least—the implied relation between writer and reader. Tone in a poem corresponds to tact in a conversation; it takes into account every aspect of the occasion, and respects it. Students would much prefer to be given a meaning and invited to discuss that, apart from the poem itself.

The last problem I'll mention is a prejudice. It is emotivism, which Alasdair MacIntyre has described as "the doctrine that all evaluative judgments and more specifically all moral judgments are *nothing but* expressions of preference, expressions of attitude or feeling, insofar as they are moral or evaluative in character."[11] Most students are born emotivists and they grow up possessed by this prejudice. They are barbarians in the sense in which Santayana called Browning and Whitman barbarians: they have no doubt that their passions are sufficiently justified by the fact that they have them. They see no reason to do anything with their passions except to express them: no reason to interrogate them for point or cause or justice. Many educational forces conspire with this blindness, not least the ideology of workshops in "creative writing"—the most popular classes in any English department these days—according to which every student's feelings are to be treated with emphasized tenderness lest a sensibility be made to doubt itself. It is not uncommon in such classes that students write more than they read. Similar tenderness obtains in classes that require students to read other authors than themselves. When students complain that they "can't relate" to a particular poem or novel, they regard that complaint as critically decisive. They see no reason why they should relate to it if they don't do so spontaneously. They are not to be asked to imagine being different: they are concentrated on being the same and persisting in that state, at one with themselves. The ideology of individualism in America has a lot to do with this self-regarding prejudice, even if the students haven't read Emerson.

But I should acknowledge that my aesthetic theory is vulnerable in at least two respects. It does not clarify what the act of imagining being other entails, or the extent to which such acts ought to become constituents of one's life. It's easy to claim that sympathy for someone's plight, or empathy as a stronger version of sympathy, requires an act of imagination: you have to imagine what it would be like to be in that person's condition. Sympathy is easy, and it feels good. Belief is harder, especially since it comes in several degrees of seriousness. Lionel Trilling argued that "it is characteristic of the intellectual life of our culture that it fosters a form of assent which does not involve actual credence." Many among us, he claimed, "find it gratifying to entertain the thought that alienation is to be overcome only by the completeness of alienation, and that alienation completed is not a deprivation or deficiency but a potency."[12] He had in mind the cultivation of madness as the recovery of lost truth, a project recommended by R. D. Laing and David Cooper. Trilling's distinction between assent and credence implied that credence is the force of belief on which one is prepared to act, to the extent of changing one's life: assent is a weaker degree of belief, such that the verb "to entertain" indicates that the assent is merely notional and won't make a real difference. It is a defect of my aesthetic theory that it does not indicate how far the imagining of being different should go. If, reading "This Last Pain," I imagine what it would be to be an agnostic and to hold my agnosticism, as Empson seems to hold his, sardonically, should I entertain the experience merely as a notion to be discarded at the end of the poem, or take the risk of letting it stay in my mind as a possibility or a temptation?

The second vulnerable point may be indicated by an intervention by one of my graduate students. He said, in effect: "the logic of your aesthetic is that anything goes; it can't provide you with a defense against a book that includes the vilest thoughts and sentiments; you are bound to receive *American Psycho* just as cordially as *The Portrait of a Lady;* and then there is the politics of pluralism and multiculturalism." When I had stopped wincing, I tried to think of a respectable answer. The following is as far as I've got. If, like me in my reading, you allow for free speech, you have only yourself to blame when you find yourself (as you will) inviting to the platform or the seminar an adept of hate speech. All you can do is hope that he will lose the rhetorical fight because the audience will find his sentiments, his manners, and his tone disgusting. You're obliged to hand him the microphone and not to interrupt him, but you're not obliged to take his rhetoric seriously enough to change our own values. It's only fair to listen and to imagine what it would be to hold such views, but it is most unlikely that you will be convinced by views so alien to your own. But doesn't this undermine my practice of reading, since it sets a limit in advance on the degree to which I will let myself be persuaded? It does, but this consideration is not lethal. When I talk about imagining what it would be to be different, I envisage two extreme degrees of imagining. One extreme would entail identifying myself with the other person, as Miranda in *The Tempest* identifies herself with the people she saw suffering the shipwreck. The other extreme is that of maintaining my distance. Adam Zachary Newton allows for these extremes, in *Narrative Ethics:* he refers to "a mode of active engagement with the other which mediates between identification or empathy on the one hand, and objective respect at a distance on the other."[13] My decision to stand at one point rather than another between these extremes would depend on many factors: my sense of the merits of the case, my response to the general tone of the appeal, my judgment on the issues at stake. I would stand at a notable distance from *American Psycho*. But even in that case I would end up not quite as complacent in the possession of my values as I was before I listened to my opponent.

Notes

1. William Empson, *Collected Poems* (New York: Harcourt, Brace, 1949), 33–34.

2. Ibid., 97–98.

3. Cf. Philip Gardner and Averil Gardner, *The God Approached: A Commentary on the Poems of William Empson* (London: Chatto & Windus, 1978), 120.

4. Quoted in Gardner, *The God Approached*, 123.

5. "William Empson in Conversation with Christopher Ricks," *The Review*, nos. 6 and 7 (June 1963): 26–35. Quoted in Gardner, *The God Approached*, 126.

6. William Empson, *Argufying: Essays on Literature and Culture*, ed. John Haffenden (Iowa City: University of Iowa Press, 1987), 16.

7. Søren Kierkegaard, *Either/Or*, translated by D. F. and L. M. Swenson (New York: Anchor Books, 1959), 1:143.

8. Gabriel Josipovici, *On Trust: Art and the Temptations of Suspicion* (New Haven: Yale University Press, 1999), 28.

9. Empson, *Argufying*, 198.

10. M. M. Bakhtin, *Art and Answerability: Early Philosophical Essays*, ed. Michael Holquist and Vadim Liapunov, trans. Vadim Liapunov (Austin: University of Texas Press, 1990), 87.

11. Alasdair MacIntyre, *After Virtue: A Study in Moral Theory*, 2d ed. (Notre Dame: University of Notre Dame Press, 1984), pp. 11–12.

12. Lionel Trilling, *Sincerity and Authenticity* (Cambridge: Harvard University Press, third printing, 1973), 171.

13. Adam Zachary Newton, *Narrative Ethics* (Cambridge: Harvard University Press, 1995), 85.

15 | Teaching and Religion in Sociology

ROBERT WUTHNOW

"Should teaching reflect the religious perspective of the teacher?" This is the question that several of us were asked to address at one meeting of the Lilly Seminar on Religion and Higher Education. I'd like to start with a few prefatory comments about my own approach to this topic. First, I will be drawing from personal experience, using anecdotal examples to prompt reflection from others who may have had similar experiences. Second, to me teaching means many different things, so I will want to deal with various aspects of the teaching task. Third, I want to talk more about "religion" than "religious perspective." I am not quite sure what is meant by "religious perspective" but I am convinced that "religion" is a part of my being. Finally, in order to address the "should" question posed above, I have to start with a prior question, namely, *"Does religion affect my teaching?"* I will then reflect on whether that is a good or bad thing.

Working with Students

When I was phoned and invited to participate in a panel on this topic I was in the middle of meeting with a prospective graduate student. So I will use this as my first example and then go on to give examples of my approach to teaching in other contexts.

The student with whom I was meeting on this occasion was a young woman who had graduated from Barnard College a few years ago and was considering whether to go to graduate school in sociology or politics. She was interested in sociology of religion or religion and politics, so she had made an appointment with me to get some advice. I use this example because I am in charge of graduate studies for the sociology department, and a lot of my "teaching" is like this. This woman was especially interested in religion as a result of research she had done for her undergraduate thesis on the role of the religious left in the Spanish Civil War. Her question to me was primarily about the comparative differences between politics and sociology departments. She asked me to tell her about various graduate programs, and I reviewed about a dozen programs with her. We also talked a bit about the job market in sociology of religion, and we discussed the application process. I thought the time was well spent. Neither she nor I said anything about our respective religious backgrounds or beliefs. This woman was from Princeton, and I occasionally see her parents at a particular Catholic church in Princeton, so I am fairly sure that she was raised Roman Catholic. But this only occurred to me later. It did not seem to be relevant to the conversation. In fact, what struck me most about the conversation was its ordinariness. Yet this is a big part of what I do as a teacher, especially in my capacity as director of graduate studies in the sociology department. I am paid in part to do this kind of advising of prospective students. To me this is teaching. When I ask myself whether my religion influenced how I related to this student, the answer, I hope, is yes. I did not question her sanity about being interested in religion. At the same time, I was quite straightforward with her about the possible job market in this area as opposed to others.

This was a fairly typical encounter, but let me reflect more briefly on two other situations concerning my work with graduate students. A few years ago, I spent a great deal of time helping a sociology graduate student from another country. She had basically been disowned by her family, had no fellowship support, and as a result was not eating or functioning very well. While this student was taking one of her qualifying examinations, the department secretary went into the room and found her unconscious on the floor. In the aftermath of this incident I spent a considerable amount of time creating a support network to make sure that she survived. For example, I called the dean's office repeatedly, talked to people at the infirmary and in the hospital, conversed with other faculty who knew her better than I did and tried to arrange for some other women in the community from the same country to meet with her. Did religion affect that encounter? I would like to think that compassion was part of it. But I also suspect that any reasonable person would have responded much the way that I did.

Another student came to me one day in tears because it appeared that a close relative of his had suddenly contracted an illness and the doctors were unsure how serious it was. He told me that he was scared and was coming to me because he had nobody else to talk to. My relationship with this student had more of a religious dimension to it because we were from similar backgrounds and had talked about church activities. The student asked me if I would pray for him. I said I would keep him in my prayers. I also encouraged him to talk frankly with the relative who was ill. He had been afraid to say anything in case his own fears would make matters worse. This student later told me that the ensuing conversation with the family member was helpful.

I also work with undergraduates involved in various independent projects. At Princeton all seniors write senior theses, and all juniors write junior independent papers. This has been a very important part of teaching for me because it usually provides the opportunity to get acquainted with a student on a deeper level. One works with a student over a period of months, and quite often this develops into a meaningful relationship that is remembered on both sides over the course of years. In fact, as I was putting these thoughts together I happened to get a phone call one day from a student who had been my senior thesis advisee fifteen years ago. She was a very bright but quiet African-American woman who is now a medical doctor running a clinic for poor people in the South. Among other things she said to me in the course of this phone conversation, "I remember you as a person of faith, and I want you to know that I pray every day and ask God for strength as I deal with the patients in my clinic." This is not the kind of relationship I have with all students, but it happened to be something that this particular student remembered.

The example I want to focus on, however, is a very interesting case that intrigued me all of last year. It concerned a junior, an African-American woman who was interested in writing about revivalism. She said that her interest in revivals stemmed from the fact that she lived in Pensacola, Florida, and attended the church there that has had much revival activity in recent years. We did not discuss her personal religious experience, but I gave her a number of historical books and articles that dealt with sociological theories on the subject of revivals. I encouraged her to sort through the various explanations for revivals that were presented in this literature. We met throughout the year, and I got to know her a bit better. It was not the kind of relationship where I disclosed anything very explicit about my own religious views except to encourage her to think that she had had a legitimate religious experience and that she was working on a legitimate topic for her junior paper.

During the course of the year she started raising questions about what would be appropriate to include in her final sociological paper, specifically whether it would be acceptable to include some of her personal experiences. I encouraged her not to focus exclusively on these experiences because she had not done any systematic observation at the church, but I also affirmed that her own experience was a piece of evidence, a form of data. When she submitted the first draft of the paper (about twenty pages in length), I was surprised to see that it was all from the Bible—biblical passages from both the Old and New Testament about revival.

Reflecting on this episode, I realize that there would have been a time in my department when she would have been "read the riot act" for submitting a paper quoting extensively from the Bible. It would have been deemed completely inappropriate. But I thought, why not? She was treating this biblical material as evidence, and she was making arguments based on this evidence rather than taking a purely subjective approach to her topic. She seemed quite systematic in reviewing what the Bible said about revivals. When the second draft came in there was another long section about her personal experiences. At this point I insisted that she include some sociology in the paper, and she eventually did. The final version was divided about equally among each of these elements—the Bible, her observations about what was going on at the church in Pensacola, and a summary of relevant sociological and historical literature. It was not remarkably well put together. As I recall, she got a B on the final product. But she had been given permission by me to include elements that were meaningful to her from her own personal background.

At first I thought it was probably just because of who I am that I had permitted her to do this. But all of these papers have a second reader. In this case the second reader was a faculty member with quite different religious views from my own, and this other faculty member independently came to exactly the same conclusion about the paper, i.e., that drawing on the Bible and her personal experience was perfectly reasonable. Neither of us gave her grief for having a lot of the Bible in the paper. Both of us simply pushed her to use the occasion also to demonstrate her knowledge of the relevant research literature.

So when I ask myself how much my religion affected that encounter, I come up with a mixed view. The principles governing this encounter were twofold. First, I respected what this student was bringing to the subject matter and what she wanted to do. Second, I attempted to respect the discipline of sociology by recognizing that the student needed to be stretched— to learn some things and to think in some new ways. I felt it was legitimate from my own personal view, whether religious or otherwise, to push her more into doing sociology than she might have done on her own. But my colleague's response made me wonder, did I really respond from my religious views or was this what any reasonable person would have done?

The Classroom Setting

My other examples are from classroom teaching. Over the years I have taught a number of different courses, and when I am carrying heavier administrative responsibilities I do relatively little classroom teaching. Thus, it is difficult to make generalizations about the ways in which my religion may influence my teaching. If I am teaching a research methods course, I do not see that my religious views make much of a difference there at all to the subject matter. Religion simply does not come up very much in such a course. If I am teaching other courses, religion sometimes emerges unexpectedly, often as one of many factors relevant to understanding social behavior.

Occasionally, however, I teach an undergraduate sociology of religion course. A number of years ago I decided that one of my goals for this course would be to show that religion is a significant dimension of human behavior, and that it is therefore worth taking seriously. Indeed, this is often an issue with which undergraduates are struggling personally. If they have been raised in a religious tradition, they are probably asking whether or not religion is important enough to continue thinking about; if they have not been raised in a religious tradition, their encounters with other students may make them wonder if religion is something they should regret having missed and should consider exploring. In a sociology of religion course at Princeton, it is certainly not a matter of teaching from a particular tradition or encouraging students to pursue a particular tradition, but simply taking the subject matter of religion seriously. Nor does this mean that I focus only on religion's positive aspects: some students may conclude that religion is worth taking seriously because it has been a source of war or because it reinforces views about abortion that they oppose. But I do expect students to treat religion with respect, and for the most part I model this by treating it with respect myself. For example, I talk about reductionism in the social sciences and the differences between trying to "explain" something sociologically and "explaining it away." I have them read Robert Bellah's essay on symbolic realism in his book *Beyond Belief* as a springboard for discussion because it makes more complex some of the relationships between religious belief and social science.[1] Some students are critical of the inclusion of such material while other students find it valuable.

I include some selections about religion from Karl Marx in the undergraduate course as well. One way in which my teaching of Marx may differ from that of some others is that even though I emphasize Marx's view of religion as the "opium of the people," I also give equal time to the preceding phrase, "religion is the heart of a heartless world."[2] We talk about what that means, especially the ways in which religion responds to the problems of pain and alienation that afflict the human experience. I try to give a more complex view of Marx's thinking, especially his early thinking, including some of the ways in which he writes almost tenderly about the role of religion. I then try to put these passages into the broader framework of Marxist thought.

When I teach about the work of Max Weber in this course, I emphasize Weber's interest in the theodicy problem—in the ways in which questions about the sources of evil and suffering arise in the world's major religious traditions, and I probably emphasize this problem much more than sociologists who teach Weber in a theory course do. We discuss Weber's arguments about the relationships among views of evil in world religions, views of salvation, and the implications of these views for ethical behavior. For undergraduates I find that Weber's discussions of theodicy are a bit abstract. So I deliberately reach outside the sociological literature, often using Annie Dillard's *Holy the Firm* as a way to prompt their thinking.[3] The book consists of Dillard's struggle to understand why a little girl gets badly burned in an airplane accident; theodicy questions come up very vividly for the author. It is certainly not a sociological treatise, but I have no qualms about including it.

Similarly, when I teach a section on American fundamentalism, I some-times use at least part of James Ault's film "Born Again." I use it because there is very little interpretation in the film. Yet it is possible for students simply to see the characters for who they are. For example, there is a vivid moment in the film when a man is encouraging his brother to repent; the film captures the brother's tear-filled eyes as he says he would like to know God but somehow cannot. There is another moving episode in which a pastor is talking to a couple who are on the verge of being divorced, counseling each one separately, going back and forth, encouraging each to work harder to preserve the marriage. The film itself prompts virtually all of the discussion. I simply let the students run with it. My goal is nei-ther to defend nor to criticize fundamentalism, but to encourage the stu-dents to grapple with it seriously.

In the smaller discussion sections associated with this course I encour-age students to introduce themselves to one another by including some information about their religious background if they feel comfortable doing so. On more than one occasion I have been the only Protestant in the room. I generally say something to the class about the fact that I grew up as a Protestant, and it becomes evident to them sooner or later that I know more about that tradition than other traditions. So in a classroom context my religion certainly makes a difference, but in different ways in different contexts and in different ways even from week to week.

Some Reflections

Thus far I have emphasized specific examples from my personal experi-ence, partly in the interests of candor, and partly to demonstrate that situ-ations matter, that knowledge of one's motives is seldom conscious or explicit, and that outcomes depend as much on practice as on principle. In conclusion, then, let me summarize four general factors that influence my approach to teaching.

First, *context* is extremely important. I work in a social science depart-ment within a religiously diverse institution. Those are realities that reflect the many previous choices I have made about training, investment of energy, and so forth. I am comfortable with this context, recognizing that it provides freedom to do many things even though it restricts me from doing other things. I am quite conscious of the fact that I do not teach at a church-related college or at a divinity school and that I am not a professor of Christian studies. In my situation, religious beliefs are necessarily more private than publicly expressed, and embracing norms of respect for religious diversity is something that I largely take for granted. Yet if asked to speak at a seminary or to write something for a particular denomination, I happily recognize and avail myself of the opportunity of being in a different context.

Second, *identity* is very important. If one works in a given field long enough, one leaves traces of oneself; you gain a reputation. People who know my work can fairly quickly see that I am interested in churches and religious beliefs. I have worked mostly on things that are not especially prestigious in the wider field of sociology, and those are choices I have been willing to make. But I am also aware that I have a complex identity, and I want to keep it that way. For example, I generally do not present myself as being from within one particular branch of Christianity.

Third, *upbringing* is also quite important. This might not be exactly the right word, but by upbringing I mean the self or perhaps the deep self, as opposed to the professional roles one plays. I am puzzled by people who have creedal statements they want professors to sign, as if signing a document that someone else has written means much about who one is. (Thus I find myself amused by a Jewish professor who annually adds his name to the creedal statement at the evangelical Christian college where he teaches.) In our contemporary cultural milieu, as Peter Berger has shown, the relationships between selves and creeds are problematic.[4] The self goes far deeper than creeds and theories. It does so because the self emerges slowly in the course of our upbringing. It reflects the embedded religious practices that associate faith with the rich sounds, tastes, and smells of our youth as much as with mental processes.[5] In my own case, I had a very "heavy duty" religious upbringing. In fact it still shapes the dreams I dream at night, and lyrics or verses that I have not heard for thirty years sometimes pop full-blown into my head. My upbringing continues to influence my fears and anxieties. It has shaped my ability (or lack of ability) to trust people, my view of life in general, and even why I've written this essay and the particular examples I presented earlier.

Finally, *reflection* is crucial. It is one thing to be shaped by childhood religion; it is another to reflect on that experience. One does this by reading hundreds of books in many fields but also by engaging in an ongoing process of self-interpretation, by thinking about the meaning of one's days. The great virtue of the academic life is that it gives one excuses for reflection of this kind—perhaps not the unrestricted access to opportunities for self-examination that monastics enjoy, but every academician I know finds ways to work on projects that are partly journeys of self-exploration. Encouraging students to pursue the examined life is one of the greatest joys—and challenges—of teaching.

In light of all these considerations I find it difficult to be prescriptive about the question, "Should a teacher's teaching reflect the teacher's religion?" It does. It simply *does*. There is no way we can escape it. It is like asking the question "Should the grass be green?" Being green is not a choice for grass to make. Unlike grass, however, we are self-reflective individuals. We choose. "Should one's ideas be shaped by living in the United States?" They simply are. That does not mean that one just affirms being xenophobic; nor does it mean one somehow transcends all cultural influences. It is still possible to choose *how* one lives and thinks and behaves as a citizen of the United States. But one does so within limits—limits imposed by one's upbringing and one's previous choices. In closing, then, I must admit that I have trouble with generalizations on this subject, and I am certainly not trying to suggest that my way is the best or the only way. Thankfully, my religious upbringing taught me a lot about vanity. So, if anything, I struggle to avoid vanity while at the same time remembering that the greatest vanity is to imagine oneself being free of vanity.

Notes

1. Robert N. Bellah, *Beyond Belief: Essays on Religion in a Post-Traditional World* (New York: Harper and Row, 1970), 216–29.

2. See also Robert Wuthnow, *Meaning and Moral Order: Explorations in Cultural Analysis* (Berkeley and Los Angeles: University of California Press, 1987), chap. 2.

3. Annie Dillard, *Holy the Firm* (New York: Harper Collins, 1999).

4. Peter L. Berger, *A Far Glory: The Quest for Faith in an Age of Credulity* (New York: Free Press, 1992).

5. Robert Wuthnow, *Growing Up Religious: Christians and Jews and Their Journeys of Faith* (Boston: Beacon Press, 1999).

16 | Does, or Should, Teaching Reflect the Religious Perspective of the Teacher?

JEAN BETHKE ELSHTAIN

A quick answer to *should* teaching reflect the religious perspective of the teacher is impossible. A quick response to *does* teaching reflect the religious perspective of the teacher is in order. The answer is yes, necessarily and always, because no deep commitment can ever be shed completely when a teacher enters the classroom. The term "reflect," however, is ambiguous—no doubt intentionally so. "Reflect" is a rather gentle term by contrast, say, to describing the religious perspective of a teacher dominating her teaching, or controlling it in an overwhelming and total way. "Reflect" calls to mind the way our shadows give indication of the sun's rays or our image in a photograph reflects what we "look like." That teaching thus reflects a religious perspective, or a political perspective, or some other powerful perspective should be no occasion for lamentation but, instead, for critical assessment of what this "reflection" is all about. We rightly cavil at the use of a higher-education classroom for what is almost always pejoratively called "indoctrination": that is not what "reflect" is all about.

My experience of twenty-eight years in the classroom tells me two things: First, that those who unashamedly used their classroom for explicit purposes of indoctrination were political ideologues of one sort or another, not persons with strong religious belief; and, second, that the by-far most common form of indoctrination or inculcation was neither political nor religious but, instead, *methodological and epistemological*. Let me hasten to add that "indoctrination" need not be cast entirely in pejorative terms. Literally it simply means to bring into a doctrine, to form a person's beliefs or character in some way. That said, I will reserve "indoctrination" for a way of pushing a perspective that is, by definition—for the purpose of this paper—problematic insofar as it leaves little or no room for challenge, interpretation, and critique. "Reflect," by contrast, will be a shorthand way of indicating that we cannot shed our deep commitments and beliefs like so many outer garments doffed when we enter the front door of our homes. We can, however, and should, reflect on what it is we are reflecting and how it is we are reflecting it.

Let me take the reader back to graduate school in the mid-1960s. This was not a calm time, culturally and politically speaking. The civil rights movement was in full swing. President Kennedy had been assassinated. Protest surrounding the war in Vietnam was heating up. The counterculture was preaching its "make love not war" gospel. Many of us were struggling to understand what was going on and to sort out just where we "fit" in the midst of all this. Who were we anyway—as a people, as singular persons? But, with a few rare exceptions, none of my graduate courses in political science addressed any of these matters. We were, in fact, more or less obliged to leave such burning concerns off to one side when we entered the classroom. It wasn't that our teachers weren't politically engaged: some were, some weren't. But the reigning orthodoxy in political science—called *behaviorism*—proclaimed that the study of politics could be cleansed from the smudginess, messiness, and taint of "values." What political science was about was the search for law-like regularities in political life—laws of political "behavior"—and it was always behavior, rather than action or commitment or engagement, as a way of reducing what human beings did politically to discrete pieces or bits of "behavior," not unlike the laws that were said to dominate in the natural sciences.

The goal of the behaviorist way of doing things was neither understanding human beings and their social and political worlds, nor interpreting the world of self and others, but the construction of "verifiable hypotheses" with the power to predict. In order to predict, so the gospel according to behaviorism went, one assumed behavioral regularity on the part of human beings that, at least from time to time, followed an inexorable logic. It followed that behavior could be said to be *caused*, not unlike a causal explanation in the natural sciences. The political and social context within which behavior was to be tested and reduced to law-like regularities was simply taken as a given rather than itself being a subject for interpretation. When human beings got together, they did so as members of "interest groups" in and through which the pooled self-interests of a particular group could be made known. The "incentive" for human coming-together was presumed to be self-interested all the way down.

Another feature of this perspective was the privileging of a positivistic epistemology within which description and evaluation were presumed to be entirely separable activities. Those who mixed the two were fuzzy-minded, impressionistic, and incapable of rigorous analysis. This split between descriptive and evaluative statements further impoverished the study of political science because human understanding, as embodied in language, could never itself be an occasion for reflection. There were either facts—and a kind of translucent relationship between a fact and its expression was assumed—or there were "subjective" things like "values, biases, emotional preferences." Notice that one was not permitted to speak of moral claims or norms or rules—no, anything of that sort got reduced to a subjective preference and thus was ruled out of the arena of rationality altogether. One wound up with a really crummy deal: reductionistic scientism, subjectivist emotionalism. Most of what people had to say politically, most of the emotions stirred up by politics, most of the language in and through which politics was conducted was consigned to a kind of conceptual netherworld. No wonder so many of us were so turned off. We had entered graduate school on fire with ideas and passions, including political passions about creating a more fair, more free, more decent America. All that had to be bracketed and set aside. You might just call it, as we were taught to do, your "biases" and let it go at that.

It is easy enough to see how there is no room for concerns flowing from religious belief or, indeed, any strong, normative commitment, to breathe within the straitjacket of behaviorism or similar approaches. For ramifications of behaviorism eroded moral theory as well. The link between political inquiry and moral imperatives presupposed by classical theorists in the history of political thought belonged outside the world of political science proper. To be sure, political theorists might still inhabit departments of political science but they couldn't claim the most cherished of all designations—scientific inquiry—for what it was they did and how it is they did it. Political theory became a refuge for many of us precisely because one could take up the "big questions"—the nature of order, justice, freedom, liberty, community itself. Complex questions arose from the great tradition, and studying the canon drew the student into a world of vital debates.

But something funny happened on the road to canon creation in political theory: the "religious thinkers" got dropped and the religious dimensions of those thinkers who weren't dropped got bowdlerized or diminished. There were even editions of John Locke's famous second treatise—from his classic *Two Treatises on Government*—that excised all of Locke's own scriptural proof-texting and references as inessential to the text! In this way, students were, in effect, being taught to avert their eyes whenever a possible Scripturally-based argument emerged. Locke's religion just didn't figure. Nor did that of any other great thinker in the canon. The thinkers whose religion couldn't be scraped off like so much stale icing from a two-day old cake were admitted to the political theory world in radically excised form. Perhaps Chapter 19 of Augustine's *City of God*, but forget his great *Confessions* as they had nothing to do with politics. Well, of course, they do—just not politics reduced to narrowly self-interested bargaining between self-maximizing units. None of the reformers appeared in this canon. In fact, I remember just how bold and transgressive I felt when I first began teaching and I actually assigned Martin Luther's "Freedom of the Christian" in the same section in which we read Machiavelli's *The Prince*, insisting, as I did so, that Luther's text was far more important over the long run of Western history, presaging, as it did, profound alterations in the structure of selfhood, our understanding of freedom, our views of everyday life, our ideas of authority and rule, on and on.

Working on my first book, I determined to put in thinkers that were always left out—Luther was one—and I further determined that religiously derived ethical matters needed to take center stage. There was a good bit else going on in that work—*Public Man, Private Woman: Women in Social and Political Thought*, published by Princeton in its first edition in 1981—that displays what it means to "reflect" a religious perspective or conviction, although I didn't recognize this back then. As I wrote that book, my own assessment was that whatever religious belief still clung to me was scarcely visible in an overt way. Oh yes, I had incorporated for discussion "religious thinkers" often omitted but I had done so because I could make the case for their *political* importance. But, looking back, I realize that my critique of various thinkers from the canon, as well as of certain schools, tendencies, and ideologies in feminism, derives directly from—reflects, if you will—religious commitments I scarcely knew I had at the time. I refer to such weighty matters as ontological presuppositions, anthropological considerations, ideals of human purpose and dignity, birth and death, the moral development of the child. It actually took others to point this out to me, most often in the form of rather nasty criticism along the lines of my alleged "false-consciousness" in holding onto and "reflecting" ideals, passions, and commitments that all those with consciousnesses raised long ago derided, then abandoned.

Let me give you an example of what I am talking about. Here are several paragraphs from the concluding pages of the last chapter of *Public Man, Private Woman*. Consider the ways in which religious commitments, or religiously derived concerns, are here reflected:

> Once we political thinkers escape the iron cage of the agora, we can say, paraphrasing a religious ideal, "Where any number of citizens is gathered in the name of acting together in common towards ends they debate and articulate in public, there is citizenship." The quadriplegic who wants simple entrance and egress from the public buildings accessible to us all, just like the black youths who sat in at the lunch counter twenty years ago, or the women struggling for equal respect, are heroes and heroines of another mold, not militarized citizens, not world-historic leaders who take the world as "their own," but individuals who fit another mold different from the Greek one. (p. 348)

> The armies of nonviolence, participatory citizens informed by reconstructive ideals that grant inalienable dignity to human beings and to their everyday lives as well as to their political commitments and ends, are ideally suited for women to join their ranks. Camus cried that perhaps we cannot prevent a world in which children are tortured but we can lessen the number of tortured children: If you do not do this who will do this? Given the concrete realities of their social life-worlds, women are uniquely placed to affirm this imperative and to make it binding on others. Finally, a reconstructive ideal must fight the enchanting lures of resentment and the poisonous destruction of rage. Martin Luther King expressed, unyieldingly, moral outrage but he never raged at others, for he hoped to draw them into his moral and political vision. A feminist politics that does not allow for the possibility of transformation of men as well as women is deeply nihilistic; it does not

truly believe in transformative possibilities nor the ideal of genuine mutuality. (p. 349)

And I concluded in this way:

> There are things we must not do for in so doing we will not only further cheapen already fragile human ties in the present but undermine the very humanitarian ends we claim to seek. Each of us has the responsibility of making judgments between competing visions of the political imagination, rejecting those which tap primitive rage from those which have as their template our earliest memories of needs met and succor provided within a social context that was our secure universe. Only in this way can envisagements of hope and compassion— private and public—ideals [that] the more clamorous picture of the rageful would expunge from our world—be kept alive. . . . The task of the political imagination is possible if civility is not utterly destroyed, if room remains for playful experimentation from deep seriousness of purpose free from totalistic intrusion and ideological control. For even when notions of sexual equality and social justice are not realized and seem far-off ideals, freedom preserves the human discourse necessary to work toward the realization of both. One day as our children or their children or their children's children stroll in gardens, debate in public places, or poke through the ashes of a wrecked civilization, they may not rise to call us blessed. But neither will they curse our memory because we permitted, through our silence, things to pass away as in a dream. (pp. 352–53)

Rereading these lines and passages, I am struck by how "Christian" they are. What do I mean? I mean, of course, the foregrounding of perduring normative concerns. But that can be done by people with many religious convictions or none at all. Something more is going on—a certain sensibility, the way key terms move through the discourse (like hope and compassion), the lifting out and up of religiously derived locutions and practices ("where two or three are gathered together," "blessing"), the refusal to sever the body from the mind, the spirit from matter, the good of persons from their location in community. So this is a reflection of religious conviction. In my own case, it brought energy, commitment, and a language of reflection to bear in making an argument in political theory. Surely there can be no objection to such "reflection."

Finally, how does all this relate to teaching? There are so many possible points of entry. Many of us—indeed, most of us in the academy—teach required courses. Mine, most often, have been courses in political philosophy. There are many inventive things one can do *even if* one is teaching, as I have at certain points, in situations in which a very rigid definition of what constitutes orthodox "political science" prevails. (I was once told by a former colleague that what I taught was "political fiction," not "political science." So much for the tradition of Western political thought!) Even if you have the leeway of political theory or philosophy to work with, the boundaries of *that* enterprise are remarkably circumscribed very often and "religious thinkers" omitted. But you can't understand *anything*—at least not anything beyond the most superficial level—about the entire scope and sweep of our history, from the late antique world to the present, if "religion" is excised. So add Luther on freedom; Calvin on order; Aquinas on a common good; Augustine on peace and how best to define a city. The modern social encyclicals offer a robust view of social justice and freedom "rightly understood." On the nature and meaning of work—central to all our lives—you can't do any better than Pope John Paul II's great 1979 encyclical, *Laborem Exercens.*

I am a lucky person, though, as my 1995 move to the University of Chicago and its great Divinity School freed me to move in many fruitful directions in my teaching that have enabled me to bring together all the dangling threads of my concern into a coherent whole. For example: I now teach what students of the Divinity School call "the war trilogy." This begins with a term on political realism that incorporates Christian realism within its purview. It goes on to a term on the "just war" tradition, followed by a course on "War and Human Identity." A favorite course of mine and of students from many departments is "Politics, Ethics, and Terror," a look at how three great and very different thinkers—Dietrich Bonhoeffer, Hannah Arendt, and Albert Camus—responded to twentieth-century totalitarianism. When I teach the basic texts in Western social and political thought, it is via the prism of ethics so that the normative questions—"How ought I to live?" "What is a good city?"; and so on—are foregrounded. In a course on "Ethics and Autobiography" we read thinkers as diverse as Henry Adams, Dorothy Day, and Mahatma Gandhi.

I am struck daily by how bringing religion *in* opens everything *up:* it is a wonderful liberation!

Scholars associated with the so-called "linguistic turn" or "language philosophy" in the human sciences often like to talk about the way language "speaks us." What do they mean by such an awkward locution? They mean that human beings—encultured creatures that they are—swim in a sea of language. Language communities exist prior to the emergence of any one of us within and out of such communities. It behooves us to pay close attention, therefore, to the linguistic resources that are ready to hand and how the ways in which we describe the world and the place of human beings within it either makes more capacious our understanding or cramps and shrivels it. Our awareness of the ways in which we are shaped to and for a way of life is no negation of human freedom; rather, it is a precondition for authentic human freedom. Our actions are never unconstrained, as they always take place in response to a material and moral environment. That what we say and do and how we say and do it must needs reflect that environment—and for those of us formed within what we now like to call a "faith tradition," that is a constitutive, central part of an environment—is not a surprise. What is surprising is the attempt, from time to time, whether in the name of reductionistic methodologies (like behaviorism) or radical revolutionary ideologies (like some forms of Marxism) to leap out of our historic skins, or to shed them, or to bracket them. Such pretense and the arrogance often attendant upon it, is a far greater danger to the integrity of the teaching and scholarly enterprise than a "reflection" emanating from a teacher's religious beliefs. So long—I should add—so long as she is prepared to examine critically her beliefs and to explain carefully what conceptual and scholarly "work" they do.

Teachers with religious convictions should not be unduly burdened because of those convictions. Nor should they be uniquely benefited. Religious convictions, if they are robust and go deep are, essential, not incidental, to who a person is and to what a person does. You can't say to someone, "I really liked class this day except for the religious references," or "Your book was terrific but I wish you'd left out the discussion of religious thinkers," and make any sense. To repeat, the references and discussion are essential, not incidental. In the Academy Award-winning film for 1981, "Chariots of Fire," we are told the story of several British

Olympians off to compete in the games in Paris in the 1920s. One of the British champions is a great Scottish runner who is also a devout Christian believer and minister. He and his compatriots go off to Paris in high hopes, awaiting their moment to shine for king and country and comrades. In the case of the Scottish runner, well, he runs *ad Deo Gloriam* as well. He believes that his running is a gift: "God made me fast." But it so happens that (as ill luck [in this case] of the draw might have it), his race, the one in which he excels and in which he is the champion of Great Britain, is set for a Sunday. He refuses to run. Even the Prince of Wales, his future king, cannot dissuade him. Finally, one of the members of the British Olympic Committee sees the light and they permit him to take the place of another runner in a different event—that runner, having already got a medal, ceding his place to afford his devout teammate an opportunity to compete without violating the Sabbath. The committee member who has seen the light tells another, disgruntled member of the committee, who is blasting the runner for not racing, something along these lines: "But he would surely lose if he ran on Sunday, don't you see. His faith makes him fast." That is, his faith is so much who he is—so much his identity—that the notion that his legs would somehow hurl him forward if the deepest part of himself were disengaged or in torment, is risible. The religious convictions reflected in scholarly and pedagogical work are a bit like that. Without them, some of us wouldn't have energy for the race and wouldn't be able to run half so fast. In fact, we wouldn't even know what the race was all about.

17 | "Stopping the Heart"

The Spiritual Search of Students and the Challenge to a Professor in an Undergraduate Literature Class

SUSAN HANDELMAN

Knowledge is not necessarily the same as . . . truth. The difference? Knowledge does not arrest the senses, but truth always stops the heart.
—Monique, student in English 379B, "Literature and Religion," University of Maryland

She has done it again. Monique has gotten in. She writes, "Knowledge does not arrest the senses, but truth always stops the heart." Wow. There is much that we could read into this statement. For starters, I must agree that there has been nothing in my studies that has ever given me sufficient reason for pause. Nothing in my life has "arrested the senses." It is true that significant revelation has caused people this sensation, but it seems that nobody has stumbled upon something so grand as to "stop the heart."
—Caleb, fellow student in English 379B

I often think of my friends and [myself] as characters in a cheaply made twenty-something angst movie. We have all of the stereotypical problems and anxieties. I wanted to write my final paper on our, or perhaps, just my, quest for some sort of direction, purpose, or meaning to our/my melodramatic existence.
—Beth, fellow student in English 379B

I begin with these quotes from my fall 1999 "Literature and Religion" class, because what I would like to do in this essay, above all, is let the voices of our students be heard. As important as our historical, academic, and theoretical reflections are about "religion and the academy," I find myself also constantly asking the question, "Where and how does it all finally matter, come to fruition?" After twenty years in academia, I begin to feel that what goes on in the face-to-face daily interaction in the classroom is the ultimate answer to that question.

I do not, of course, mean to negate the importance of our research and publishing, our continuous restless revisions of knowledge, our efforts in this book to advance scholarly perspectives on a subject that has almost been "taboo" for so long. I simply want to put them in another perspective. There is another aspect of our scholarly lives I would like to address as well. We so often write and research out of passionate personal concerns; yet these remain largely concealed as we carefully code and translate them into the discourse of our respective fields. I myself have written books about hermeneutics and epistemology, the relation of rabbinic modes of interpretation to modern literary theory, and the struggles of some of the great Jewish thinkers of the twentieth century to find a way back to Judaism without negating or sacrificing modernity. In these writings, the personal religious concerns that had impelled my scholarly projects were expressed for the most part in a highly abstract academic mode. I kept them mostly hidden from my students as well . . . for good and obvious reasons: a belief that the academy was the forum for an unmediated free play of ideas, and that my role as a professor in a large publicly-funded state university was to generate this free play; a sense that our mission was to teach "critical thinking," and that my function was to unsettle and challenge my students, not to be their spiritual counselor, or put forth my own personal religious beliefs.

Nor, I must admit, would I have felt comfortable doing so. Yet there is also an older meaning of the word "profession" as "vocation"—of a "professional" as someone called to a "service." The word "profession" originally had a moral and even religious component, which has long been obscured by the more contemporary meaning of "professionalization as the achievement of technical skill, specialized theoretical knowledge, and admission to an elite community of self-governing practitioners."[1] Today, we take "professional" to mean removing one's own personal prejudices and emotions from the task at hand. Yet a "professor" is also etymologically defined as one who "professes": from *pro-fateri*, to "declare loudly," publicly; one who "makes open declaration of his statements or opinions, one who makes public his belief." "Con-fess" and pro-fess share this same Latin root; and so one also "professes" one's faith, love, or devotion.[2]

Many of my colleagues teaching feminist and postcolonial theory, or gay and lesbian studies quite passionately "profess" their personal beliefs on those issues. Yet professing beliefs on religious issues in the classroom tacitly seems to have been deemed illegitimate. The discourse in English departments these days, as in much of the humanities, often centers around issues of "gender, race, and class." The thrust has been to insert texts back into their political and ideological matrices, to analyze them as part of larger "cultural practices," to try to hear voices which have been "marginalized," to challenge the canon, and so forth. One of my students, who loved poetry and was an English major, was surprised when we talked one week about Emily Dickinson's struggles with faith. "I never studied her or thought of her as a religious writer in my American literature classes," she said. We have elided religion as one of those factors that goes into making of identity—not even hearing it as a "marginalized voice." While we encourage a very free discourse about political and sexual identity, we are silent about our spiritual sides. As a colleague commented to me when I told him I was writing this essay: " 'Religion'— that's the Last Frontier in the academy these days!"

My courses in the English department at a large state university are on topics such as the Bible as literature, literature and ethics, literary theory. Over the years, I have indeed challenged my students to "think critically." The classes were interesting, and for the most part successful. Yet I always had the nagging feeling that somehow, something was missing. For I also knew from my students' private comments to me (after class, in the office, in the halls) that many of them, too, were deeply searching spiritually and at a very vulnerable time in their lives. At the end of the semester, after the profusion of ideas, questions, and debates to which I exposed them, they often expressed a frustrated need for help in sorting it all out, knowing where to take a stand, a feeling of being left hanging. As one bright student in a recent undergraduate seminar on the "Bible as Literature" said on the last day of class: "It was an excellent course, don't get me wrong, but we cleverly avoided talking about God, didn't we?" "Yes," another student added, "and, you know—He is a major character in the book!" These comments affected me strongly, and I began to rethink my stance.

Needless to say, over the past several years, postmodern thought, feminist theory, and cultural studies have relentlessly critiqued the notion of an objective subject, of an ability to speak above or beyond ideology. Interest in the relations among power, knowledge, and institutions also started to refocus theoretical attention on the classroom as the site where all this came to a head. But could there possibly be a way to stop "cleverly avoiding talking about God" in these skeptical and critically sophisticated classrooms? I myself had written academically at length about the ways postmodernism philosophically opened a new path for "religion" to "return" to the academy. But still I wondered if there was a way I could somehow bring a discourse of—for want of a better term—"spirituality" to my classroom without sacrificing my goals of challenging critical thinking and the free play of ideas. I am not, of course, the first to raise these questions or struggle with these issues. Writers like Jane Tomkins and Parker Palmer have bravely preceded me. Jane Tomkins says it well when she writes that despite all our professed educational goals of critical thinking, or social change, or transmission of cultural heritage, or professional training,

> I have come to think that teaching and learning are not preparation for anything but are the thing itself. . . . The classroom is a microcosm of the world; it is the chance we have to practice whatever ideals we cherish. The kind of classroom one creates is the acid test of what it is one really stands for. And I wonder, in the case of college professors, if performing their competence in front of other people is all that amounts to in the end.[3]

Palmer supports his attempts to recreate the classroom by using postmodern notions of epistemology, rightly stressing that our models of epistemology—of what knowledge is and what the relation of knower to known is—contain implicit pedagogies that either undermine community or foster it. As he writes in his book, *To Know as We Are Known,* "To teach is to create a space in which the community of truth is practiced":

> In truthful knowing we neither infuse the world with our subjectivity (as premodern knowing did) nor hold it at arm's length, manipulating it to suit our needs (as is the modern style). . . . In truthful knowing, the knower becomes co-participant in a community of faithful relationships with other persons and creatures and things, with whatever our knowledge makes known. We find truth by pledging our troth, and

knowing becomes a reunion of separated beings whose primary bond is not of logic but of love.[4]

II

A wonderful vision indeed. The reality of trying to implement it, of course, is another matter. As I began to write the next sentence of this paragraph, to describe the new course on "Literature and Religion" I had decided to teach in fall 1999, to try finally to face these issues head on, a typo spelled the words "new curse." At times, it did feel like that. In the rest of this essay, I would like to describe my experience with this course, and mostly let the voices of its students be heard. For our students also often hide from us *their* own most passionate concerns, their spiritual struggles. Not often are they afforded an opportunity to express them in a large state university; and they are quite tentative about doing so, fearing retribution from relentlessly skeptical professors and seemingly cynical fellow students.

I, too, was quite unsure how I was going to be able to create some kind of new space or new language for such discussion in the university classroom. I had been struck by a recent article in my Smith College alumna magazine about "Religion on Campus" in which a Smith religion major was quoted as saying that in her religion courses, "we talk about spiritual experiences as if no one in the classroom could possibly have had one."[5] I knew I wanted to try to give my students the freedom to talk about religious issues, but I did not want to force this upon them, nor did I feel it was my role either to resolve their doubts or challenge their beliefs. I did not want them to battle each other over whose religion was "true," or attempt to proselytize each other. I wanted them to be stimulated and broadened by literature that would show them the paths others had taken on spiritual quests, and to learn from each other. I realized, in retrospect, that I did want somehow to encourage and confirm them in their spiritual quests, to affirm their searching until they each found what she or he needed, each in her or his own way. I agonized endlessly over the reading list and course description, and finally came up with the following:

Literature is one of the best vehicles for exploring those questions of "ultimate meaning" we all ponder. This course will examine the relation of literature and religion from a variety of angles: representations and quests for the Divine in literature; spiritual autobiographies; the relation of issues of faith to the academy; literature as substitute for religion; the relation of the literary to the sacred in myth and story. We will read poetry, fiction, and drama that explores the religious experience in Christian, Jewish, Eastern and Native American traditions.

When finally it came to putting together the fourteen weeks of reading, among the texts I ended up with were Dostoevsky's "The Grand Inquisitor," Tolstoy's "The Death of Ivan Ilych," selections from the Bible (some chapters of Genesis and Matthew, all of the Book of Job and the Song of Songs), selections from Emerson, Dickinson, Alfred Kazin's review of the American Transcendentalists in his *God and the American Writer*, stories by Flannery O'Connor, Tony Kushner's play about the AIDS epidemic, *Angels in America*, Viktor Frankl's holocaust memoir, *Man's Search for Meaning*, the modern Yiddish and Hebrew writer Chaim Grade's story on the holocaust, "My Quarrel With Hersh Rasseyner" (along with the film version of the story), Generation-X writer Douglas Coupland's *Life After God*. At mid-semester, after evaluating together with the students our progress in the class, I responded to their expressed intense desire to read non-Western religious literature by adding such Native American material as *Black Elk Speaks*, Buddhist and Hindu tradition via Herman Hesse's *Siddhartha,* and African religion through Chinua Achebe's *Things Fall Apart.* Speakers were invited to talk about Zen Buddhist poetry and practice, and Native American healing rituals. It was quite clear to me by then that what the students wanted was material that spoke *straight* to their hearts and souls, that addressed on their own level what burned inside them—issues such as faith and doubt, good and evil, intellect versus emotions, the meaning of suffering. Writing which did not do this, or which was circuitous, such as Emerson's—they simply ignored, or sat in stony silence when I tried to get a discussion going.

Who were the students? The course was open, had no prerequisites, and so gathered its members from a variety of disciplines and backgrounds. There were business and accounting majors, science majors, premeds, literature majors, psychology and communications majors, one philosophy student, undecideds, transfer students new to campus. They also reflected the rich multicultural nature of my university, which is very close to

Washington, D.C. and Baltimore. The roster included students whose backgrounds were Vietnamese-American Catholic, Russian Eastern Orthodox, Korean-Christian, Jewish, African-American Baptist, old-line American Protestant, African-American Pentecostal, agnostics, atheists, *plus* the president of the campus "Pagan Student Union" (an organization I had certainly not heard of till then!) and some of his friends from this unusual club.

III

Now, of course, this was a self-selected group, for only those students who had some special feeling for religious issues would choose such a course. Yet I must say, that in other courses I have taught, such as "Literature and Ethics," or even regular literature classes (and graduate seminars as well), I have always sensed that underneath those pulled-down baseball caps and Walkman headphones, many of the students were burning with issues of faith and doubt, or were passionate believers—but all this was just often glimpsed indirectly, and kept under wraps. So here, finally, I would try to see if some of it could be brought to the surface in an academic setting.

It was a much more difficult task than I anticipated, with many ups and downs. The initial readings on American Transcendentalists did not catch their hearts—they were withdrawn, cautious, wary, seemed confused, bored, and restless. I struggled. Moreover, I myself was cautious; I did not feel comfortable revealing myself as an Orthodox Jew. I had just returned from a two-year fellowship in Jerusalem and was readjusting to America as well. The real work, and eventual success, of the class came to take place in our "class letters." Over the years, I have developed a certain pedagogical technique of having students write letters instead of journals.[6] They are asked also to make copies of their letters for the whole class, to distribute, and read them aloud at the beginning of each session. In essence, the rhetorical directness and informal form of the letter frees them to write in a more personal, engaged way. Knowing they will "mail" the letter, i.e., read it aloud and give it to their colleagues, makes them put in special effort. We also discuss the letters in class in small groups; other students can then write back, respond to the letter in the next session or later. They can also write in the persona of a character, or to a character in the reading, as well as to a fellow student.

At mid-semester and at the end of the semester, I ask them to read the whole pile of letters accumulated over the course of the semester and pick several quotes from other students' letters, and from their own, which were most meaningful to them—to copy them, comment on why they picked them, copy them for the whole class, or post them on the class e-mail list. In place of a final exam, they write for my eyes only, a final review essay about "How My Mind Has Changed" as result of the course, using all this material, as well as quotes from the reading. As one of the more cynical and perplexed class members (the philosophy major) wrote to the class at the end of the semester in this review-letter exercise,

> Finally, I would like to comment on the letters in general. There were so many little things in each letter that could be commented on that it would take years to discuss every detail and give it the attention it deserves. What made this class so effective was the honesty and thought everyone put into the letters and discussions. That personal insight gave this class a depth that most courses lack and I thank you all for sharing. I hope you all find the answers you are looking for. And if you do please e-mail me because I am so tired of asking paradoxically unanswerable questions that at this point I'm pretty much open to anything you got. Future cult leaders take note.
>
> —Ever the Absurd Man, Nat

By the end of the semester, behind those slightly jaded looks, behind those quiet, enigmatic faces, I did find souls on fire with extraordinary passion. Their letters gave me an unusual glimpse into where so many of our students are—how there is so much "religion in the academy" in ways of which we are quite unaware. As Mary Rose O'Reilly writes: "The question for me is, how do we teach people who are profoundly, and even stubbornly, spiritual brings? I think we assume that spiritual beings is the last thing they are (because it is perhaps the last thing they will let us know)."[7]

My students were indeed spiritual beings who had vivid spiritual experiences. Aaron, a nonobservant Jewish student, artist, and musician, told the class about an experience he had undergone that previous summer in California, after some extended time at a Jewish studies institute. It had changed him, he said, and he was still trying to recapture and understand it. In his final paper, he copied for me his detailed journal entry from that day:

8/15/99—Night. Navigating a crooked cliff-top road fifty feet above the Pacific. We pull off the road, seaside, gravel crunching under radial tires. We clear a patch of ground and spread a tarp on the dirt. The air is cool, crisp, and clear. The glow of the milkyway shimmers in the glass-like calm of the ocean, framed by the soft curve of the horizon. We bed down for the night; feet to the Pacific, eyes to the sky. Meteor-shower—Falling stars seem to punctuate our conversation. I hear the hum of cars in the distance. The conversation continues and I wish for a tape recorder. My companion informs me that the traffic I hear passing is the lapping of waves on the shore fifty feet below. A veil is lifted. In my mind's eye, I am transported skyward. I see myself lying on the edge of the continent, bustling nation at my back. A brilliant flash of light arches across the sky and drops into the Pacific just beyond my reach. I am floating in the center of the universe.

He then writes: "It was a once-in-a-lifetime experience. I felt as though I had tapped into some universal truth." He had, indeed, for once, found a "truth that stops the heart."

These startling voices of my students are what I would like now to share at length. First are some passages from a "How My Mind Has Changed" final exam essay written to me from one of the brightest class members, a hard-working premedical student:

Most of the thoughts that have inspired me this semester have connections to Existentialism, and I think I have related that philosophy to just about every book we have read. The articles that you gave me put a name to ideas that I have believed for a long time. One of the religious experiences which I had as a child, long before I grasped the word "holy" as anything other than a prefix to the word "bible," was a conviction that the physical world around me was sacred. We did not have a television when I was very young, and I would spend hours lying in different nooks and crannies in my house, memorizing the layout of the physical objects in front of me. I agree with Simone Weil that "Attentiveness without an object is the supreme form of prayer." Today I know the house where I grew up in the same sense of the word which Mary Rose O'Reilly meant when she said she knew two things. It is real to me unlike any other place. I know the walls, the ceilings, the floorboards, the way the sun slants through the windows, the way the doorknobs have tarnished and the way they turn, the clamminess of the unfinished basement floor on bare feet, the squeak in the kitchen floor, which makes the whole house seem to shake when you jump on it.

This is the sort of awareness which I think might save me from the fate of the man in Kierkegaard's anecdote, "so abstracted from his own life that he hardly knows he exists until, one fine morning, he wakes up to find himself dead." It explains the appeal of Bonhoeffer's theory of faith that manifests itself not in intellectual assent to certain propositions, but in action. Siddhartha experienced a similar awareness when he stopped to learn a place thoroughly: "the river is everywhere at once, at its source and at its mouth, at the waterfall, at the ferry, at the rapids, in the sea, in the mountains, everywhere at once, and only the present exists for it, and not a shadow of the future. . . ."

I am disappointed at myself for some of the last letter that I wrote, when we read books dealing with Eastern philosophy. I wish I could have had the resource and creativity to try to convey the feelings and ideas that they inspired in me, rather than pull out my crude Western analytical devices. Christianity invites analysis and debate: two thirds of the New Testament is interpretation, and not all of it charitable! When I try to approach a Buddhist essay with the same questions and objectives, however, it feels like I am using a pair of forceps to examine a bubble. . . . There is one sentence from Anne Lamott's essay, "Why I Don't Meditate," that seems to me supremely beautiful: "You're going to be vulnerable anyway, because you're a small soft little human animal—so the only choice is whether you are most going to resemble Richard Nixon, with his neck jammed down into his shoulders, trying to figure out who to blame, or the sea anemone, tentative and brave, trying to connect, the formless fleshy blob out of which grows the frills, the petals."

I am not ashamed of my forceps, but I wish I could have the soft outstretched tentacles of the sea anemone as well.

Already before beginning this class, I had encountered most of the cosmologies and theologies that we explored. The change that has taken place in my mind has arisen from an awareness of the omni-present religious dimensions of our everyday lives. It comes from discussing the ideals of community, tradition, knowledge, faith, and innocence. I have learned from my classmates that I am not the only one with a persistent fear of not realizing what I idealize, of finding no meaning. I hope I do not lose this awareness, and I hope that I may continue to find good books to read.

Linda here articulates what haunted so many of these students, and what they often wrote of—a fear of finding no meaning, no purpose, no enduring love, and no just and good God in the universe. Rachel, another very bright science major (and member of the Pagan Student Union), writes of some of the same struggles as Linda did in the following passages from her final review letter to the class. Like the others, it was posted to the class on our e-mail list during exam period:

Dear Class:

I've really learned a lot from each and every one of you. Most of all, I have found that not one of us has the answers; we are all struggling with the details of life and God. We laughed and talked a lot about all of the things that have perplexed us. We've even shared donuts, Twizzlers, and I think everyone's favorite, coffee. . . .

As the semester wore on I often thought about Nat's statement, "As Prozac is the second most prescribed drug in America, I imagine that there are quite a few discontented people out there. It seems reasonable that in the big rat race that occupies forty hours of our weeks, we can forget the meaning of it all" (during our discussion of *Man's Search for Meaning*). That's what this class was all about, right, finding the meaning of life and possibly stumbling on God's real cause for putting us here. Nat had a real way of expressing those, I'm not sure how to put this, uncomfortable truths. Sure, no one really wants to admit it but I think we all wonder why we "bother waking up at all." I worry that one day I will be the woman in line at the prescription counter complaining that I have to wait forty minutes to pick up my medication. Frankly, the thought terrifies me. . . . I can only hope that having an understanding of the meaning of life will help me steer clear of such a predicament. I think that at least to some degree, we all decided to take this class for that reason.

If only there were some way to intellectualize the situation, to turn understanding God's intent into an exact science. I'm sure that if knowing, say for instance Calculus, would give us the understanding of God's intent, life would be a lot easier. I say this because there is only one right answer to an optimization problem and best of all, if it's an odd problem we can look up the answer in the back of the book. Unfortunately, religion and philosophy take some real thought and you never know if you're on the right track.

I just wanted to find some logical answers to the questions that plagued me. But I think our consensus is that there are no answers right now. As Vanessa said: "We all have to cope with the questions that cannot be answered and with the distance that may never diminish"(Nov. 12, 1999). I guess this has really been the hardest part for me. I wish far too much that I could sit down with the Bible, a pen, and some paper and write a really good outline of what God intended the "meaning of life" to be. It would be great to go out, solve a couple problems, do my job and maybe get a progress report in the mail. Even better; how about one of those visions people are always having in great books about religion.

As it is now, all I have to look forward to is Judgment Day and that's just too late. Still, I have acknowledged the fact that God cannot or will not give me the answers that I want in a form that I can understand . . . And what's more annoying: why won't this great all-powerful being intervene on behalf of the innocent and oppressed? I feel like a child saying that, but it's just not fair.

Mike, a very bright English major, close friend of Rachel, and fellow member of the Pagan Club was also in our class. Mike described himself to me as an "ex-Christian" ("I finished with all that in high school," was how he put it), and had become fascinated by kabbalah (Jewish mystical tradition). His initial letters were highly intellectual, theoretical, abstract mini-essays full of technical information about the history of religions; they had the unintended effect of intimidating the rest of the far less knowledgeable students. Only towards the end of the semester did he begin to speak a bit more personally. During exam period he contracted what he later found out was pneumonia, and was in a feverish state of illness when he wrote his final review letter to the class on e-mail. This condition, however, made him write intimately in a way he had never done before during the semester:

Dear Class,

. . . I feel a little like a mad prophet. You know: one of those semi-mythical priests who lived at the riverbank, cackling out insane divinations, scratching at unclean and ragged clothes, all the while my neighbors might point at me and say "touched in the head" and "touched by God" in the same sentence. And even if my style is a little less cohesive tonight than normal, I wonder what this makes you all think of me. And how different it is from whatever-God-I-choose-in-any-moment thinks of His-Her-Its erstwhile creation?

"Are we really what you had in mind that immortal day you gave us breath?" Monique wrote on November 8th, 1999. "More than life, you also gave us reason and intellect, which became barriers to you, not bridges."

. . . What does it take for us to strip away a shell of false-logic? Does our formulaic knowledge and intense concentration prohibit us from attaining some secret realization of God? I don't know. But I know that all the training I've received in my life makes me want to cling onto that rationality like a drowning swimmer clutching his life raft. . . .

That could be my mistake though; I'm—thinking—too hard. I'm really trying to bring my intelligence to bear on the issue. I'm trying to use the force of my college-trained intelligence against the puzzle of God, Tao, and Buddhism, until I break open the lock and can find out the secret.

Sometimes, I can feel that epiphany in the corner of my consciousness, like a very distant light, blinking in and out of existence with a faint heartbeat. I usually try and reach out to the epiphany, grab hold of it, and yank it back to me. You know: hold it close to my chest, and never, ever let go. Like a loved one, or a family member. It almost brings tears to my eyes; the deep longing that I want to fill with almost anything I can. Just something to cut the pain, and take the edge off it for a while.

. . . I've tried to be honest, and I've tried to be as clear (and maybe aesthetic) as this sickness would let me. I don't think I've found much in the way of an answer, but this one, small piece. That is to say, the same quote that Melanie used from Coupland's *Life After God:*

My secret is that I need God—that I am sick and can no longer make it alone. I need God to help me give, because I no longer seem to be capable of giving . . . to help me love, as I seem beyond being able to love.

Love,

Mike

PS: Keep in touch, everyone. Drop me a line. We'll have a big "God & Lit" party or something, and wait for God to wake up and notice us again.

In his final essay written after he had recovered, on how his mind had changed, Mike cited this conflict between intellect versus emotion as the issue on which he had most moved:

I forget which philosopher said "An unexamined life is not worth living." But that's been a huge hallmark in my development. I've tried to keep virtually nothing about myself "unexamined" and unexplored. Why do I feel this way about death? Why do the holidays make me feel the way they do?

After the months of studying religion through literature, though, I think I should relax that tight, rational grip. While I'm not ready to completely let go of my intellectual self-examination, I think that a more emotional connection is due to my religion.

I can't help but think of our discussions about Buddhism and the Tao in relation to this. It seems that it directly relates, actually, in that the Tao is about just "letting it flow." Whereas I seem to be blocking that flow every step of the way. If "the flow" is a river, I'm missing important things by "filtering" it through my rationality.

Studying religion through literature is probably a huge part of the reason I have come to this decision. Literature has always been emotional for me, even though I've been rationally trained as a New Historicist. So, viewing the subject through a different, emotional "filter" has instigated the change.

Most profoundly, Coupland's *Life After God* has been in my thoughts. It speaks to me, with that deep melancholy and over-riding, questioning angst. It echoes my own thoughts; not so much any despair about the nature of God, but a simple question. I see myself asking it all the time, and I don't know when I stop. I just turn my face sky-ward, stare into the night, and ask, "Are you out there?"

Of course, there's not an answer. But sometimes, I can feel a little spark, deep in my emotions. Maybe that's the reply, and it's one that my rational mind wouldn't accept.

This has been the biggest change, and probably the most profoundly affecting one. It's a radical difference in the way I think about God. I've been trying to think God, and now I wonder if I shouldn't just feel God, instead.

Mike's struggles with intellect versus emotion were strongly paralleled by those of another equally bright and analytical student, Isaac. He was thirty-one years old, had grown up in an Orthodox Jewish family, but eleven years earlier had left Judaism and dropped out of College (Yeshiva University, a modern Orthodox Jewish institution in New York) when he could not find answers to his intellectual questions about suffering, evil, the meaning of "Chosen People," and a perceived conflict between science and religion. He had spent time as a scientific research assistant, then run his own business, traveled the world, and was now returning to finish a B.A. Isaac wrote often of his struggles with doubt and faith. Initially, he had a hard time, like Mike, being able to write a letter that would speak about his real concerns. I encouraged him to be honest about what he personally thought and felt, and to share with the class some of the things he had shared with me in after-class conversations. In his third class letter he did so, quoting a line from an Emily Dickinson poem we had read, "Doubt like the mosquito buzzes around my faith," and vividly described his life after he left Jewish observance. He ended it by writing:

What I could not discover, amidst my conclusion that Judaism as I knew it was "bogus," was an answer. As my life went on without any sort of spiritual or religious faith, I became unfocused and lived a completely hedonistic and undirected life. I lived only to fulfill my primitive drives. My life became unmanageable and without any sort of faith. I was powerless to change it. I had become spiritually and morally bankrupt. I needed a buoy, something to keep me afloat. After turning away from religion so adamantly, I found that to survive, I needed a spiritual basis to my life. As such, I have to find tolerance and understanding where before there had been cynicism and rejection. Even though I can still intellectually reason against faith, in my deepest being I know faith is necessary and real for me. I am still searching for a spirituality, but somehow the search eliminates some of the doubt, and has meaning in itself.

This letter was eagerly and warmly received by the other students. On the last day of class, Isaac gave out a makeup letter that I would describe as a "bombshell," one which many of the students would quote and write about in their final reviews. The letter did not overtly relate to any reading for the class. I have found, however, that this kind of explosive personal revelation often happens on the very last days of class, or in finals weeks on the class e-mail list. It is as if the students feel this is their last chance to say what is really important to them, and it is safe to do so since we will not see each other again. I have also learned to attend carefully to these sudden eruptions—be they angry ones, or appeals to the heart, or confessions. For here, I think, we get a glimpse into where the students have really been "living" all semester, what really has been preoccupying them during the class, and perhaps what they will ultimately take from it. (Physicians and therapists report a similar phenomenon: just as the session ends and the patient is about to walk out the door, she or he turns and says, "And by the way, Doctor" and throws out the key piece of information.)

Isaac's letter simply began, "I am writing this letter to convey an experience I have been thinking of recently." On a meditation retreat in the Shenandoah Valley mountains a few weeks prior, he had received news that a close friend of his of his own age, named Mike, had passed away in California of ALS, Lou Gehrig's disease, which Mike had been struggling with for a few years. Isaac wrote of being together with Mike in California, and Mike having asked him to go with him to Las Vegas to visit his parents.

Selfishly, I did not want to go but my girlfriend accepted and I did not argue. Instead I got into the van at six in the morning with a terrible attitude. Little did I know that my experience over the next three days-the last of *my* vacation-would be one of the most memorable in my life. The whole ride through the desert Mike had me take care of him. I would massage his hands and feet to help keep his circulation going. I would feed him and help him use the bathroom. I even had to clean out his nose with a Q-tip every half hour so that he could breathe easier.

During that trip, I was not thinking about myself. For the hours we passed in the van, my self-centeredness was removed from me. I cannot recall laughing so much as I did during those three days. When we arrived in Las Vegas, Mike asked us to come with him as he needed to run an errand. It turned out that we were going to the funeral home and cemetery as Mike made the arrangements for his own funeral. I cried like a baby once I realized what was going on, but Mike kept our spirits up and reassured us that everything was going to be OK. He had made his peace with God and he accepted his situation unconditionally.

When I reflect back on this experience I am so grateful that God allowed me to be a part of Mike's life. Whenever I get caught up in my own petty problems, I try to remember those three days and that all my problems disappeared when I got out of myself by helping somebody else. . . . I hope I never forget that weekend.

Writing about this letter a week later in his final-exam review essay for me, Isaac said:

In this letter, I expressed the feelings and experience that I had regarding my faith, not just what I thought about faith. All doubt was removed from me during those three days. . . . When I was with my friend Mike I learned that through action I could remove that nagging doubt that is constantly in my head. I learned that God is in me and everyone around me. I just have to give of myself for him to be revealed. . . . I now seem to have an answer that works for me on a day-to-day basis. When I can remember to stop worrying about myself and give to another person all my doubts fade in both my heart and head. During those times I am no longer tormented by the meaning of my existence.

In the end, it was not a piece of literature we had read, or any intellectual argument that helped Isaac find what he was searching for, though these had helped him on his way—it was, instead, a living experience with

another person. . . . a truth that "stopped the heart." Linda, the very bright
pre-med student I quoted earlier, who wrote the most eloquent survey of
all our readings, revealed in her very last review letter to our class e-mail
list during exam period something quite personal as well:

> The words and ideas of the Bible resonate with me, but this is not
> the only reason that I am Christian. I am Christian because of the love
> of my neighbor, who took me to Baptist Bible school with her daugh-
> ter as I grew up, and because of the faith of my grandmother. Both of
> them have fundamentalist convictions that, with the scientific and hu-
> manist upbringing of my parents, I cannot entirely and honestly accept.
> I have the feeling that if I charged at the truth like a bull, declaring my
> freedom to believe as I wish and my unwillingness to accept any half-
> answers, any faith that blinded, I might find more answers to suit my
> personal need, but I would betray my responsibilities to the community
> where I find myself. Ultimately, humans do not have the truth, and I
> think there is honesty in recognizing that and accepting the limitations
> of our creativity, generosity, and imagination.

Despite her superb intellectual grasp of the course material, ultimately it
was also an encounter with a person that has made the critical difference
in her spiritual life. I found that the students in the course who were least
tormented by doubt and most attached to their faith, were those who also
had figures such as these in their lives.

There are, I think, important pedagogical consequences from these last
pieces by Isaac and Linda. As professors, we usually focus on "critical
thinking" and "disciplinary knowledge"—important and worthy goals,
needless to say. But we so easily forget in the rush of the semester to
cover our material, and to train those minds, that the mind is not the
whole person, and people do not, in the end, really learn and internalize
unless other parts of their selves are brought into play. As Joseph Schwab
has written:

> Eros, the energy of wanting, is as much the energy source in the pur-
> suit of truth as it is in the motion toward pleasure, friendship, and fame,
> or power. . . . The movement of Eros and the movement of the mind
> cannot take place separately, converging only at the end. In the person,

the student, they interact and interpenetrate. They must be treated so in interactions with a person. They must be moved together. . . .[8]

A postmodern theorist might phrase it differently and say that knowledge is always social, dialogical, and embedded in a concrete material situation. Or as Parker Palmer, in the quote I cited above, put it: "In truthful knowing, the knower becomes co-participant in a community of faithful relationships with other persons and creatures and things, with whatever our knowledge makes known." So these letters, though seemingly unrelated to the readings of the course, were as important for Isaac and Mike to have a chance to write as their more analytical, objective epistles.

I am glad that Isaac and Mike came to ease some of their intellectual torments. (As it turned out, they even teamed up to do a joint website on kabbalah for their final project. In one of the links, Isaac made a further revelation: his great-grandfather had been a learned and practicing kabbalist in Yemen and Egypt!) Yet I am pained that all their years of education (religious or secular) and their college experience, have not helped them to integrate intellect with spirit with emotion—that they still see faith and intellect as opposites. Perhaps this is a necessary stage in their development, but I think it also reflects a failure in contemporary university teaching. I have sensed that more often than not, students in a large public university like mine keep a distance between the intellectual exercises they are asked to do in the classroom and the real passions and interests of their lives. As if they think this is what expected of them, and almost live "double lives." If we keep the development of their intellectual faculties separate from the other parts of their being, it stands to reason they will do so as well.

Several students wrote with great anguish about their disappointment in and alienation from the university. Monique, one of the best students in class, and an African-American journalism major, wrote in her first letter responding to Mary Rose O'Reilly's essay:

> What, then, is the treatment for a decapitated educational system, the result of violent removal of it spiritual head, replaced by thought without feeling, feeling without perception, perception without insight? It is a crude mass of speculation and skepticism. . . . I am convinced that a spiritually dead person can never truly grasp the meaning of canons of

literature intended to reacquaint us with our spiritual selves. Cognitive reasoning and spirit are now polar binaries, perhaps evolved from the same abyss of un-knowing. *Was it always meant to be this way?*

In her midterm review Monique picked a sentence from an essay by Emerson we had read: "The invariable mark of wisdom is to see the miraculous in the common," and commented:

> I grow tired of the academic institution. My mind has worn out its elasticity in trying to wrap itself around the demands of professors and the claims of the scholars they teach. What began as a very engaging cerebral experience has given way to mental nausea, made feverish by indifference. But in the still and quiet, the ordinary, walking to class, or sitting on the side of the bed, I have moments of clarity. A speck of chipped paint suddenly becomes a metaphor for my entire life! I think this quote actually describes the scope of Emily Dickinson's poetry. She pushed conventional social constructs with planks of wood that bridge doubt and belief, or teeth that nibbled at her faith while a mosquito buzzed around it.
>
> I imagine her suddenly cut off in mid-sentence to gaze up at the way the light is peeking through her window. I think she probably sat and stared for hours at rain falling. Emily became the common, and it elevated her thoughts to a higher aim, more deeply and richer than any scholarly musing ever could. . . .

Their sense of fatigue and disillusionment with college troubles me greatly.

IV

As the students gradually opened their hearts and souls to each other, I played the role of sympathetic facilitator, but I did not, in turn, convey my own personal beliefs except in a few private conferences and after-class conversations. I could tell, however, that they sensed I had my own passionate beliefs and struggles. Why was I so reluctant, in addition to all the reasons I cited at the beginning of this essay, to share them more openly?

Was this a lack of nerve or a necessary stance, or both? I have been pondering this issue for some time. Just as I have also been wondering how some of the more traditional Jewish ideas of teaching and learning might be transferable to the contemporary academy. In what ways is the classroom itself a kind of "sacred space"? In what ways might the tension between withholding and giving be itself a spiritual act?[9]

For many years, I have been inspired by a model in the Jewish mystical tradition, the idea of *tzimtzum*—God's "self-contraction," a concealing or withdrawal of the divine light as the essential first step in God's creation of the universe. *Tzimtzum* ("contraction," "condensation") is the name given to the process of withdrawal of the infinite divine light in order to leave an "empty space" (*halal panui*), a space which can allow for finite beings, who otherwise would be overwhelmed and nullified by this light. In the kabbalistic scheme, a trace (*reshimu*) of the divine light remains in the void created by the *tzimtzum*, and further emanations illuminate into this void to allow for the creation of finite independent beings. There are interesting Chassidic texts which also explain the divine self-contraction using the analogy of the teacher-student relation. That is, the teacher first has to "withdraw," contract her or his intellectual light to the level at which it can be absorbed by the student, before the student can then develop to try to reach the concept on the more complex level on which the teacher herself conceives it. If the teacher would try to transfer her or his ideas directly on the level she or he conceives them, the student would be overwhelmed. The concealment, however, is ultimately for the purpose of revelation, just as the *tzimtzum* is made for the purpose of a new independent creation.

I have used this model till now to frame my teaching stance; that is, I have conceived of my role less as expansive self-expression or revelation of my religious positions, than as leaving a "trace" (*reshimu*) of them in the space I create for my students. A trace that hints, points, invites, but does not compel. My students should also have the freedom to withhold their personal beliefs. Yet the class should sense the *tzimtzum*, the fuller life beyond.[10]

On a larger scale, I wonder if this is not true of all the deepest pedagogical acts. Rabbi Nachman of Bratslav, a great Chassidic leader of the nineteenth century, in his own brilliant way, wrote that this act of emptying out, this *tzimtzum* in the teacher-student relationship is also deeply productive for the teacher. For in the act of teaching, contraction, of giving over knowledge, the teacher, so to speak, also "empties" him or herself of their own knowledge, and so creates an open space within him or herself that enables entirely new knowledge to enter the mind. The bestower then becomes the receiver.

Ultimately, then, this concept of *tzimztum* and necessary contraction reminds me of what my many years of teaching have also led me to conclude: *one can never really teach anything "directly."* The teaching that is truly received and absorbed by the student is done via indirection. And the arousal of the desire to know itself also comes so often through indirection, through a lack which prompts desire, through a glimpse of a trace which tracks a glimmering light. Indirection, as Rabbi Nachman understood so well, was also the secret power of stories. Stories, in his description, help people who have "fallen asleep," who are sunk in an existential darkness to awaken and, as he puts it, "find their face," without the light overwhelming and blinding them. Stories "garb" and "enclothe" the light so it can be received, enable the sleeper to awaken gently, like a blind person healing and slowly coming to see illumination.[11] And that is one of the best descriptions of the relation between literature and religion I have ever come across. (R. Nachman was also himself a master creator of parables, stories, and songs.)

Yet while this model has well served my act of "withholding" as a teacher in a state university, and helped me formulate the relation of literature to religion, there are times, I confess, when I feel the need to take a risk and reveal more. I am always questioning myself: Did I reveal enough of myself, or not? When is the right time? Did I give enough guidance? Only once during the semester did I also write a class letter, though in the past I have tried to do so much more frequently. By mid-semester, my students were beginning to open up to each other so honestly and taking risks, that I felt the need to somehow reciprocate, to be more than the neutral traffic director. In other words, ethically I also owed them something more of myself. I finally gave out a letter of my own when we had been discussing Tolstoy's "The Death of Ivan Ilyich," a wrenching story about a complacent Russian bourgeois magistrate who injures himself one day while decorating his house, then goes into a progressive physical decline. As he sinks closer and closer to death, he finds himself facing the truth of his shallow life, alienated from his superficial friends and self-absorbed members of his family, tormented by the question of what his life has meant.

That day, I gave to the class an e-mail letter I had received the year before, while still in Jerusalem, from my office mate, colleague, and friend, Jamie Robinson, who was then in the final stage of a nine-year battle with colon cancer. He passed away a few months after writing it. Jamie was fifty-three years old then. During the course of struggling with his illness he had tried to see it as a "spiritual journey," and he had the many ups and downs of all such journeys, several of which he shared with me in talks in our office, between or after class. Jamie's letter indeed "stopped my heart":

Dear Suzie,

Your erstwhile office mate lives (by the skin of his teeth), and so he assumes doth you. These must be particularly exciting times in Israel with the 50th anniversary of its founding—I've been reading about it in *The New Yorker* and elsewhere. . . . I would love to see Jerusalem, and envy you being there, clearly thriving in such an intense intellectual and political atmosphere.

I'd give you news on the department these days, but I'm a particularly barren source since I'm hardly ever there (average once/month) since I went on sick leave after a bunch of hospitalizations and another surgery in November. We've run out of chemotherapies, so now I'm in home hospice care (their nurse comes in 2–3 times/week to change dressings, adjust my morphine pump, etc.), and also attended by an LPN, a large woman named Josephine who hails from—ironically enough, since I served in the Peace Corps there—Ghana. She feeds me lunch, bathes me, and is around to help me take things easy, which I didn't find all that necessary at first, but which has been more required lately as my energy wears down gradually.

The tumor grows incrementally on my lower left side, whose front looks like a '56 Cadillac bumper breast (you may have to be into car culture to catch that reference), and clearly is sapping strength from me—had a transfusion last week in prep. for a trip with the children to Williamsburg and it helped me through the weekend there, but it's taken me 4 days to recover. So that may well be my last trip, which saddens me. One of the things I miss most is the opportunity to travel and see places I've never seen, like Jerusalem (op cit), the Grand Canyon, Yosemite, Provence, Maine. But I've really been pretty privileged in that regard (I've taught or lectured on 5 continents, and lived for years in Africa and Europe), so I'm not complaining, just yearning.

All told, the past four months have been a pretty weird time, "laying low" back at the house, considering how my life has been spent, balancing off the professional things undone . . . and challenges avoided, against . . . I'm not sure what, exactly. I could break into a chorus of "I did it my way," but that seems a bit too grand, and not entirely accurate. Anyway, I've achieved some spiritual growth, and probably nudged a few students in some good directions, and encouraged a lot of the average ones to love literature enthusiastically and see it as a way of framing life (a bit passe in these post-Deconstruction days). I persuade myself I've done more good than harm.

And I know you have, Suzie, and wanted to let you know while there was still world enough and time. [deletion of more personal remarks] For these and all the other things you've generously shared with me, I thank you, friend, and pray that God blesses you as He has blessed others by making you part of their journeys.

I'd like to see you "next year in Jerusalem," but reckon that's not in the cards. In the meantime, my Susan joins me in sending,

Love, Jamie.

I read the letter to the class and felt their hearts stop too. I chose not, however, to share with them my response to this message. But I have decided to print it here . . . for as Jamie faced the ultimate meaning of his life in the university, and stopped my heart, he helped me think about the meaning of mine as well. I close with these words:

April 27, 1998

Dear Jamie:

. . . You describe your process of thinking about and reviewing your life these past four months and what seems to have really counted—the effect on your students, your spiritual growth . . . I was indeed so grateful for your words to me, about how you think I have helped my students, and how somehow I have helped you in your journey. Because I often wonder what remains of all those years of mine at the University. From my perspective here in Jerusalem—a 3,000-year-old-city, the focus of so much pain and yearning where you do indeed have "intimations of immortality"—I, too, think from afar about what that life in academia is finally all about, and it seems to me it is not ultimately about the "career" part—the publications, the latest theories—all of which become obsolete fairly quickly. But the enduring things are those human relations we were able to construct almost in spite of the University—those moments of touching each other's souls somehow, even obliquely.

Someone gave me a copy of an interview with Grace Paley in which she talked about teaching writing and said, "To me, teaching is a gift because it puts you in loving contact with young people."

How many moments of loving contact do I remember in my years of teaching—with students and colleagues? In the end, that is what it is about, I think. They redeem everything. I can remember some very specifically; I missed opportunities for others, but I want to try to remember that as my ultimate goal. The course material, the literature, the theories, all the rest of it is just a means.

And I have to tell you, too, Jamie, I know you, too, created many of those moments with those around you. I always sensed that in your approach to your students, in the many kindnesses you did for them, in the ways you related to everyone in the Department. Perhaps that is why I always felt drawn to you

And in the family you had built. . . . and built with such difficulty. I saw in you a man with a special gift of love—especially how you brought into your life the several children not originally your own. . . . In Judaism, the building of a family and home is the ultimate success, and part of eternity—in this, you are a real model. I think others feel this about you too—when Janet last wrote me about you in February, she said she had seen you in the office, and that though you were quite thin, you had, as she put it, an "aura" about you. Perhaps in this whittling down, is also being further revealed the core of your essential self—that man of luminous soul and love.

Spiritual teachers say that there aren't any coincidences in life—and I don't think it was coincidental that we came to share an office, you and I. You too have touched me deeply in my life . . . given me comfort and solace and done kindness. Our office was often a little oasis in the Department.

So do we all live by the skin of our teeth—I think that phrase comes from the Book of Job. I still don't know how Job found comfort after all his tribulations, and I still don't understand God's answer to Job and I don't understand a lot of what God does, but being here in Jerusalem, one is fortified in faith despite all the difficulties, terror, conflict, bloodshed, and sense of fragility. . . .

I thought I sensed in the tone of your message that you too, despite all the pain, have been sustained by faith, made your way to certain peace with yourself and your God. In this too, I admire you so greatly.

I always loved the teaching of one of the great Chassidic masters, Rabbi Nachman of Bratslav who lived about 150 years ago and endured much. He had a famous saying, that he wrote a famous melody to—"All the world is a very narrow bridge, a very narrow bridge, and the main thing is . . . not to be afraid . . . not to be afraid at all." Thanks for being a warm companion to me on that bridge.

Love, Susie

Notes

On August 2, 1998, my colleague and friend Jamie Robinson, whom I write about at the end of this essay, passed away. I dedicate this essay to his memory. Before he died, he endowed "James A. Robinson Awards for Excellence in Undergraduate Teaching" to be awarded yearly to teaching assistants in the English department of the University of Maryland, College Park. One month after his death, a memorial program was held for him by his colleagues at the university. Some months before, he himself had chosen pieces of music and poetry to be read at that occasion, which he knew was coming. For the cover of the program, he picked the following quote from the playwright Eugene O'Neill, about whom he had written a book: "It isn't the end. It's a free beginning—the start of my voyage."

1. See Lee S. Shulman, "Theory, Practice, and the Education of Professionals," *The Elementary School Journal* (98:5): 511–26. That turn of the century "ideology" of professionalism, writes Shulman, valued the technical "objective" and "scientific" but also had an equally strong moral and "service" aspect that we need to recover.

2. The dictionary I used for these definitions is the online http://www.dict.org which is the DICT Development Group: Online Dictionary Query, a database of several dictionaries. I also used the online Middle English Dictionary http://www.hti.umich.edu.

3. Jane Tomkins, "Pedagogy of the Distressed," *College English* 10 (1990): 659. See also her *A Life in School: What the Teacher Learned* (Boston: Addison-Wesley, 1996).

4. Parker Palmer, *To Know as We Are Known: Education as a Spiritual Journey* (San Francisco: HarperSan Francisco, 1993), 19, xvii, 8–9.

5. Quoted in Karen Fischer, "The Soul of America: An Increasingly Fractured Society Sends the Nation on a Quest for Faith," *Smith Alumnae Quarterly* (Spring, 1997): 7–12.

6. For an in-depth description, see my essay, "Dear Class," in *Essays in Quality Learning: Teachers' Reflections on Classroom Practice*, ed. Steven Selden (University of Maryland: IBM Total Quality Learning Project, 1998), 17–32.

Melanie, a straight-A award-winning English major in my class, wrote at the end of the semester, "It is so refreshing to take a course in which I have the opportunity to write letters such as these, for in letters, I am more apt to struggle with ideas, which is why I feel more comfortable writing letters than papers. Formal papers scare me because the assumption is that I will unlock every mystery. My language has to be strong, no use of the first person, and I have to avoid shaky ground. In this class, however, there are no theses to prove and no definite answers." Sadly, what this comment shows, and what my years of teaching experience also confirm, is that often our formal writing assignments, which are intended to help students "struggle with ideas," instead have the opposite effect. Very often, the same students who write eloquent, complex, and stunning letters turn in final "research" papers that are the opposite: stilted, monotonous, uninteresting, forced.

7. Mary Rose O'Reilly, "Silence and Slow Time: Pedagogies from Inner Space," *Pre-Text* 11 (1–2): 135.

8. Joseph Schwab, "Eros and Education," in *Science, Curriculum, and Liberal Education: Selected Essays*, ed. Ian Westbury and Neil Wilkof (Chicago: University of Chicago Press, 1978), 109, 126.

9. For my further reflections on these matters, both theoretical and practical, see my essays "The Torah of Criticism and the Criticism of Torah: Recuperating the Pedagogical Moment," *Journal of Religion* 74:3 (1994): 356–71, reprinted in *Interpreting Judaism in a Postmodern Age*, ed. Steven Kepnes (New York: New York University Press, 1996), 221–42; " 'Find(ing) Yourself a Teacher': Opening the Discussion on Pedagogy at the Association for Jewish Studies Conference," *Association for Jewish Studies Newsletter*, Spring 1995 (45): 8–9; " *'Emunah'*: The Craft of

Faith," *Crosscurrents: Religion and Intellectual Life* 42:3 (1992): 293–313, reprinted in *The Academy and the Possibility of Belief*, ed. M. L. Buley-Meissner (New York: Hampton Press, 2000), 85–104; " 'Crossing and Re-crossing the Void': A Letter to Gene," in *Reviewing the Covenant: Eugene Borowitz and the Postmodern Renewal of Jewish Theology*, ed. Peter Ochs (New York: State University of New York Press, 2000), 173–200; "We Cleverly Avoided Talking About God: Personal and Pedagogical Reflections on Academia and Spirituality," *Courtyard: A Journal of Research and Thought in Jewish Education* 1:1 (1999): 101–20; " 'Just as All Their Faces Are Different': The Jewish, the Personal, and the Pedagogical," in *The Social Character of Scholarly Writing,* ed. David Bleich and Deborah Holdstein (forthcoming; Salt Lake City: University of Utah Press).

10. I thank R. Tzvi Blanchard of the Center for Leadership and Learning in New York for helping me formulate this idea.

11. R. Nachman of Bratslav, *Likkutei Moharan* (Jerusalem: Agudat Meshek Ha-Nahal, 1811; reprint 1969), "Patakh R. Simon" #60.

Concluding Reflections on the Lilly Seminar

FRANCIS OAKLEY

While the remarks that follow emerged, like the chapters preceding, from a three-year seminar on Religion and Higher Education sponsored by the Lilly Foundation, unlike those chapters they were not framed as a formal paper or delivered as such at the public conference held as a supplement to the seminar. Nor were they generated by way of commentary on those chapters. What occasioned their composition, instead, was an invitation to say a few words at the concluding meeting of the seminar about the wide-ranging discussions in which we had all been engaged during the three years preceding. They represent then, simply my own retroactive "take" on that stimulating set of discussions. They were addressed directly to a group of colleagues whom I had come very much to like and admire, and they retain the voice and form appropriate to such a moment of *viva voce* deliverance.

Having been invited to reflect upon and speak about the full array of our wide-ranging discussions in the Lilly Seminar over the past three years, I decided to prepare for my assignment by reading the splendidly meaty reports on each of our sessions routinely circulated as reminders immediately prior to the meetings that followed. Andrea Sterk wrote most of these reports, and I should like to begin by congratulating her on their impressive quality—full, clear, accurate, and intellectually generous. I mention this last admirable quality because she usually succeeded somehow in perceiving glimmers of insight in even the more occluded or obfuscatory moments that occasionally punctuated our discourse.

What immediately caught my attention as I read through these reports were the issues that were raised more than once but never quite succeeded in making it into the center of our discourse, or the issues that were only fleetingly alluded to and never made it further than a sort of off-stage presence on the margins of the group's consciousness—moths, as it were, banging against the outer screen of our consciousness but not quite able to get to the light.

Of these, essentially failures as issues, at least so far as our dominant discourse was concerned, three in particular caught my attention. I find it interesting that two of the three were essentially institutional in nature and the third administrative. Despite their fate, all three, I believe, really are pertinent to our various discussions about religion and what was referred to as the "formation" of students; about the intersection of religious commitment and classroom teaching and whether or not that was something to be deplored or affirmed; and about the impact—desirable, undesirable, or essentially irrelevant—of a scholar's religious beliefs upon the nature of the research he or she pursues and the scholarship he or she produces.

What I should like to do, then, is to begin by describing these three quasi-"failed" issues before turning to say a few words about religion and student formation, religion and classroom teaching, religion and scholarship. (On the topic of divinity-school education to which we did devote a session, having failed myself to get any sort of intellectual traction on the specific issues involved, I am afraid I have nothing to say.)

I

The first of these quasi-failed issues concerns the institutional makeup of the world of American higher education. At our Pasadena meeting, Clarke Cochran adopted a firmly institutional approach and spoke interestingly about the role institutions play in embodying meaning, sustaining it in the people who belong to them, mediating it to their initiates, and manifesting it to the larger world.[1] For me, at least, he was sounding harmonics of the sort of notes Mary Douglas strikes in her little book, *How Institutions Think*.[2] But Cochran was something of an exception and I haven't sensed that, as a group, we have really been all that interested in hearing about institutions. (Or, at least, I had not thought so until Gene Lowe and Richard Mouw got into the matter during our discussions yesterday.)

No big surprise, of course. One does not have to do much more than paddle in the shallows of the vast ocean of controversialist commentary on the state of American higher education, the corruption of the academy, the decline of the humanities, and so on, without becoming gloomily conscious of the speed with which academics, when throwing themselves into such controversy, tend to abandon their painfully acquired habits of disciplined scholarly inquiry, reaching instead, and it seems instinctively, for the provincially autobiographical, and substituting for empirically informed argumentation great gusts of disheveled anecdotage.

But that, of course, won't do. There are, after all, more than 3,500 institutions of higher education in the United States, big and small, public and private, religiously affiliated and not, different enough in institutional mission, sources of funding, makeup of student body, quality of faculty, and so on as to induce the Carnegie Corporation to come up with a classification system that allots them to one or other of no less than ten different categories. And while on some issues one can, of course, generalize across the lines separating those categories in reasonably meaningful fashion, on others it is really misleading to do so.

One might have thought that all this institutional variety and differentiation would induce a measure of careful specification in those delivering themselves of generalizations about the state of higher education today. But not so. Read enough of the vigorous controversialist, culture-war type of literature about our campuses, penetrate the surface skin of incantatory accusation, probe the underlying soft tissue of endlessly recycled anecdotage, and one finds that the supportive skeletal frame would appear to extend no further than the situation prevailing (or allegedly prevailing) at no more than a dozen or so of our leading research universities and liberal arts colleges—all of them in some respects highly privileged institutions and far from being representative of the whole.

Admittedly, in our own discussions in this seminar we've done somewhat better than that. Richard Hughes helpfully reminded us of the different modes of Christian education to be found even in the small universe of colleges and universities with an explicitly Christian identity. Alan Wolfe also alluded to the same matter. And Richard Bernstein properly complained about the uncritical way in which we kept using the word "secular," as if we really knew what it meant. But I cannot recall anyone's having brought those two things into any sort of constructive configuration—not enough, at least, to raise the question of what exactly we mean when by way of contrast to religiously affiliated colleges, we apply the word *secular* to the larger institutional universe, to all those thousands of disparate campuses, from leading private research universities to obscure community colleges, institutions operating under vastly different conditions, pursuing quite disparate missions, possessed of very different histories. And yet, if Berkeley and Yale are both of them secular universities they are, surely, secular in different ways. Similarly, Evergreen State and, say Swarthmore. Such differences in modes of secularity are unlikely, I suspect, to have all that much of an impact on the deportment of faculty as teachers, still less in what they do in their scholarly work—if, that is, they are accustomed to doing any on a regular basis (most American academics, after all, are not). But those differences will, I am pretty sure, affect what is done in the way of "student formation" on a particular campus, and whether or not, indeed, such a thing is even talked about.

The second of our quasi-failed issues was that pivoting on the matter of differences among disciplines. The academic disciplines as we know them are historical deliverances reflecting the institutionalization of contingent selections of academic and intellectual presuppositions and practices, and I classify them as institutions. And, even if we bracket the natural sciences, and concern ourselves only with the arts, humanities, and social sciences, I am struck by the degree to which these institutional forms shape the way in which we severally react to talk about "the warranting process," "the rules of the relevant epistemic community," the demand for "intersubjective testability" in our intellectual endeavors—again, a fact to which Alan Wolfe alluded yesterday. But in our earlier discussions it was Denis Donoghue who returned to this issue again and again, and with considerable insistence, even objecting that the criterion of intersubjective testability was being given "a kind of totalitarian force in its application." And Jean Elshtain, I believe, surfaced cognate worries in a different context.

But I don't think, by and large, that we fully engaged that issue or came to grips with it properly or with a sufficient degree of specification. If, as Denis Donoghue pointed out, truth claims involving statements about how the world *is* play little or no rule in art, literary criticism, musicology, and so on, then talk about intersubjective testability is likely to smack of boiled-over scientism, and some other sort of warranting process has to be called for. For example, is a given work competent, productive, significant, interesting?

It's a pity that we did not discuss such disciplinary differences a bit more probingly. I would be curious to know, for example, if we could all agree that talk of intersubjective testability is the sort of warranting talk that should be confined to the empirically-based disciplines. I would also like to know if Nicholas Wolterstorff, Richard Bernstein, and Eleonore Stump would definitely want to exclude philosophy from its purview. And I would like to know, too, if the firm line Denis Donoghue has drawn *between* disciplines is not really a line that can be seen to run *through* such disciplines as art, musicology, and literary studies. Surely one would want to evoke some sort of criterion of intersubjective testability in assessing the product of the sort of historian who finds a disciplinary home in a history department. But would not one also want to do the same for a scholar who tells us that he or she is a "new literary historian" as opposed to a person pursuing a formalist-cum-aesthetic approach to literature? And the same, I think, and for the same reasons, would apply to art history and musicology.

I see a good deal of art historians and museum curators, and I cannot help noticing the growing condescension evident in both groups toward the more aesthetic and formalistic approaches to evaluating works of art. Those they sometimes find possible to dismiss as "mere connoisseurship"—though no museum, of course, could function without some curators blessed with that richly mysterious capacity. The art historians and curators who adopt such a posture of condescension are usually themselves pursuing historical or sociological approaches, and I can't help thinking that it would be a healthy discipline for them to have to respond to the demand for intersubjective testability in much the same way as the work of ordinary, honest-to-God historians is subjected to it.

Moreover, even if one evokes by the way of substitute warranting criteria like "competent," "significant," "productive," "interesting" (what in one of our sessions David Hollinger referred to, engagingly, as "mush words"), it would still seem to me that, if empirical data are adduced in defense of the proposition that such-and-such a work is, say, "significant," then, thus far at least, the warranting process would properly have to involve some sort of "intersubjective testability."

The third of our quasi-failed issues was our lack of interest in the insights afforded by the administrative perspective. Richard Mouw made a noble effort to introduce it into our discussions and Gene Lowe,

Jeanne Knoerle, and I dipped an occasional tentative toe in the same waters. But the issue didn't fly (or swim!). Again, no big surprise. At these seminars we have heard many an explicit or implicit affirmation of faith, but the only robustly explicit affirmation of a lack of faith that comes to mind was that of a lack of faith in university administrators. The prevailing gulf in the academic world between faculty and administrators seems to be so wide as to tempt faculty to conclude that there doesn't even exist anything as stable or coherent as an administrative perspective.

This was brought home to me about twenty years ago when, after several years of hard work as dean of the faculty, I was fortunate enough to be invited to spend a year as a member of the history school at the Princeton Institute for Advanced Study. During that year I quickly learned not to let drop too readily the fact that I had been serving as an administrator. After all, what serious scholar would do anything so foolish? But, then, I had a mirror-image experience when the year was over and I went on to spend six weeks during the summer as a participant in the Institute for Educational Management at Harvard. There, to let drop the fact that you were a faculty member still involved in teaching and research would clearly have the effect of calling into question your credentials as a card-carrying member of the administrative guild. To most of the participants at the Harvard institute the great enemy in academe, the alien other, appeared unquestionably to be the faculty.

All this is too bad, and for many reasons that I can't go into here. Suffice it to say that in the context of this seminar it is too bad that the administrative perspective was not a more central presence in our protracted but somewhat desultory discussions of student formation. I sense (or, at least, suspect) that many of us as faculty members were not really all that interested in (and, perhaps, even a bit suspicious of) all that talk about issues pertaining to the formation of students. But no one who has been in an administrative leadership position on a campus—or, at least, on a small campus—can for a moment doubt that a richly textured, complex, and largely uncoordinated process of student moral formation is going on. Nor can such a person, especially if he or she is president, indulge for a moment the illusion that he or she has properly no role to play in that process, or can in conscience avoid the responsibility of attempting in some measure to shape it. He or she, after all, and willy-nilly, is the bearer, shaper, mediator, even embodier of the institution's purpose, mission, meaning. That is to say, to borrow the language of some commentators on the phenomenon of leadership, one of his or her most testing challenges is undoubtedly that of "managing the institution's meaning."[3] I'll return to this in a moment.

II

Thus far, I have talked of three of the things that failed to make it into the center of our discourse. And it should be clear that all three are pertinent to one or more of the topics we have discussed at considerable length: religion and student formation, religious commitment and classroom teaching, religion and scholarship. And, while trying to avoid repeating myself, I would like to say a few further words about each of those three topics.

First, the matter of formation. This topic strikes me as not a very rewarding one to address unless one is prepared to distinguish among both institutional settings and institutional responsibilities. So far as settings go, this includes distinguishing between institutions with a confessional religious identity and those without one, for the former differentiating (as Richard Hughes did) by particular confessional tradition; among the latter differentiating, if you wish, by degrees of secularity or detachment from a religious tradition; among all of them distinguishing between big universities with extensive commitments to graduate and professional education and small, face-to-face college communities with a predominantly undergraduate teaching mission. It includes distinguishing also between institutions catering for a body of full-time students drawn from the traditional collegiate age-group, and those catering much more to older students and part-time students; and between those with a predominantly residential student body and all the others—by far, incidentally, the majority. Only a fifth of our undergraduates nationwide now have a residential experience at college.[4] And so on. And, so far as institutional responsibilities go, I think we need to distinguish between the instructional corps and those with administrative and/or leadership responsibilities pertaining in some measure to the quality of student life.

It is usually, I think (and understandably so), those involved in religiously affiliated institutions who are prone to raising to the level of conscious deliberation knotty questions pertaining to student formation, but some such formation is, of course, going on in the full range of our institutions of higher education, whether religious or secular. I would guess that in big universities catering in large degree for graduate and professional education and/or for older, nonresident, and frequently part-time, students, that formation is likely to be confined largely to the classroom setting, where, whether we want to admit it or not, students do take their cues, whether by imitation or reaction, from the intellectual/moral deportment of their instructors. And, at one of our sessions, an interesting exchange among Denis Donoghue, Peter Steinfels, Eleonore Stump, and Richard Bernstein reflected a clear recognition of that fact, with Richard noting that even though Denis "was saying what he didn't want to do, he had in fact described a distinctive, important way of mentoring."

In my own institutional setting, which is basically secular though with some religiously blunted edges (or, if you wish, religiously eroded contours), I don't think I had thought all that much about the formation issue until I became president of the college. (Though I had thought a great deal, as dean of the faculty, about the mentoring of faculty, for that job did involve a certain amount of pastoral care of one's colleagues.) But, as president, though I cannot recall ever having used the term, I simply could not sidestep the issue of student formation. I had in some way to try to shape the ethos of the place, to shape student behavior—or, at least, to set limits to it.

A strong stream of sewage flows beneath the surface of even the most benign of campuses (so much so that, in our own case, reading on Monday mornings the security reports of weekend mayhem resurrected memories from my distant past in the British Army of reading similarly the duty officer's reports of weekend goings-on in a garrison town—who was in jail for disturbing the peace, who had to be bailed out, and so on). From time to time, that stream of sewage is prone to surfacing, and when that occurs, one has to work to prevent it from leaking into and polluting the general stream of campus life, as well as to reduce the incidence of such occurrences. And that not only means maintaining a firm, equitable, equitably-administered and credible disciplinary system, but also making (or grasping) the occasion to articulate the standards of community behavior expected of students, as well as explaining, discussing, and, if necessary, arguing about, those standards. With that in view, we instituted at

Williams regular class meetings, individual and separate assemblies for the first year, sophomore, junior, and senior classes; in addition, during the nine years of my presidency I also went along every month with the dean of students, dean of the faculty, and provost to each of our residential houses in turn for an after-dinner open discussion, at which students could raise whatever questions they wished. While these sessions were sometimes quite boring, on other occasions they were deeply moving and compelling, and one sensed a real and growing hunger for an adult presence in student life. At times the issues raised were trivial, at other times far from that. They ranged from matters like complaints about parking space, or about campus lighting, to questions about the college's alcohol policy or investment practices, to hand-wringing about the behavior of fellow students (for instance, the vomit level at such and such a residential house after a weekend party), all the way to quite sensitive, probing, and affecting discussions about race- or gender-related problems, or the complexities of sexual-identity issues, or even about curricular matters and the challenges of the life of the mind.

Clearly, a great deal of our effort was devoted to articulating, modeling, and inculcating attitudes of tolerance, decency, and mutual respect among students with very different backgrounds in an increasingly multiracial and culturally plural community. But, as Jim Heft properly reminded us at one of our sessions, thoughtful explication of the life of the mind, and of the type of freedom and restraint it presupposes, is itself a formation. And, recognizing that within the nation at large the life of the mind is itself a countercultural form which the academy must vindicate and celebrate, we sought to multiply the occasions on which we could do precisely that.

But what, you may be thinking, has religion got to do with all of this? That is not at all easy to assess. The fact that I myself had had what Robert Wuthnow would probably call a "heavy-duty" religious upbringing undoubtedly imparted to me some of the passion I brought to this particular responsibility, as well as the level of comfort with which I went about the task on the explicitly religious occasions which still occur on a voluntary basis on our sort of campus, or in such explicitly religious settings as the college chapel or the college's Jewish Religious Center—a synagogue which I myself had built in response to the rising level of religious observance among our Jewish students. In evoking the college's

ethos and affirming its commitments on such occasions and in such settings I did so, I suspect, with an unself-consciously religious charge. And
I can't believe I was unique in so doing, given the variety of conditions
and complex, shifting accommodations covered by the term when we
designate a university or college as "secular."

But what, in the second place, about the relationship between one's
teaching and one's personal religious commitments? On this matter I really
don't have a great deal to add to what has already been said in our discussions. So far as the descriptive side of the matter goes, it seems to me a
simple matter of fact that the religious background or continuing religious
commitments of academics have frequently drawn them to the particular
subject they teach, led them to focus on some particular dimension of that
subject, and/or encouraged them in the particular emphases they impart to
the subject in the course of teaching it. And I believe that fact to be an important one. Here, I was much taken at one of our sessions by Frank
Turner's argument that scholars and teachers of religious commitment may
well function within the academy, as it were, counter-cyclically, keeping
alive certain types of questions, topics, interests that the prevailingly dominant academic norms may have had the effect of delegitimating, sidelining,
or, at least, extruding into the academic shadows.

Further than that, I am inclined to think that certain types of religious
commitment may lead a teacher to emphasize or convey to students by his
or her own intellectual or pedagogic deportment the degree to which there
is a moral dimension to learning, the fact that we don't do our thinking as
disembodied intellects but as real, sentient human beings burdened with all
the normal freight of vanity, fear, ambition, insecurity, laziness, and pride.

And if one turns to the prescriptive side of the coin—the affirmation
in the classroom of one's faith or, at least, the explicit identification of
oneself as a believer in this or that—I thought I detected at least in our
particular small-discussion group a sort of cleavage in sensibilities between evangelicals and Catholics, with the former more prone to favoring
forthright self-identification and the latter more comfortable with a rather
oblique or even occluded stance. Certainly, even though I myself teach a
lot of religiously-related material, my own classroom practice does not involve any such self-identification. But, then, as David Hollinger pointed
out, we all participate in "multiple solidarities," and I'm not in the habit in
the classroom of foregrounding any of them. If a student asks (and that

is an unusual occurrence), I am perfectly willing to respond in forthright fashion. But I am anxious for students to avoid substituting identity for argument or stereotyping for understanding. I worry that too much focus on the teacher or the teacher's commitments may serve to distract them from paying close attention to the matter at hand—a text, a body of evidence, logical or illogical chains of reasoning, and so forth. Subject-matter matters. It matters a great deal.

Third, and finally, the matter of Christian scholarship. Of all the issues we have addressed this was the one that interested me most. And yet, as our discussions wore on, this was the issue that came to puzzle me most. I have not read Warren Nord's book to which reference has more than once been made, but, after hearing him speak and from talking with him, I did not come away with any clear sense that he was arguing for the sort of redefinition of epistemic community or opening up of warranting conventions, or "turn from cognitive to constitutional analysis" that David Hollinger attributed to him at one of our sessions. On the other hand, rightly or wrongly, I did get that impression of George Marsden's project from the last chapter of his *Soul of the American University* which we have also had occasion to discuss. But if that was, indeed, his original project, he certainly seemed to have moved away from it in his later book, *The Outrageous Idea of Christian Scholarship*. And nothing that he said when he spoke to us at one of our meetings suggested anything to the contrary.[5]

I am left, then, with the impression, as I indicated last time, that what some of the advocates of Christian scholarship may be doing is not so much asserting some sort of epistemic *privilege* for Christian scholarship as expressing (perhaps unwittingly) a type of epistemic *resentment* stimulated by the degree of marginalization or condescension they may have experienced at the hands of a highly secularized mainstream academic establishment. And, from an interesting set of remarks he made at the end of our last meeting, I venture to think that Mark Schwehn might not altogether disagree with me on that.

That said, where do I stand? Well, after reflection, I think I stand in a rather uncomfortable place—uncomfortable because I find myself attempting the stretching maneuver of trying to stand in two places at the same time. And I conclude that that may be the case because, over the years, and in my historical work at least, I have pursued two rather different sets of interests—the first of which has given me good reason to worry about the assertion of claims to epistemic privilege (or, better, the tacit assumption of such a privilege), while the latter leads me off in a different direction and induces me to wonder a bit about the nature of the structures of plausibility sustaining the epistemic norms dominant in contemporary academic scholarship, and to wonder also if they are not destined, as time goes on, to erode and to become increasingly the exclusive possession of a beleaguered cognitive minority. Let me at least try to explain what I mean.

The first is the easier matter to address. I have worked for years on a topic in the history of the ecclesiology of the Latin (i.e., Roman) Catholic church. That topic concerns the external structure or constitution of that church as a visible, hierarchical organization. And I have come to the conclusion that side by side with the familiar high papalist, absolutist monarchical understanding of the church's constitution favored classically by Italian theologians, there existed, deeply-rooted in earlier canon law but with a clear prominence from about 1300 onwards, a rival constitutionalist understanding which emphasized the community-based consensual and conciliar (or, if you wish, "parliamentary") nature of the church's supreme authority. And that constitutionalist tradition, I now conclude, was no revolutionary and merely evanescent product of an era of crisis, which is the way in which for the past century or so it has usually been portrayed, but one with a continuous history in the Latin church, side by side with the high-papalist monarchical view, all the way down to the First Vatican Council in 1870, after which, by a sort of politics of oblivion or triumph of an essentially ultramontane historiography it was extruded into the outer darkness of heterodoxy and stuffed down a kind of Orwellian memory hole so that it is well-nigh forgotten today. But I found myself arriving at that conclusion in the teeth of a dominant historiography, largely Catholic in provenance, in which, even in the work of some very fine ecclesiastical historians, theological and canonistic criteria had been permitted, on admittedly neuralgic points but still anachronistically and improperly, to trump arguments framed in accord with the normal canons of historic endeavor.[6] Epistemic privilege, it seems with a vengeance. Others, doubtless, would disagree with me on this. But I've thought about it a lot. That is where I am. *Ich kann nicht anderes.* As a result, when I hear any talk about claims for epistemic privilege, I tend to rally instinctively to the side of the skeptics.

The second matter is a more tricky one to address. It stems from my teaching in the history of ideas, which has been fairly broad-gauged, as well as from a long-standing research interest of mine pertaining to the complex intersection across time of natural theology, natural philosophy, and natural-law theory. This is the matter I took up briefly in a letter I wrote to Jim Turner after our last meeting and which, I believe, he circulated to the group. It is also the matter that led me to suggest that we might all profit from a reading or rereading of Hans Jonas's lucid little essay, "Jewish and Christian Elements in the Western Philosophical Tradition."[7] In that essay, you will recall, and evoking what he dubs "the well-worked theme of the Judaeo-Christian component of Western thought," he asks in what sense that component, self-confessedly based on revelation rather than reason, can really be considered a part of the *philosophical* tradition. In other words, "can religion enter philosophy without either disrupting it or forsaking itself?" And to that question he gives an unambiguously affirmative answer. "Since philosophy is the work of thinking men," he says,

> the philosopher's participation in the common heritage of faith asserts itself in his philosophizing. As a result, certain ideas, motifs, and choices of revealed religion pass over, open or concealed, into the patrimony of philosophy itself and—eventually dissociated from their origin in revelation and its authority—become genuine parts of the modified philosophical landscape. This is not merely a matter of insinuation of extraneous ideas into philosophy through the all-too-human psychology of the philosopher. Rather it is a matter of the legitimate continuation in the medium of philosophy, of existential insights and emphases whose original locus is the world of faith, but whose validity and vitality extend beyond the reaches of faith.[8]

In so arguing, Jonas does not purport to be pursuing a species of "faith-based" scholarship and certainly makes no claim to any sort of epistemic privilege. His project revolves, instead, within the intellectual orbit characteristic of the history of ideas. If it is to be distinguished at all from the normal run of work in that subfield, it is because it is so markedly "internalist" in its approach and because he brings so commendably high a degree of philosophical literacy to his task. His claims, in effect, are straightforwardly historical in nature and, as such, are subject to the criteria for assessment normally accepted among historians at large—what David Hollinger has in mind, I assume, when he uses the term "intersubjective testability."

That said, the plot thickens if one turns from scrutinizing the epistemic status of Jonas's claims and begins to engage instead their explicit content. For what he claims happened in the distant past as ideas of biblical provenance came gradually to subvert the prevailing archaic and Greek common sense, would appear to be something that the more secular-minded among us would probably feel very threatened by if we sensed that it (or something cognate to it) were beginning to happen today.

After all, if Jonas is in general historically correct (and I have long since come to the conclusion that he is) then, in the more distant reaches of our own intellectual history, the rise to prominence of a religious tradition rooted in the nonphilosophical beliefs and practices of a mass of ordinary faithful succeeded, in the course of a slowly unfolding encounter with the Greek philosophical tradition, in raising new questions and postulates that came eventually to be naturalized as *philosophical* questions or postulates right at the very heart of the European and Western philosophical tradition as it has come down to us.

But if that is so, and if the outer membrane of philosophy has not become (as Jonas also implies) less permeable than once it was, then should we not be open to the possibility that something similar could happen again, and should we not, therefore, be more attentive today to shifts in the religious thinking of the broad masses of ordinary believers in society at large beyond the intellectual ramparts of the academy? And should we not be open also to the possibility that the claims for "faith-based" scholarship that people like Warren Nord and George Marsden appear to be making might well be straws in the wind, the moral equivalent of leading economic indicators, signaling the advent of fundamental intellectual changes to come?

Finally, the profound reshaping of the ancient philosophical common sense that Jonas delineates was clearly a very slow and complex process, and appears to have presupposed the gradual spread from the mass of believers into the thinking of the intellectual elite (through the agency, for example, of people like Philo Judaeus or the Greek and Latin Church Fathers, all the way down to St. Augustine) of religious ideas that would have been laughed out of court by their Greek philosophical predecessors. But if that was indeed the way in which some of our Western tradition's most fundamental philosophical ideas developed in the past, should we not at least be open to the possibility that some comparable, religiously driven development could well occur in the future? And does not that very possibility serve to underline the historically contingent, institutionally conditioned, community-sustained nature of the plausibility structures that undergird the epistemic norms currently regnant in our contemporary scholarly world? If so, and again, should that not in prudence dispose those of us who tend instinctively to skepticism on such matters to be somewhat more open than we currently seem to be to the claims being advanced for faith-based scholarship? Or, at the very least, should it not encourage us to keep our dialectical powder dry and to await with a measure of equanimity the gradual unfolding of what promises to be an intriguing epistemic drama?

Notes

1. See above, Part II, chapter 10.

2. Mary Douglas, *How Institutions Think* (Syracuse, N.Y.: Syracuse University Press, 1986).

3. See, e.g., Linda Smircich and Gareth Morgan, "Leadership: The Management of Meaning," *The Journal of Behavioral Science* 18, no. 3 (1982): 252–73.

4. See *Three Thousand Futures: The Next Twenty Years for Higher Education*, Final Report of the Carnegie Council on Policy Studies in Higher Education (San Francisco: Jossey-Bass, 1980), p. 19, n. 6. Note that as recently as 1960 some 60 percent of the total student population lived on campus.

5. George M. Marsden, *The Soul of the American University: From Protestant Establishment to Established Nonbelief* (New York: Oxford University Press, 1994), and *The Outrageous Idea of Christian Scholarship* (New York: Oxford University Press, 1997); Warren Nord, *Religion and American Education: Rethinking a National Dilemma* (Chapel Hill: University of North Carolina Press, 1995).

6. See, e.g., Hubert Jedin, *Bischöfliches Konzil oder Kirchenparlament? Ein Beitrag zur Ekklesiologie der Konzilien von Konstanz und Basel*, 2d ed. (Basel and Stuttgart: Helbing and Lichtenhahn, 1965), and Joseph Gill, "The Fifth Session of the Council of Constance," *Heythrop Journal* 5 (1964): 131–43, and "Il decreto *Haec sancta synodus* del concilio di Constanza," *Revista di storia della Chiesa in Italia* 12 (1967): 123–30.

7. Jonas's essay appeared originally in *Commentary* 44 (November 1967): 61–68. It was reprinted in somewhat altered form in *Creation: The Impact of an Idea*, ed. Daniel O'Connor and Francis Oakley (New York: Scribner, 1969), 241–56.

8. Ibid., in *Creation*, 241–43. The insights and emphases Jonas focuses on concern especially the novel conception of God, along with the congruent reinterpretation of the notion of creation, that emerged in the writings collected together in the Jewish Bible/Christian Old Testament. "The doctrine of creation," he notes (244), "with all that flows from it concerning the concepts of nature and man, was thematically close enough to the terms of natural philosophy to fall, as an issue, within the philosophical domain and thus *had* to be taken up by philosophers, whether affirmatively or negatively."

Epilogue

NICHOLAS WOLTERSTORFF

As Andrea Sterk, the editor, explains in her preface, two-thirds of the essays in this volume were composed by members of a three-year long seminar on religion and higher education sponsored by the Lilly Endowment; and all but one were delivered as papers during the course of the seminar meetings or at a public conference held as a supplement to the seminar. It now falls to James Turner and me as the two leaders of the seminar to offer, as an epilogue, our joint reflections on what emerged from the seminar's discussions.

To read the elaborate summaries of the seminar discussions carefully prepared by its staff and now available on-line (at www.nd.edu/~lillysem/) is for us, the co-directors, to be reminded of how rich, insightful, eloquent, passionate, pointed, and good-humored these discussions were. This was academic discourse at its finest!

The members of the Lilly Seminar were not selected because they represented some shared point of view. Quite to the contrary; we the co-directors picked people highly respected in their fields whom we knew to have interesting but distinctly different things to say about religion and higher education. We were looking for a group of people all of whom had thought seriously about the issues but who approached them from divergent angles.

One would expect the resultant discussions to be "all over the place." And so, in a way, they were; the diversity of insights and ideas was invariably fascinating and refreshing, sometimes even astounding. Nonetheless, in retrospect, one can discern an important line of thought emerging from the discussions which, so far as we can tell, all the participants shared. By no means could everything said be construed as a contribution to this line of thought; it's rather that, among the diversity of points made, this line of thought emerged as a persistent theme. There were

247

particular points around which there continued to be disagreement; nonetheless, the convergence is unmistakable. What we propose to do in this epilogue, then, is to trace out that line of thought, paying due attention to the points of disagreement.

We don't expect that all the participants will want to own our particular way of formulating the line of thought we claim to discern; given the intellectual independence and imagination of the group, any such expectation would be folly. Neither do we expect that all of them would pick out this particular theme for emphasis. But we do expect that they will all acknowledge that we have put our finger on one very interesting point of convergence.

Some historical background presented by historians who were members of the group made the participants very much aware of the fact that the place of religion in American higher education is very different today from what it was in the nineteenth century and on into the early part of the twentieth. The Protestant hegemony which then characterized American higher education is now gone; "educational Christendom," as one participant characterized it, is over in this country. It's very tempting for Protestants—at least those of certain stripes—to interpret this change as decline. But whenever some member of the group would, however tentatively, employ the language of declension, others would quickly challenge this description. For the Protestant hegemony had its undeniable dark side: Catholics and Jews were excluded, and the representation of women and ethnic minorities was minimal. The inclusion of such groups in the academy, everybody agreed, is not declension but its opposite.

A standard way of describing the changes with respect to religion that took place in American higher education over the course of the twentieth century is to say that higher education in America became secularized. Though probably everybody in the group felt that this description was getting at something important, nonetheless nobody in the group felt happy with this way of putting it. For one thing, if one were to give much weight to this description, one would have to have an articulated account of what it is that constitutes secularization; and that has become a much contested issue. But more basically, even operating with an intuitive understanding, if one looked at that entire *sector* of American society constituted by higher education, it's clearly not correct to say that American higher education in general has become secularized. Not only are religiously oriented colleges and universities thriving; when one looks inside a good many of our most prestigious universities, one discerns that a great deal of what takes place is quite explicitly religious in its orientation. No doubt it's true that, in some appropriate sense of the word "secularized," American higher education in its totality is *more* secularized today than it was one hundred years ago; but it would be much too simplistic to describe higher education in its totality as "secularized." One of the historians in the group observed that present-day American higher education exemplifies the *failure* of secularization!

This is not only true if one looks at teaching and research, but also if one looks at what the group came to call "formation." Religious and moral formation were once the quite explicit project of the faculty and administration of American colleges; how effective they were is another matter! If one looks at the entire sector of American higher education, there's obviously much less of that today than there was a century ago. But putting aside for the moment the explicitly religious colleges, what one sees is not that religious and moral formation have disappeared from the scene of the public, and the nonreligious private, universities, but that it's been taken over by a multitude of para-university organizations who are perhaps doing it more effectively than the educational institutions themselves ever did: Hillel Foundations, Newman Clubs, Inter-Varsity groups, Campus Crusade organizations; on and on goes the list.

There were some members of the group who were inclined to use the language of "victimization" when describing what has been happening to Protestants in particular, and to Christians more generally, in the major research institutions of American higher education. Christians, both faculty and students, are being victimized *on account of* their Christianity. A good many other members of the group boggled at this language. Nobody denied that some of this goes on; and everybody agreed in finding it reprehensible. Nonetheless, to use victimization as a basic category in thinking about these matters is to use the language of identity group politics; and nobody in the group was a defender of that.

The fact that everybody in the group agreed that it was wrong in any way to victimize students or faculty on account of their Christianity—or Judaism, or Buddhism, or whatever—brings us to that line of thought on which there was convergence. There may be some who celebrate the end of the hegemony of Protestantism in American higher education on the ground that that makes room for the hegemony of some favored alternative comprehensive perspective—"comprehensive perspective" being John Rawls' term; some, for example, might favor the hegemony of naturalism. Or some might favor the hegemony of the view that comprehensive perspectives are to play no role in the workings of the academy, or more pointedly, that those comprehensive perspectives that are religious are to play no role. Undoubtedly there are present-day members of the academy who favor one or another such hegemony.

What was striking about the seminar, however, was that no participant was of this view. Instead, a phrase introduced into the discussion by Richard Bernstein seemed to capture everybody's conviction as to what it is that should replace the old Protestant hegemony: "engaged fallibilistic pluralism."

Pluralism proved to be a prominent theme in the discussions. Rather often it was pointed out that for the purposes of our discussion it was important to keep in mind the extraordinary diversity of the institutions of American higher education; different things have to be said on the topic of religion in higher education depending on whether one is speaking, for example, of religiously oriented colleges and universities, or speaking of the state universities and such private universities as Yale, Princeton, and Stanford. Likewise it's important to keep the diversity of disciplines in mind; what's to be said about the relation of religion to physics is certainly different from what's to be said about its relation to the humanities and social sciences. While keeping in mind the importance of these two sorts of pluralism, the pluralism Bernstein had in mind with his phrase "engaged fallibilistic pluralism" was the pluralism of comprehensive perspectives, whether religious or otherwise. His thought, shared by all members of the seminar, was that the academy, rather than favoring any particular comprehensive perspective, and also rather than favoring the elimination from any role in the academy of the comprehensive perspectives of its members, should be *pluralistic* in this regard. Allow, and even encourage, a plurality of voices: the Catholic, the Protestant, the Jewish, the Muslim, the humanist, the naturalist, all of them and more. Give faculty and students the freedom to let their comprehensive perspectives shape their work in whatever way seems to them appropriate, provided it satisfies the standards of the academy. We'll be getting back to that phrase, "satisfies the standards"; it was especially at this point that disagreements arose within the group.

It must be an *engaged* pluralism. That is to say: to be a member of the academy requires that one engage in the give and take of argumentation rather than each simply speaking his or her mind. And that requires a commitment to *fallibilism* of a certain sort. One must be open to a serious consideration of the arguments offered by others against the positions one has developed within some field of learning, and vice versa. This is not to expect consideration of any old argument, obviously, for that would be much too stringent a requirement, but arguments that are carefully developed and seriously offered. For a fuller explanation of what he meant by "engaged fallibilistic pluralism," the reader is referred to Bernstein's article in this collection: "Religious Concerns in Scholarship: Engaged Fallibilism in Practice."

Different participants had different reasons for favoring pluralism of the sort described. What Alan Wolfe and Jean Elshtain regularly emphasized is that the absence of the religious and the humanistic voices in their fields results in a certain superficiality and blandness. Richard Bernstein, George Marsden, and Richard Mouw each in their own way offered an argument that amounted to a blend of anthropology and ethics. Academic learning is unavoidably perspectival, in that it is shaped by the convictions, the commitments, and the goals of the person engaged in the activity. To some extent these will be convictions, commitments, and goals shared by virtually all members of the particular academic discipline. But often, especially in the humanities and social sciences, these will be convictions, commitments, and goals rooted in the comprehensive perspective, be it religious or nonreligious, of the individual scholar. And these, given the diversity of our comprehensive perspectives, will differ from person to person. Few, if any, in the group thought that this perspectivalism implied that we have to give up on the idea of an objective reality; but all agreed that it is impossible to turn oneself into a generic human researcher. The rest of the argument is that if this anthropology is correct in its claim that it is impossible to remove one's perspective and become a generic human being, it is unjust in a democracy to allow into the academy those whose scholarship is shaped by, say, their commitment to naturalism, while disallowing those whose scholarship is shaped by, say, their Christianity or their Judaism.

It was typical of some Catholics in the group to offer yet a third argument for pluralism, focusing less on the comprehensive perspective of the scholar and the ways in which it shapes certain kinds of research, and focusing more on religious traditions: our religious traditions, it was argued, are a treasury of insights, diverse approaches, and so forth, that would enrich the academy if they were brought into the discourse.

It was that matter of the *standards of the academy* that caused the most disagreement in the group—disagreement in a number of different directions. George Marsden, who was a guest of the Lilly Seminar during its final year, has become well-known as a spokesman for Christian learning and for its place in the American academy, not just in the Christian colleges and universities but in the public universities and in those private universities that see themselves as no longer religious in their foundations. There were some in the group who understood him as not only making an anthropological argument, to the effect that academic learning is perspectival in character, but as also making an epistemological argument to the effect that Christian scholars do have, and should be allowed to have, their own criteria for what constitutes acceptable scholarship. This would also be the case, then, *mutatis mutandis*, for the scholarship produced by those committed to other comprehensive perspectives.

A number of participants reacted strongly against this understanding. David Hollinger insisted, for example, on the importance of distinguishing the context of discovery from the context of justification. It makes no difference to the rest of us in the academy whether it's something in a person's religion that accounts for her insights, for what it is that she is interested in, for how she makes her judgments of significance, and so forth; what we care about is only the "warranted assertibility" of her scholarly claims—whether they're justified by the evidence. And for the making of such judgments we appeal to the shared standards of the guild. If, judged by the standards of the guild, it's good history, then it's to be accepted no matter what its origins. A discussion of origins is of only autobiographical interest. When judging the acceptability of a piece of scholarship, nothing at all has any epistemic privilege except the standards of the guild.

Marsden declared, to the surprise of some, that he agreed with this position. He would prefer to talk about the shared *craft* of history writing rather than about shared epistemic standards; but those who interpreted him as arguing for some epistemic privilege for Christians had misunderstood him. It was instead mainly the philosophers in the group who dissented and offered a different picture, arguing that not only do the standards of the guild change, a point everyone conceded, but that they are themselves often the topic of argumentation and contestation. Disagreements within scholarship are not confined to whether or not some piece of scholarship fits the standards; we disagree about the standards themselves. Furthermore, though such disagreements are often themselves rational disagreements, that's not always true; the philosophers felt that some of their historian colleagues were operating with an unduly idealized picture of what lies behind the way in which the academy discriminates between what it regards as acceptable and what it regards as unacceptable scholarship. Sometimes what determines standards is power in the service of prejudice.

Denis Donoghue, who was unfortunately our sole representative from literature and the arts, posed yet a different sort of objection. The vocabulary of "evidence," "warranted assertibility," "justification," and so forth, seemed to him irrelevant to the work of the literary critic. When he reads his fellow critics, he's not making judgments as to whether they have offered sufficient evidence for their truth claims. He's looking to see whether they have interesting, promising, significant, and such like things to say about literature. It's not truth but meaning, in some sense of that word, that the literary critic is after. The corresponding question then is whether there are shared guild standards for the determination of such matters. It seems evident that there are not.

The seminar ended with some participants expressing unhappiness over the fact that we had not been able to deal satisfactorily with this fundamental epistemological issue: Must we expect that, over the long haul, a diversity of comprehensive perspectives in the academy will result in a diversity of "epistemic communities," or can the role in the academy of comprehensive perspectives be confined to the "context of discovery" and kept from invading the "context of justification"? Will differing comprehensive perspectives tend over the long haul to yield different judgments as to when the craft of history is being well practiced—alternatively, when a piece of history measures up to appropriate standards—or in the midst of a pluralism of comprehensive perspectives can we hope for shared standards of the guilds rationally arrived at? One finds this unhappiness coming to the surface in Francis Oakley's contribution to this volume. And of course it would have been gratifying if the seminar had been able to analyze this issue in sufficient depth to be able to come to some agreement. Nonetheless, as co-directors, we find it quite amazing that, in the context of coming to a shared understanding of the academy which is very different from the traditional understanding, the Lilly Seminar was able, with such insistence and acuity, to identify this issue as among the most important of those that remained to be analyzed and discussed in depth. This is more than we had hoped for. We regard it as an important contribution.

Members of the Lilly Seminar on Religion and Higher Education

Nancy T. Ammerman (Hartford Seminary)
Michael Beaty (Baylor University)
Richard Bernstein (The New School for Social Research)
Barbara DeConcini (American Academy of Religion)
Denis Donoghue (New York University)
Craig Dykstra (Lilly Endowment)
Jean Bethke Elshtain (The Divinity School, University of Chicago)
Philip Gleason (University of Notre Dame)
Nathan Hatch (University of Notre Dame)
Stephen Haynes (Rhodes College)
James L. Heft (University of Dayton)
Monika Hellwig (Association of Catholic Colleges & Universities)
David Hollinger (University of California, Berkeley)
Richard Hughes (Pepperdine University)
Jeanne Knoerle (Lilly Endowment)
Eugene Y. Lowe, Jr. (Northwestern University)
Richard Mouw (Fuller Theological Seminary)
Mark Noll (Wheaton College)
Francis Oakley (Williams College)
Mark Schwehn (Valparaiso University)
Douglas Sloan (Teachers College, Columbia University)
Peter Steinfels (New York Times)
Eleonore Stump (Saint Louis University)
Frank Turner (Yale University)
James Turner (University of Notre Dame)
Diane Winston (The Pew Charitable Trusts)

Alan Wolfe (Boston College)
Nicholas Wolterstorff (The Divinity School, Yale University)
Robert Wuthnow (Princeton University)